CONTENTS

UNDERSTANDING, PREPARING FOR, AND PRACTICING

Christian Worship

SECOND EDITION

UNDERSTANDING,
PREPARING FOR,
AND PRACTICING

Christian Worship

SECOND EDITION

Franklin M. Segler
REVISED BY Randall Bradley

BROADMAN
& HOLMAN
PUBLISHERS

Nashville, Tennessee

4211-68
0-8054-1168-2

Dewey Decimal Classification: 264
Subject Heading: Worship
Library of Congress Card Catalog Number: 95-15291

Typography by TF Designs

Library of Congress Cataloging-in-Publication Data

Segler, Franklin M.
    Understanding, preparing for, and practicing Christian worship, second edition / Franklin M. Seger, C. Randall Bradley.-- [Rev. ed.]
        p. cm.
    Includes bibliographical references and index.
    ISBN 0-8054-1168-2
    1.Worship. 2.Public worship. I. Bradley, C. Randall, 1960-. II. Title.
BV10.2.S4 1996
264—dc20   95-15291
                                                                  CIP

1 2 3 4 5 6 01 00 99 98 97 96

PREFACE

S ince the first edition of this work, worship has experienced unprecedented interest; worship has certainly been a foremost discussion topic for church leaders during the 1980s and 1990s. Worship conferences and hundreds of books and journals now are devoted exclusively to the subject of worship. While Franklin Segler was well ahead of his time in realizing the importance of worship, worship has undergone many changes since 1967. The revised edition retains all but one of the original chapters: "Form and Freedom in Worship" has been incorporated into "Planning the Order of Worship," and "Worship and Church Renewal" has been moved earlier in the book since it serves a foundational role. Five new chapters—"Children and Worship"; "Architecture, Acoustics, and Worship"; "The Christian Year and Other Special Days"; "Drama and Worship"; and "Rites of Passage" have been added as well as numerous other sections within existing chapters. Various appendices were added to provide an added practical dimension. The bibliography has been completely updated.

INTRODUCTION
(1967 EDITION)

E C. Dargan, a leading Baptist theologian of the nineteenth century, declared that a study of worship is indispensable for an understanding of the church and its ministry.[1] One of the duties and privileges of the Christian church is that of providing for and maintaining the worship of God. The first order in the church's mission is worship. All other aspects of ministry are motivated by worship, and without worship the church will die.

The purpose of this book is both theological and practical. It is written with the hope that it will help to interpret the meaning of worship and provide guidelines for planning and leading worship. It is meant to be a sourcebook for pastors and other leaders in the churches, and especially for college and seminary students, pointing to treasures both old and new in the literature of the church.

Part 1, "The Meaning of Worship," interprets worship from the standpoint of its biblical and historical foundations, its theological basis, and its psychological principles. The attitudes involved in the act of worship are also discussed.

Part 2, "The Means of Expressing Worship," discusses the elements used in expressing worship and shows how these elements are related to the

---

1. E. C. Dargan, *Ecclesiology* (Louisville: Charles T. Dearing, 1897), 517.

entire worship service. These include music, prayers, preaching, the reading of the Scriptures, and others.

Part 3, "Planning and Conducting Worship," proposes to provide principles for relating form and freedom in worship. Form should never be so rigid as to restrict the spirit of freedom or spontaneity. Neither should a spirit of spontaneity ignore the need for some concrete form for the expression of our common praise.

There is no set form suggested which Christians must follow in worship. However, it is natural, indeed inevitable, that they will use some form in their efforts to commune with God. It is better to use sound principles than to be careless and indifferent. God is a God of order, and we live in a universe of law and order. Worship will of necessity follow some form and order.

There are various types of worship—formal and informal, public and private, planned and spontaneous. The spirit and motive are always the same: the desire to commune with God, to have a new and fresh encounter with the Lord of life. The attitude and spirit are primary. The form, as a secondary essential, is meant to aid in disciplining and expressing the attitude.

Chapter 6, "Worship and Church Renewal," shows worship to be the motivating dynamic for the life and mission of the church. Worship is the lifestream of the church. Vital worship motivates us and inspires us for righteous living, fervent evangelism, and the total stewardship of life. The hope for church renewal depends upon a renewal of genuine worship.

PART ONE:

THE MEANING OF WORSHIP

CHAPTER 1

WHAT IS WORSHIP?

*W*orship is an end in itself; it is not a means to something else. Karl Barth has appropriately declared that the "church's worship is the *Opus Dei*, the work of God, which is carried out for its own sake." When we try to worship for the sake of certain benefits that may be received, the act ceases to be worship; for then it attempts to use God as a means to something else. We worship God purely for the sake of worshiping God.

To worship is:

- To quicken the conscience by the holiness of God,

- To feed the mind with the truth of God,

- To purge the imagination by the beauty of God,

- To open the heart to the love of God,

- To devote the will to the purpose of God.[1]

Why do we worship? Because we cannot help worshiping. Worship is not a human invention; rather, it is a divine offering. God offers himself in a

---

1. William Temple, *The Hope of a New World* (New York: Macmillan, 1942), 30.

personal relationship, and we respond. God's offer of love elicits our response in worship. A vision of God demands a worship response because God is worthy of worship. We discover that when we seek God, God has already found us.

Defining worship is difficult; however, a study of historic words closely related to our term *worship* can assist in the interpretation of worship.

PRELIMINARY TERMINOLOGY

The English word *worship* is derived from the Anglo-Saxon *weorthscipe*—"worth" and "ship"—meaning one "worthy of reverence and honor." When we worship, we are declaring God's worth. The angels sang, "'Worthy is the Lamb who was slain,'" and every creature answered, "'To him who sits upon the throne and to the Lamb be blessing and honor and glory and might for ever and ever!' And the four living creatures said, 'Amen!' and the elders fell down and worshiped" (Rev. 5:12, 13–14).

The biblical term *glory* is often attributed to God as God is worshiped. The Hebrew term *kabod*, translated "glory," means the "honor" or "weight" of God. When Isaiah saw the Lord high and lifted up, he declared, "the whole earth is full of his glory" (Isa. 6:3). The New Testament term *doxa*, translated "glory," expresses that God is worthy of praise and honor. At the birth of Jesus the angels sang, "Glory to God in the highest, and on earth peace among men with whom he is pleased!" (Luke 2:14).

The principal Old Testament term translated "worship" is *shachah*, which means to "bow down" or to "prostrate" oneself. When the people of Israel heard that God had spoken to Moses, they believed and "bowed their heads and worshiped" (Exod. 4:31).

The Greek term most often indicating worship in the New Testament is *proskuneo*, meaning literally to "kiss the hand towards one" or to "prostrate oneself" before another in reverence. Jesus used this word when he said to the woman of Sychar, "God is spirit, and those who worship him must worship in spirit and truth" (John 4:24).

The term *liturgy* is derived from the Greek *leitourgia*, translated "ministry" or "service." In the New Testament, liturgy does not occur in connection with ceremonial affairs. It denoted the work of the priestly office under the old covenant (cf. Luke 1:23, Heb. 9:21) and also the ministry of Christ (Heb. 8:6) and the worship of the church (Acts 13:2). Literally, *leitourgia* means an "action of the people," and more particularly the service which the Christian renders to God in faith and obedience.

For Paul the true *leitourgia* of God is a life of faith that shows forth fruits of the Spirit (Gal. 5:22). Worship is meant in Paul's exhortation, "I appeal to you therefore, brethren, by the mercies of God, to present your bodies as a living sacrifice, holy and acceptable to God, which is your spiritual worship [*leitourgia*]" (Rom. 12:1). In later centuries the term *liturgy* came to mean the order of worship in the churches.

Without a clear concept of the meaning of service, worship is difficult to understand. Although the term *cult* in English often has a negative meaning, its meaning in Latin and Romance languages, such as French and Italian, is much more positive. According to James F. White:

> Its origin is the Latin *colere*, an agriculture term meaning to cultivate. Both the French *le culte*, and the Italian *il culto*, preserve this Latin word as the usual term for worship. It is a rich term, far richer than the English word "worship," for it catches the mutuality of responsibility between the farmer and his land or animals. If I do not feed and water my chickens, I know there will be no eggs; unless I weed my garden, there will be no vegetables. It is a relationship of mutual dependence. . . . It is a measure of giving and receiving, certainly not in equal measure, but by being bound to each other. Unfortunately, the English language does not readily make the obvious connection between cultivate and worship that we find in the Romance languages.[2]

DESCRIBING WORSHIP

Christian worship defies definition; it can only be experienced. For the Christian, theology is an attempt to describe the experience of God's grace applied in a redemptive relationship. A living experience may be analyzed, but it can never be completely contained in formulas, creeds, and liturgies.

Worshipers may identify with Paul: "I had such an experience that it cannot be told; in fact, it does not seem appropriate to speak about it" (see 2 Cor. 12:3–4). Certain experiences in worship are so intimate that the worshiper cannot share them. Although the majesty and holiness of God cannot be comprehended, and the feeling of awe cannot be strictly defined, worshipers cannot help reflecting on the meaning of worship; therefore, the clearer our understanding of worship, the more meaningful will be our experience of worship. Even though the *esse* (reality) of worship cannot be defined or contained in formulas, the *bene esse* (well-being), or those things which aid worship, can be discussed.

Although the innate desire to worship is universal, there is often confusion about the meaning and nature of worship. While efforts at defining worship seem inadequate, certain aspects of worship need to be described. The essence of worship as inner experience and the outward acts of worship which aid in the experience are interrelated. The following descriptions may aid in clarifying this relationship.

Mystery. Worship is both revelation and mystery. A worshiper experiences the presence of God in revelation and stands in awe of God in the face of mystery. God both reveals and withholds at the same time. While we can be

---

2. James F. White, *Introduction to Christian Worship*, rev. ed. (Nashville: Abingdon Press, 1990), 32.

conscious of God in our lives, we can never comprehend the ultimate meaning of God. In worship we experience both mystery (God's transcendence) and revelation (God's immanence).

Communion with God is a miracle, just as the revelation of Jesus Christ and the continuing work of the Holy Spirit in the church are miracles. According to Samuel Miller, the miracle of worship is the "sight of God seen through earthly circumstance; it is the glory of God shining through darkness; it is the power of God felt when all other strength fails; it is the eternal manifested in time." Worship becomes more meaningful when churches approach worship with a sense of mystery, awe, and wonder. Worshipers can know God in worship, but they can never fully comprehend his nature nor fathom the mystery of his ways.

Celebration. Worship is essentially the celebration of the acts of God in history—God's creation; God's providence; God's covenant of redemption; God's redemptive revelation through Jesus Christ in the Incarnation, the Cross, and the Resurrection; and the manifestation of God's power through the coming of the Holy Spirit. Von Ogden Vogt sees worship as the interruption of work to praise and to celebrate God's goodness. Worship is indeed a celebration of the gospel.

Worshipers worship in appreciation for what God has done. As Henry Sloane Coffin affirmed, we worship for sheer delight. A worship service is a celebration.[3] Martin Luther said, "To have a God is to worship him."

Life. Worship is not limited to acts of devotion, rites, and ceremonies. For the Christian, worship is synonymous with life. In its broadest aspect, worship is related to all human action. As a part of God's creation, humankind responds in gratitude to the Creator. Every area of life belongs to the kingdom of God; therefore, worship is practicing the presence of God in every experience of life.

There is a sense in which we may think of the "whole life of the universe, seen and unseen," as an act of worship, glorifying God as its Creator, Sustainer, and End.[4] Paul claimed the whole universe for Christ—the world of things, the world of persons in time, and the world of the eternal (1 Cor. 3:21–23). Because Christ is the Lord of all life, he is to be worshiped in every sphere of life. Acts of worship are more meaningful if the whole of life is devoted to God.

Dialogue. Worshipers experience God in a conscious dialogue. Worship is both revelation and response. God takes the initiative in revelation, and humankind responds in worship. God is revealed to the worshiper's spirit through the Bible, through persons in the fellowship of believers, through

3. Henry Sloane Coffin, *The Public Worship of God: A Source Book* (Philadelphia: Westminster Press, 1946), 15, 16.
4. Evelyn Underhill, *Worship* (New York: Harper & Bros., 1937), 3.

music, through symbols, through human actions, and through God's Spirit. Humankind responds to God through words and music and acts of celebration and dedication.

Worship is more than conversation: it is also encounter. In this encounter, God confronts and makes demands upon the worshiper. In his dream, Jacob was conscious of God's coming to him in the presence of angel messengers who were ascending and descending on the ladder. When Jacob awoke from his sleep he said, "'Surely the LORD is in this place; and I did not know it.' And he was afraid, and said, 'How awesome is this place! This is none other than the house of God, and this is the gate of heaven'" (Gen. 28:16–17). For the apostle Paul, it was important to know God, but it was more important "to be known by God" (Gal. 4:9). Meaningful worship leads to decisive experiences with God.

Offering. The purpose of worship is not primarily to receive blessings from God but to make offerings to God. Ancient peoples presented offerings in the form of sacrifices. In the Bible, the Hebrews made offerings in various ways. The psalmist exhorted, "Ascribe to the LORD the glory due his name; bring an offering, and come into his courts!" (Ps. 96:8).

The New Testament also emphasizes giving as central in worship. Worshipers are to offer their gifts in sincere faith and total obedience, as in the days of Abel and Cain (Heb. 11:4). The "holy priesthood," the congregation of believers, is to "offer spiritual sacrifices acceptable to God through Jesus Christ" (1 Pet. 2:5). Worship is more than speech: it is action. It is acting on the word of God in faith. As God has acted toward believers, so believers are to act toward God.

Worship is primarily the offering of our total selves to God—our intellects, our feelings, our attitudes, and our possessions. Our outward gifts are the result of our inward dedication. Paul saw the gifts of money from the Philippian church as "a fragrant offering, a sacrifice acceptable and pleasing to God" (Phil. 4:18). The highest expression of giving is offering yourself, presenting "your bodies as a living sacrifice, holy and acceptable to God" (Rom. 12:1). What God wants is our selves. Coffin declares, "We present him our thoughts, our penitence, our thanksgiving, our aspirations for our own lives, for those dear to us, for our land and our world. Our selves is the gift he seeks."[5]

Eschatological fulfillment. Worship is the eschatological function of the church. According to Delling, "It is, in its very essence, the continuing decisive working out of salvation in history, which ends in the eternal adoration of God."[6] The church is charged to continue its worship. Paul said, "As

---

5. Coffin, *Public Worship*, 21.
6. Gerhard Delling, *Worship in the New Testament*, trans. Percy Scott (Philadelphia: Westminster, 1962), 182.

often as you eat this bread and drink the cup, you proclaim the Lord's death until he comes" (1 Cor. 11:26). In worship humanity anticipates that coming time when we shall be gathered together around God's throne in heaven.

REALITY IN WORSHIP

There is no possibility of the church's being Christian without worship. The essence of worship is the self-portrayal of the congregation, whom God has called to be his people in the world. In fact, worship is the power from God that enables the church to be the church. W. T. Conner states, "The first business, then, of a church is not evangelism, nor missions, nor benevolence; it is worship. The worship of God in Christ should be at the center of all else that the church does. It is the mainspring of all the activity of the church."[7]

People too often attend church with the mistaken idea that when they worship they leave the "real world" behind. Willard L. Sperry says, "A service of worship is a deliberate and disciplined adventure in reality. In Church, if anywhere, we are under moral bonds to be real."[8]

The term *reality*, to be intelligible, must have certain points of reference. Religious experience is a real experience. There are at least three essential points of reference: (1) To Christian philosophy the ultimate reality is personal, and to Christian theology and experience the ultimate expression of the personal is God's manifestation of himself. Worship is in the realm of the personal. (2) Another point of reference is historical manifestation. Christian worship is related to the acts of God in history. These acts are observable in time and place. The experience of God in history verifies the reality of divine revelation, especially in the person of Jesus Christ. (3) Worship may also be judged by the reality of its dynamic effects. Serious dialogue with God produces transforming results. A clear vision of God brings a realistic picture of a person's needs and a desire for God's cleansing and forgiveness. Life is most real when a person finds his or her true self in Christ.

Finally, to reiterate, definitions and descriptions cannot adequately delineate the experience of worship, for worship is an act of faith. Worship is the lifting up of the heart in willing response.[9]

Worship is not a mere preparation for action. It is the *Opus Dei*, the adoration of God as humankind's highest privilege. God will be served for God's glory alone, not as a means to an end.

---

7. W. T. Conner, *The Gospel of Redemption* (Nashville: Broadman Press, 1945), 277.

8. Willard L. Sperry, *Reality in Worship* (New York: Macmillan, 1925), 206.

9. Carl Michalson, "Authority," *A Handbook of Christian Theology*, eds. Arthur A. Cohen and Marvin Halverson (Cleveland, Ohio: World, 1958), 28.

Such a utilitarian approach is not valid even if the end is as admirable as service to the community, building the morale of a nation, or the making of individuals with greater integrity, health, or sensitivity. While genuine worship may cause persons to be drawn into a church's fellowship, worship, not church growth must be the church's priority. At all costs churches must resist the temptation to embrace all cultural norms and innovative worship forms without first considering how God will be honored. Worship used for any purpose other than God's glory is not true worship. God must be worshiped for God's own glory, or worship is idolatry, however worthy its motivations.

CHAPTER 2

BIBLICAL FOUNDATIONS

C hristians generally consult the Bible for the norms of worship. Churches of strong ecclesiastical traditions believe that the Bible provides the basic principles for worship, and Free Churches particularly stress biblical authority for their principles of worship. However, all churches tend to develop their patterns of worship partly from biblical principles and partly from tradition. Patterns and practices in public worship should be continually tested by the spirit and practice of leaders who have faith in the Bible, especially in New Testament Christianity.

ANCIENT BACKGROUNDS

Humankind is by nature religious and must have some object of worship. Therefore, worship in some form is universal, ranging from superstitious fear or fetishism in paganism to the highest spiritual exercise in Christianity. Primitive history indicates that all people have worshiped some object. The oldest monuments of civilization contain evidences of religious convictions, inspirations, and worship.

Primitive practices often took the form of nature worship. This was usually polytheistic, making a god of every object; or pantheistic, considering everything in nature of divine essence. For example, the Egyptians worshiped Ra, the sun-god, and Osiris, the god of the Nile and of fertility.

Primitive worship usually took the form of sacrifices and superstitious rites intended to ward off evil spirits or to placate angry gods. Primitive worship was prompted by the innate needs of humankind. People created gods as objects of worship in order to fulfill their needs. For example, Baal was imagined to be the god of the crops who provided for material needs. The worship of this god of materialism was often encountered by Old Testament peoples (see Judg. 2:11–14; 1 Sam. 7:3–4; 1 Kings 18:17–19).

Archaeologists and anthropologists have discovered artifacts and other indications of the types of worship practiced by ancient peoples. Many primitive peoples did not distinguish between spiritual deities and natural phenomena. There were gods of the fields, of rivers, of the sun and moon, of fertility and barrenness, and of birth and death. Certain groups even believed in the hope of reincarnation. Humankind has always had a sense of the supernatural in its struggle with the problem of good and evil.[1]

In some ancient cultures, human beings were offered as sacrifices, slain upon altars, burned, or buried alive. For example, some Canaanite people worshiped the god Moloch by offering their own children as sacrifices to him on an altar of fire. Although the facts are too meager to give definite conclusions about many of these rituals, it is clear that humans worshiped from ancient times. People have always sought to understand themselves and the complex world in which they live. However paganistic or polytheistic their attitudes, people have always searched for the "unknown god."

WORSHIP IN THE OLD TESTAMENT

The worship of the people of God in the Old Testament was distinguished from Oriental cults as follows: (1) Israel's God was the only God; (2) God was a personal God who intervened in history; (3) Israel had no image in its worship.[2]

G. Ernest Wright also contrasts the worship of Israel with that of the polytheistic religions: "In the faith of Israel the basis of worship lay in historical memory and in spiritual communion."[3] Although there are no strict lines of demarcation, it is evident in the Old Testament story that worship

---

1. See James F. Frazier, *The Golden Bough*, 1 vol. (New York: Macmillan, 1930); Sigmund Freud, *Totem and Taboo*, trans. A. A. Brill (New York: Moffat, Yard, and Co., 1918); Edward B. Tyler, *Primitive Culture*, 2 vols. (New York: Holt, Rinehart, & Winston, 1874); and Mircea Eliate, *A History of Religious Ideas*, 3 vols. (Chicago: University of Chicago Press, 1978).

2. Roland De Vaux, *Ancient Israel: Its Life and Institutions*, trans. John McHugh (London: McGraw-Hill, 1961), 271ff.

3. G. Ernest Wright, "The Faith of Israel," in *The Interpreter's Bible*, ed. George Buttrick (Nashville: Abingdon-Cokesbury Press, 1952), 1:375.

in the life of Israel developed over time; from an original cultus, various practices of worship developed throughout the history of Israel.

The ancient story always assumes that God desires to commune with humankind. In the garden of Eden God asked, "Adam, . . . Where art thou?" (Gen. 3:9, KJV). The sons of Adam, Cain and Abel, worshiped God. Cain was a tiller of the soil, and Abel was a keeper of sheep. Cain brought the fruits of the soil as an offering to the Lord, and Abel brought the firstlings of the flock as an offering. The Lord accepted Abel's offering but rejected Cain's, evidently because of their differing motivations (Gen. 4:2–5; see Heb. 11:4).

Enoch lived in constant fellowship with God. "Enoch walked with God; and he was not, for God took him" (Gen. 5:24). The Hebrew word *walked* suggests an intimate fellowship between Enoch and God. The literal translation is they "walked back and forth together." Enoch not only worshiped God at stated times, but he lived in continuous relationship with his Creator.

Several generations later, we find Noah worshiping God. God again took the initiative and called Noah to serve and represent God before the people. Noah obeyed God and built an ark of safety into which he took his family. After the flood, at God's command, Noah left the ark and "built an altar to the LORD . . . and offered burnt offerings on the altar" (8:20) in celebration of his deliverance. This episode of communion between God and Noah was sealed with the rainbow of promise (9:11–12).

THE PATRIARCHAL PERIOD—PRIVATE AND FAMILY ALTARS

The atmosphere of worship pervades the whole Pentateuch. Its design and religious symbolism, hallowed by centuries of worship, produce a solemn sense of the holiness and majesty of God. God created humanity to commune with him and took the initiative in seeking them. Their worship responses included building altars and dedicating places and objects.

God appeared to Abraham and called him to leave his own country and go to a land of promise. He promised to bless Abraham, to make of him a great nation, and to make his name great (12:1–30). Abraham responded with faith and obedience and built an altar unto the Lord and worshiped him (12:7). Later Abraham worshiped God when he indicated his willingness to sacrifice his own son Isaac to the Lord (22:9–10).

Abraham taught his son Isaac to worship God. Isaac built an altar and called on the name of the Lord (26:24–25). Jacob's experiences in worship were as numerous as they were glorious. He dreamed that God appeared to him through angels descending and ascending a ladder that reached up into heaven. In the morning he declared, "Surely the LORD is in this place; and I did not know it. . . . How awesome is this place! This is none other than the house of God" (28:16–17). He set up a stone for an altar which he dedicated to the Lord and called it Bethel, "house of God."

Thus, even before the ritual law of Leviticus was given, the Old Testament stresses the necessity of worship.

THE MOSAIC PERIOD–THE COVENANT OF REVELATION AND RESPONSE

Israel's worship consisted in the celebration and proclamation of the covenant that God ordained. God revealed himself to Israel as Jehovah, the covenant God. The covenant was delivered to Moses in Sinai as God's claim upon Israel (Exod. 20:1–18). God demanded sincere worship: "You shall not bow down to them [idols] nor worship them, for I the Eternal, your God, am a jealous God" (Exod. 20:5, Moffatt). Jehovah, who delivered the tablets to Moses, is the God who acts in history. From that time forth the tablets of stone became for Israel the revealed Word of God. Perhaps the matrix of the meaning and purpose of worship in the Old Testament is best summed up in Deuteronomy 6:4, "The LORD our God is one LORD."

The people of Israel observed public worship in the wilderness under the direction of Moses. The primitive sanctuary or "tent of meeting" probably resembled an ordinary shepherd's tent, having both outer and inner compartments. The tent of meeting seems to have been pitched outside the camp (Exod. 31:7; Num. 11:26).

Ultimately God directed Moses to build a sanctuary for worship and an ark in which the Ten Commandments should be kept (Exod. 25:26). With the building of the tabernacle, congregational worship was established as an institution. God then commanded Moses to consecrate Aaron and his sons to the office of priesthood (28:2–3). The duties of the priests were set forth in detail. The people were to bring offerings to God continually as an act of worship (29:30).

THE PERIOD OF THE JUDGES

As Israel proceeded with the conquest of Canaan, they encountered the worship of nature deities known as the "Baalim." In this environment, God's people were influenced by the tribes who worshiped false gods, and Jehovan worship was corrupted. Some of the people forsook the God of their forbearers. Many of them transferred the rituals and ceremonies of the popular shrines, where false gods were worshiped, to the worship of Jehovah. Doubtless, Hannah's prayers were genuine (1 Sam. 1), but the corrupt acts of priests (1 Sam. 2:12–17, 22–25) and the fetish value placed upon the ark (1 Sam. 4:3) indicate false acts of worship.[4]

---

4. Horton Davies, "Worship in the Old Testament," in *The Interpreter's Dictionary of the Bible*, ed. George Buttrick (Nashville: Abingdon Press, 1962), 4, 882.

Some of the people remembered Jehovah, and Jehovah worship continued at numerous shrines during the period of the judges. Gilgal was likely the first place established for the worship of Jehovah in the new land of Canaan. Saul was crowned in the Gilgal sanctuary, and annual celebrations of Israel's crossing into Canaan may have taken place there. Altars at Gilgal (Judg. 2:1), Ophrah (Judg. 6:24), Shiloh and Dan (Judg. 18:29–31), Hebron (2 Sam. 5:3), and Gideon (1 Kings 3:4) indicate that Israel's conquest of the land for Jehovah was constantly going forward.

TEMPLE AND CULTUS

In the historical books the king appears several times as the leader in worship, for he was a holy person, sanctified by his anointing and adopted by Yahweh. David set up the first altar for Yahweh in Jerusalem (2 Sam. 24:25) and also conceived the plans for building Yahweh a temple (2 Sam. 7:2–3).

In Solomon's temple at Jerusalem, Old Testament worship reached its climax. Of Israel's holy places dedicated to the worship of God, the temple was the most magnificent and elaborate. The temple was erected in Jerusalem, where God had previously appeared (2 Sam. 24:16–25); thus, it became the central sanctuary of Israel. King David desired to build a house of rest for the ark of the covenant of the Lord and for the footstool of God (1 Chron. 28:2). Although David made elaborate preparations for the building of the temple, God would not allow him to build the temple. God informed David that his son Solomon, who would succeed him as king, had been chosen to build the house of God. When David delivered elaborate plans for the building of the temple to Solomon, David said, "Be strong and of good courage, and do it. Fear not, be not dismayed; for the LORD God, even my God, is with you. He will not fail you or forsake you, until all the work for the service of the house of the LORD is finished" (1 Chron. 28:20).

The temple was elaborately furnished with dedicated vessels: "the golden altar, the tables for the bread of the Presence, the lampstands and their lamps of pure gold . . . the flowers, the lamps, and the tongs, of purest gold; the snuffers, basins, dishes for incense, and firepans, of pure gold; . . . and the sockets of the temple, for the inner doors to the most holy place and for the doors of the nave of the temple were of gold" (2 Chron. 4:19–22). When the building was complete, Solomon commanded the elders and the Levites to bring up the ark to the temple.

Second Chronicles gives an account of the dedication of the temple. The priests and the Levitical singers—arrayed in fine linen, with cymbals, harps, lyres, and trumpets, together with many singers—offered praise and thanksgiving to the Lord. They sang, "For he is good, for his steadfast love endures for ever" (2 Chron. 5:13). The house of the Lord was filled with a cloud, and the priests could not stand to minister, because the glory of the Lord filled the house of God (2 Chron. 5:13–14). Then Solomon knelt before the assembly and prayed a prayer of dedication, and God's glory filled the temple. When the people saw the glory of the Lord upon the temple, they bowed their faces to the earth and worshiped and gave thanks to the Lord. Solomon and the people offered sacrifices before the Lord, the priests offered praises, the Levites sounded their trumpets, and all Israel stood (2 Chron. 7:3–6).

With the magnificent temple came a further development of the ritual which had developed largely around the feasts celebrated throughout the land. For example, the Feast of Unleavened Bread was celebrated annually, with the eating of unleavened cakes, the offering of first fruits, and the waving of the sheaf of first fruits preceded by the Passover with its slain lamb and the blood-sprinkled doorposts. The Feast of Booths was the greatest of all celebrations. It was a harvest of thanksgiving which included the use of lights and dancing (Isa. 30:29). Israel lived in booths for seven days and celebrated the new year, offering prayers for the coming of the rains.

The temple at Jerusalem was the central place of worship for the entire land. The people came up to Jerusalem to rejoice before God. They brought their tithes and sacrificial offerings to the sanctuary. Their acts of worship included music, solos, anthems, shouting, dancing, processions, playing instruments, preaching in elementary form, sacred recitations of the stories of Israel—her forebearers, heroes, saints, and soldiers—interspersed with petitions, prayers, vows, promises, sayings of creeds and confessions, sacred meals, and washings.

There was silence also in Israel's worship. Habakkuk exclaimed, "The LORD is in his holy temple; let all the earth keep silence before him" (Hab. 2:20). The psalmist spoke for God: "Be still, and know that I am God" (Ps. 46:10).

Elaborate rituals and ceremonies, with feast days and sacrificial offerings, were developed to remind the people of their sinfulness and also of God's mercy and love. The entire book of Leviticus is devoted to this sacrificial and priestly system. Sacrifice was understood to be a necessary condition of effective worship.[5]

Israel's ritual of sacrifice included (1) the "holocaust" or burnt offering "taken up" to the altar, whose smoke "goes up" to God (1 Sam. 7:9; Deut. 33:10); (2) the "communion sacrifice" in which the victim is shared between God and the persons offering the sacrifice (Lev. 3); (3) the "expiatory sacrifice," offered for sin (Lev. 4:1—5:13) and as reparation for sin (Lev. 5:14–26); (4) the "vegetable offerings," presented as a memorial of a

---

5. See John B. Ascham, *The Religion of Israel* (New York: Abingdon Press, 1918), 92. Part of this priestly code probably goes back to more ancient times. See John Bright, "Modern Study of Old Testament Literature," *The Bible and the Ancient Near East*, ed. G. Ernest Wright (Garden City, N.Y.: Doubleday, 1961), 18.

pledge made (Lev. 2); (5) the "offering of shewbread" or "bread of the presence," symbolizing a pledge of the covenant between God and Israel (Lev. 24:5–9); (6) and the "offering of perfumes" or incense (Exod. 30:34–38; Lev. 16:12–13), fragrant aromas presented to God. Paul speaks of the gifts of the Christians at Philippi as a "fragrant offering, a sacrifice acceptable and pleasing to God" (Phil. 4:18).

THE PROPHETS AND THE PSALMS—PERSONAL AND ETHICAL RELIGION

Numerous prophets vigorously protested the empty ritualism and mixed motives of the people in their acts of worship. The herdsman Amos abhorred the Israelite's feast days, solemn assemblies, burnt offerings, and meat offerings, and called Israel back to a sincere worship of Jehovah (Amos 5:21–24). Hosea prophesied for God, "I desired mercy, and not sacrifice; and the knowledge of God more than burnt offerings" (Hos. 6:6, KJV). The book of Micah conveyed a similar exhortation: "With what shall I come before the LORD, and bow myself before God on high? . . . Will the LORD be pleased with thousands of rams, with ten thousands of rivers of oil? . . . He has showed you, O man, what is good; and what does the LORD require of you but to do justice, and to love kindness, and to walk humbly with your God?" (Mic. 6:6–8). This does not mean, however, that the prophets rejected the forms and content of all ritual. They called not for the abolition of ritual, but for sincerity in the performance of the ritual.

Several of the prophets called for a general reformation of worship. Jeremiah insisted on personal or experiential worship. Jehovah is personal and desires that his people worship in sincerity. "My people . . . have forsaken me, the fountain of living waters, and hewed out cisterns for themselves, broken cisterns, that can hold no water" (Jer. 2:13). Both blessings and judgments are connected with Israel's worship. "Blessed is the man that trusteth in the LORD, and whose hope the LORD is" (17:7, KJV). "'Woe to the shepherds who destroy and scatter the sheep of my pasture!' says the LORD" (23:1).

Ezekiel, priest and prophet, also called for reform: "Because you have defiled my sanctuary with all your detestable things . . . therefore I will cut you down" (Ezek. 5:11). False prophets were prophesying peace for Israel when there was no peace (13:16). Individual responsibility of parents and children was declared: "The soul that sins shall die" (18:20). Because false shepherds were concerned only about feeding themselves, the hungry sheep looked up and were not fed (34:8).

Having denounced their sins and condemned their false worship, Ezekiel challenged Israel to return to genuine worship by means of a vision that God revealed to him. This magnificent vision of the measureless God's temple includes a detailed account of meaningful rites—a chamber for washing the offering (40:38), tables for slaughtering the sacrifice (40:39–41), chambers for the priests' preparation (40:44–46), the most holy place (41:4), carved likenesses of cherubim and palm trees (41:17–18), the table before the Lord (41:22), chambers where the priests consumed the offering (42:13), the priests' holy garments (42:14), a visitation of the spirit and a vision of the glory of the Lord filling the temple (43:4–5), the voice of God speaking God's Word (43:6ff.), the altar for the burnt offerings with details for making the sacrifice (43:18–27), detailed instructions to the priests concerning their garments, their consecration, and their ministries (44:15ff.). The vision of the temple and the acts of worship climax with the blessings of God flowing out from the sanctuary like fresh waters to bless the land with ever-bearing trees producing fruit for food and leaves for healing (47:1–12).

A popular example of worship is found in the experience of Isaiah recorded in Isaiah chapter 6. In a vision of the temple of worship, Isaiah saw the Lord in all majesty and glory. Confronted by God, Isaiah confessed his sins, received cleansing, and committed himself to the will of God.

The book of Malachi is particularly concerned with worship. The prophet was burdened about the deterioration of worship. Their polluted bread, diseased animal sacrifices, and unrighteous attitudes had perverted God's covenant and profaned God's altar. Malachi called for repentance and dedication to the Lord. To those who turn from their wickedness and fear Jehovah's name, Jehovah promised healing and renewal of life (Mal. 4:2).

The psalms are rich in personal worship; however, *personal* does not necessarily mean individual or private, for many of the psalms were written to be used in public worship. The Psalter has always been the most used and best-loved book of the Old Testament. The psalms have been the foundation of Christian hymnody. The title of the book of Psalms in Hebrew is *Tehillim*, which means "cultic songs of praise."

Above many of the psalms appear headings or terms indicating the liturgical aim of the particular psalm, for example: Psalm 100, "For thanksgiving"; Psalm 88, "For penance" or "To humiliate" one's soul; Psalm 38, "For reminder" or "For a memorial sacrifice." "To the Chief Musician" appears above several with certain instructions as to how the music is to be offered in worship.

Many of the psalms are "songs of ascent" that pilgrims sang on their way up to the temple of worship located on Mount Zion. "I lift up my eyes to the hills. From whence does my help come? My help comes from the LORD, who made heaven and earth" (Ps. 121:1–2). "I was glad when they said to me, 'Let us go to the house of the LORD!'" (122:1). Another song acknowledged dependence upon the Lord: "Unless the LORD builds the house, those who build it labor in vain" (127:1). Still another gives assurance of

God's blessings upon those who worship him: "Blessed is every one who fears the LORD, who walks in his ways!" (128:1).

Samuel Terrien observes that the Hebrew psalms establish the core of personal prayer and corporate worship for all forms of Judaism—Orthodox, Conservative, Reform—and for all churches of Christendom—Orthodox, Roman Catholic, Protestant.[6] They were the liturgical food of the inner life of Jesus and provided support for Paul and Silas in prison (Acts 16:25). The Christians in the catacombs, the preachers of the Reformation—John Hus, Martin Luther, John Calvin—the Huguenots, the Puritans, and contemporary Christians all give a central place to the Psalms in their worship.

Terrien says the secret of the vitality of the Psalms may be explained by the following facts: (1) the sense of worship that animated their poets; (2) the poets' boldness and honesty in prayer; (3) their theological certainty concerning God's ultimate victory; (4) their sense of historical and social responsibility; and (5) their elegant literary and aesthetic form.[7] The poetry of the Psalms as the vehicle of spiritual intuition and devotion is related to the entire history of our worship.

WORSHIP IN THE NEW TESTAMENT

According to the New Testament story, Christian worship is rooted in Jewish practices. The earliest Christians were Jews who had been faithful in their worship at the temple and in their synagogues. Jesus himself followed the practices of his people in worship. To some extent, the first Christians followed Hebrew worship as they were accustomed to in the temple and in the synagogue.

From the beginning Christian worship used Jewish ideas and images. The early Christians sensed no incongruity in using Jewish liturgical forms. The raw material of Christian worship was a common religious inheritance—the practice, teaching, and symbolism of the temple and synagogue, together with the special practices and teachings of Jesus. Although Christian worship is distinctive, there is no radical discontinuity between Old Testament worship and New Testament worship.[8]

It is generally conceded that there are three merging types of worship in the New Testament: worship in the temple, worship in the synagogue, and Christian worship in the homes and other places where Christians met.[9]

---

6. Samuel L. Terrien, *The Psalms and Their Meaning for Today* (New York: Bobbs-Merrill, 1952), vii.
7. Ibid., xi–xiv.
8. See Massey H. Shepherd, Jr., *Worship in Scripture and Tradition* (New York: Oxford University Press, 1963), 32.
9. See Ilion T. Jones, *A Historical Approach to Evangelical Worship* (Nashville: Abingdon Press, 1954), 61.

THE TEMPLE—TRADITIONAL PLACE OF WORSHIP

There are numerous associations of New Testament activity in the temple: (1) Zechariah had a vision that assured him he would not die childless (Luke 1:11ff.). (2) On his presentation in the temple by Mary, the infant Jesus was greeted by Simeon and Anna (Luke 2:25ff.). (3) In his twelfth year Jesus was found talking with the temple rabbis (Luke 2:46ff.). (4) Jesus cleansed the temple of the dealers who profaned his Father's house of prayer (Mark 11:15–17; John 2:13ff.). (5) Jesus was observed at various feasts in the Temple (John 5; 7; 8; 10:22ff.). (6) Jesus spent most of the last week of his life in the temple (Matt. 21:12–16; Mark 12:41ff.; Luke 21:5). (7) At the temple Jesus announced that not one stone would be left upon another.[10]

Luke observes that the Christians were continually in the temple blessing God (Luke 24:53). (1) After Pentecost they were found in the temple day by day continuing steadfastly in prayer (Acts 2:46). (2) The apostles continued to teach daily in the temple (Acts 4:1ff.). (3) Although Paul attended the temple for ceremonial purposes (Acts 21:26), he proclaimed that "the Most High does not dwell in houses made with hands" (Acts 7:48; 17:24). (4) Jesus himself had predicted, "The hour is coming when neither on this mountain nor in Jerusalem will you worship the Father" (John 4:21). (5) The Christians no longer needed the temple in Jerusalem, for Christ himself had become their temple, their place for meeting God in worship. Paul saw the church as a "holy temple" of the Lord (Eph. 2:14, 21).

THE SYNAGOGUE—WORSHIP IN TRANSITION

The fall of Jerusalem and the destruction of Solomon's temple, the long period in exile away from the central place of worship, the decline of the prophetic ministry, and the accelerated emphasis on the Scriptures gave rise to new modes of worship. New centers of worship known as *synagogues* began to arise. Although no mention of synagogues appears in the Old Testament, they were probably established by the third century B.C.[11]

Since the temple with its majestic architecture and elaborate symbolism was destroyed in A.D. 70, its influence did not strongly prevail in the development of Christian worship. The synagogue, with its plain building and simple services, had greater influence on Christian practices. The Greek word for *synagogue* meant a "gathering-place" (Luke 7:5).

The synagogues were first established as institutions for teaching, but later they were used as places of worship for the Jews. Even in Jerusalem there were many synagogues, and in all parts of the Dispersion there were partic-

---

10. This prediction was fulfilled in the destruction of the temple by the Romans in A.D. 70.
11. *The Interpreter's Dictionary of the Bible*, 4:882.

ular synagogues for community worship (Acts 6:9). In Palestine, synagogues were scattered all over the country, the larger towns—including Nazareth (Matt. 13:54) and Capernaum (Matt. 12:9)—having one or more.

According to the Gospels, Jesus, following Jewish tradition, made use of the synagogues for teaching and worship (see Luke 4:16–21). Paul and other disciples were also accustomed to going to the synagogue for worship (Acts 14:1).

Worship in the synagogues differed from worship in the temple. The following differences have been pointed out: (1) synagogue worship was less formal; (2) the didactic or teaching element was foremost in the synagogue; (3) priestly functions were not as prominent; (4) the teacher was the central figure in the synagogue; and (5) lay participation was more prominent.

The chief elements of synagogue worship have been outlined as follows: (1) reading of the Scriptures and their interpretation; (2) recitation of the Jewish creed, the Shema (Deut. 6:4); (3) the use of the Psalms, the Ten Commandments, the Benediction, and the Amen; (4) the prayers; and (5) the Jewish Kedushah, or prayer of sanctification, which became in the Christian tradition the *trisagion* ("Holy, Holy, Holy").[12]

The practices of worship in the Old Testament have been summarized as follows: (1) Everything was prescribed, such as the prayers, the offerings, and the ceremonies. (2) Worship was built largely around a sacrificial system in which blood was a symbol representing life for the people. (3) The Hebrew year was given much prominence. (4) The priest played an important part in the system, for he dramatized the offering of sacrifices. (5) The place of worship was prominent in that it symbolized the presence of God. (6) There was a great deal of emphasis on the feasts, especially the Passover, Pentecost, Trumpets, Day of Atonement, and Tabernacles.

Obviously, the sacrificial system in Old Testament worship included many rituals which are not appropriate for Christian worship. There are, however, many abiding principles, as well as certain rituals and symbols, which are valid for Christian worship.

NEW TESTAMENT DISTINCTIVES

Although early Christian worship grew out of the Jewish practices of the temple and the synagogue, Christian worship had its own distinctions.

1. Christians used writings of their own leaders, such as the Epistles of Paul and the Gospel accounts of the life of Jesus, and perhaps verbal

---

12. W. O. E. Oesterley, *The Jewish Background of the Christian Liturgy* (Oxford: Clarendon Press, 1925), chap. 2.

recollections. These writings soon took precedence over the Law and the Prophets.

2. Although the Psalms were used to express praise in Christian worship, new hymns were added by Christian writers, such as those found in the Epistles of Paul. The classic passage on the humiliation of Christ seems to be an early hymn or a confession of faith (Phil. 2:5–11). Paul encourages the Christians to speak to one another "in psalms and hymns and spiritual songs, singing and making melody in your heart to the Lord" (Eph. 5:18–19, KJV).[13]

3. Baptism and Communion are distinctive additions to Christian worship. Beasley-Murray shows the distinction between Christian baptism and the earlier practices of baptism.[14] Oscar Cullmann believes the Lord's Supper was the "basis and goal of every gathering."[15] There are numerous references to Christians breaking bread together. The so-called love feasts seem to bear some relationship to the Lord's Supper. The prominence of the Lord's Supper in the early worship services cannot be known for certain, but we can be sure that it was a vital experience in Christian worship.[16]

4. There was a spirit of zeal in Christian worship produced by the consciousness that the Holy Spirit was present with these early Christians. Worship became primarily a celebration of the acts of God manifested in Jesus Christ. The Resurrection struck a triumphant note in the hope which the Lord himself had planted in their hearts. The spontaneous spirit of early Christian worship revealed an unbounded enthusiasm. The emphasis was upon the presence of the risen Christ. Paul expressed this in the words, "Now the Lord is that Spirit: and where the Spirit of the Lord is, there is liberty" (2 Cor. 3:17, KJV). From the first, there was a devotion to the living Christ that gave a deep sense of mystery, awe, and triumphant joy.

5. Christian worship was held at different times and places than Jewish worship. The Jewish sabbath as the day of worship was fulfilled and observed by Christ; however, the Lord's Day, the first day of the week, became the Christian day of worship in commemoration of the Resurrection. The Christian Sunday is not a continuation of the Jewish sab-

---

13. Kenneth G. Phifer, *A Protestant Case for Liturgical Renewal* (Philadelphia: Westminster Press, 1965), 23. See also Gerhard Delling, chap. 1.

14. George R. Beasley-Murray, *Baptism in the New Testament* (London: Macmillan, 1962), 27ff.

15. Oscar Cullman, *Early Christian Worship* (London: SCM Press, Ltd., 1953), 29ff.

16. See Joachim Jeremias, *The Eucharistic Words of Jesus*, trans. Norman Perrin (New York: Charles Scribner's Sons, 1966).

bath, yet it does symbolize the fulfillment of the promises which the sabbath foreshadowed.

Although the early Christians at first worshiped in the temple and in the synagogues, the place for meeting God was no longer limited to the central sanctuary. The living Christ was present wherever two or three gathered in his name (Matt. 18:20). The early Christians met in homes or "house-churches" and in other places at first. From about the third century onward, Christians began to build their own buildings for the services of worship.[17]

ELEMENTS OF NEW TESTAMENT WORSHIP

Although there is no prescribed order for worship in the New Testament, there is evidence of order and planning. As Paul warns against the excesses expressed in ecstatic utterances and speaking in tongues, he concludes with the exhortation concerning worship, "Let all things be done decently and in order" (1 Cor. 14:40, KJV). Traces of ritual are found in the New Testament, not only in the Lord's Prayer and the doxologies, but also in rhythmical passages in the apostolic writings.

No exact order can be found in the worship of New Testament times, but the following elements of worship are found throughout the New Testament:

1. Music had a central place in the Christians' expression of praise. They sang psalms and hymns and spiritual songs, making melody in their hearts unto the Lord (Eph. 5:18–20; Col. 3:16; 1 Cor. 14:15). Among the earliest Christian hymns were the *Magnificat* of Mary in Luke 1:46ff, the *Nunc Dimittis* of Simeon in Luke 2:29–32, and the *Benedictus* of Zechariah in Luke 1:68ff. These hymns were probably used in early Christian worship services. Other great hymns of the New Testament are found in Revelation 5:9, 12–13; 12:10–12; and 19:1–2, 6. These hyms are called *canticles*, which means biblical hyms other than those found in the book of Psalms.

2. The reading of the Scriptures was definitely an element in early Christian worship, for Jesus stood in the synagogue to read the Scriptures (Col. 4:16; 1 Thess. 5:27; 1 Tim. 4:13), and Paul's letters were written to be read in the churches. Doubtless Scripture reading came to be a part of regular instruction in worship. Selections from the Old

---

17. For further information, see Ralph P. Martin, *Worship in the Early Church*, rev. ed. (Grand Rapids: William B. Eerdmans, 1989).

Testament Scriptures continued as a part of Christian worship, especially passages from the Prophets and the Psalms.

3. There is abundant evidence of prayers in early Christian worship. Luke's narrative of the early church tells us they devoted themselves to teaching, to fellowship, to the breaking of bread, and to prayers (Acts 2:42). There were prayers of thanksgiving, petition, intercession, and benediction. Examples include Philippians 4:6; Colossians 2:7; 2 Timothy 2:1–2; and 2 Corinthians 13:14. One of the oldest liturgical prayers is the Aramaic *Maranatha*, "Come, Lord Jesus" (1 Cor. 16:22). The classic example of prayer is the Model Prayer given by Jesus to his disciples (Matt. 6:9–13).

4. The people's "amens" are seen in numerous places in the New Testament. *Amen* is a term used by the congregation to express approval of what the leader says (see 1 Cor. 14:16).

5. The sermon or exposition of the Scriptures was a part of early Christian worship. On the day of Pentecost, Simon Peter stood up and preached the gospel to the people (Acts 2:40). Paul exhorted Timothy to be faithful in preaching the Word (2 Tim. 4:1–4). The *kerygma*, or the acts of God in history revealed in Jesus Christ, was preached wherever Christians went.[18]

6. Exhortation was essential in worship. The writer of Hebrews felt that it was important for Christians to "provoke (one another) unto love and to good works" (Heb. 10:24, KJV; see also 3:13). Paul urged his fellow Christians to exhort one another and to reprove one another with authority in the Lord (1 Thess. 3:2; 2 Thess. 3:12; Titus 2:15).

7. Christians gave offerings in public worship. Paul exhorted the Christians at Corinth to share their material goods with their less fortunate brethren in Jerusalem (1 Cor. 16:2; 2 Cor. 9:6–7, 10–13). He implied that giving is motivated by worship of the Lord Jesus Christ who, though he was rich, became poor so that by his poverty believers might become rich (2 Cor. 8:1–8). Jesus commended the poor widow for presenting her offering in sincere worship, for out of her deep poverty she gave all she had (Mark 12:42).

8. New Testament worship is filled with doxologies. Throughout his writings Paul breaks forth with doxologies unto God. For example, Paul rejoices, "Blessed be the God and Father of our Lord Jesus Christ,

18. See C. H. Dodd, *The Apostolic Preaching* (New York: Harper & Bros., 1936).

who has blessed us in Christ with every spiritual blessing in the heavenly places" (Eph. 1:3).

9. Open confessions seem to have been a practice of Christians in the early church. There was the public confession of sin in the presence of witnesses (1 Tim. 6:12). Paul says that confession of faith in Jesus Christ with the lips is a part of the process of salvation (Rom. 10:9). James urged his fellow Christians to confess their sins one to another and to pray for one another (James 5:16).

10. Christian worship included the ordinances of baptism and the Lord's Supper. Jesus commanded his followers to practice the observance of baptism and the Lord's Supper. Baptism followed belief in Jesus Christ as Savior and Lord; it was an act of confession that Christ is Lord (Matt. 28:18–20; Acts 2:38–41; Gal. 3:27). The Lord's Supper had an important place in early Christian worship. At the institution of the Supper, Jesus commanded his disciples to practice the observance of the Supper in remembrance of him (Matt. 26:26–28). In his treatment of worship, Paul deals at length with the observance of the Lord's Supper (1 Cor. 11:20–34).[19]

Neither Jesus nor Paul proposed a particular order for worship. However, both of them implied that there is a logical order for public worship. The model prayer includes a logical sequence of attitudes in worship, and Paul insists upon orderliness and thoughtful discipline in the worship service (1 Cor. 14:40).

---

19. For further study see A. J. B. Higgins, *The Lord's Supper in the New Testament* (London: SCM Press, 1960), 70ff.

CHAPTER 3

HISTORICAL BACKGROUNDS

WORSHIP IN THE EARLY CHURCHES

*F*ew literary sources of information exist concerning the development of Christian worship in the early centuries.[1] There are few strictly liturgical manuals or texts. Clement's personal letter to the church of Corinth, written about A.D. 96, contains exhortations concerning various elements in worship services but no specific instruction concerning the worship service. Clement encourages the people to read and revere the Word of God, to repent and confess their sins, to show humility before God's majesty, to acknowledge the Holy Spirit in their presence, to acknowledge their salvation in Jesus the High Priest, to proclaim faithfully the Word of God, and to present offerings for the support of those who serve among them. The letter concludes with a prayer which would be fitting for a worship service.[2]

---

1. For a more detailed study of the history of worship see Dom Gregory Dix, *The Shape of the Liturgy* (London: A & C Black, 1945); W. Maxwell, *An Outline of Christian Worship* (New York: Oxford University Press, 1936); James F. White, *A Brief History of Christian Worship* (Nashville: Abingdon Press, 1993); James F. White, *Introduction to Christian Worship* (Nashville: Abingdon Press, 1990); and Ralph P. Martin, *Worship in the Early Church*, rev. ed. (Grand Rapids: Eerdmans, 1989).

2. See *Library of Christian Classics, Early Christian Fathers*, ed. Cyril C. Richardson (Philadelphia: Westminster Press, 1953), 1:43ff.

Pliny, Roman governor of Pontus and Bithynia, wrote to the Emperor Trajan (about A.D. 112) requesting a clear policy on how to deal with the problems Christians were creating within his province. He describes the worship of the Christians on Sunday, mentioning two rites. First, they meet "before daybreak" when a hymn is sung to Christ as God and the Christians bind themselves by a "sacramentum" to abstain from evil. They meet later to eat food described as "common and harmless"; this is the second rite.[3]

Part of a paragraph from Pliny's letter reads as follows:

> They were in the habit of meeting before dawn on a stated day and singing alternately a hymn to Christ as to a god, and they bound themselves by an oath, not to the commission of any wicked deed, but that they would abstain from theft and robbery and adultery, that they would not break their word, and that they would not withhold a deposit when reclaimed. This done, it was their practice, so they said, to separate and then to meet again together for a meal.

The *Didaché* was probably written between A.D. 120 and 150 and purported to be "The Teaching of the Twelve Apostles." A copy was discovered in 1873 at Constantinople.[4] This manual, the first of the church orders claiming apostolic authorship, was divided into two parts: (1) a code of Christian morals, and (2) a manual of church order. It gives instruction on baptism as follows: "Baptize in running water in the name of the Father, and of the Son, and of the Holy Spirit. If you do not have running water, baptize in some other. If you cannot in cold, then in warm. If you have neither, then pour water on the head three times in the name of the Father, and of the Son, and of the Holy Spirit." Moreover, it instructs the one who baptizes and the one being baptized to fast one or two days beforehand. It instructs believers to pray three times a day the Model Prayer that Jesus gave to his disciples.

The *Didaché* gives instructions concerning the observance of the Lord's Supper as follows:

Now about the Eucharist: This is how to give thanks:

1. First in connection with the cup:

   "We thank you, our Father, for the holy vine of David, your child, which you have revealed through Jesus, your child. To you be glory forever."

2. Then in connection with the piece (broken off the loaf): "We thank you, our Father, for the life and knowledge which you have revealed through Jesus, your child. To you be glory forever. As this piece (of bread) was scattered over the hills and then was brought together and made one, so let your church be brought together from the ends of the

---

3. Maxwell, *Outline*, 8.
4. See *Early Christian Fathers*, 1:161.

earth into your Kingdom. For yours is the glory and the power through Jesus Christ forever."

3. You must not let anyone eat or drink of your Eucharist except those baptized in the Lord's name. For in reference to this the Lord said, "Do not give what is sacred to dogs."

4. After you have finished your meal, say grace in this way: "We thank you, holy Father, for your sacred name which you have lodged in our hearts, and for the knowledge and faith and immortality which you have revealed through Jesus, your child. To you be glory forever.

"Almighty Master, 'you have created everything' for the sake of your name, and have given men food and drink to enjoy that they may thank you. But to us you have given spiritual food and drink and eternal life through Jesus, your child.

"Above all, we thank you that you are mighty. To you be glory forever.

"Remember, Lord, your Church, to save it from all evil and to make it perfect by your love. Make it holy, 'and gather' it 'together from the four winds' into your Kingdom which you have made ready for it. For yours is the power and the glory forever."

"Let Grace come and let this world pass away."

"Hosanna to the God of David."

"If anyone is holy, let him come. If not, let him repent."

"Our Lord, come!"

"Amen."

In the case of prophets, however, you should let them give thanks in their own way.[5]

The first broad outline of worship is given in Justin Martyr's Apology written about A.D. 140. A. H. Newman calls Justin's outline of worship "one of the most detailed and life-like views of the ordinances and worship of the early Christians that we have."[6] The following is Justin's description of Christian worship:

1. The Reading of the Scripture—On the day which is called Sunday we have a common assembly of all who live in the cities or in the outlying

---

5. Ibid., 175–76.
6. A. H. Newman, *A Manual of Church History* (Valley Forge, Pa.: Judson Press, c. 1931).

districts, and the memoirs of the Apostles or the writings of the Prophets are read, as long as there is time.

2. The Address of the President—Then, when the reader has finished, the president of the assembly verbally admonishes and invites all to imitate such examples of virtue.

3. The Prayer—Then we all stand up together and offer up our prayers, and, as we said before, after we finish our prayers, bread and wine and water are presented.

4. Thanksgiving and Amen of the people—He who presides likewise offers up prayers and thanksgivings, to the best of his ability, and the people express their approval by saying "Amen."

5. Distribution of the bread and the wine—The Eucharistic elements are distributed and consumed by those present, and to those who are absent they are sent through the deacons.

6. Collection for the Poor—The wealthy, if they wish, contribute whatever they desire, and the collection is placed in the custody of the president. (With it) he helps the orphans and widows, those who are needy because of sickness or any other reason, and the captives and strangers in our midst; in short, he takes care of all those in need.[7]

Justin states, "Sunday, indeed, is the day on which we all hold our common assembly because it is the first day on which God, transforming the darkness and matter, created the world."

In the early centuries there must have been considerable latitude, since the choice of psalms and hymns would vary and the earliest prayers were probably extemporary.

WORSHIP DURING THE MEDIEVAL PERIOD

The progression toward ritualism with an established liturgy was soon begun in the early Christian churches. In the third and fourth centuries the various forms of primitive Christianity evolved into the beginning of a formal system, which was later thoroughly developed by the Roman Catholic Church.

The emphasis upon outward form and ceremony was due to the theological system of sacramentalism and sacerdotalism. Medieval worship reverted to the priestly system of the Old Testament, with certain customs of the mystery and pagan religions added.

---

7. Justin Martyr, *The First Apology*, trans. Thomas B. Falls (New York: Christian Heritage, Inc., 1948), 107.

From the fifth century until the Reformation, emphasis was placed upon buildings designed to fit set forms of worship performed at certain times. Hence, the Mass, a certain way of celebrating the Lord's Supper was developed. The service included numerous Scripture readings, many prayers with versicles and responses, occasional hymns, and the commemoration of the saints. Several books were used to conduct the service: the psalter, the antiphonal, the hymnal, the Bible, the collect book, the processional; and for direction, the *Consuetudinary*, the *Ordinal*, and the *Directorium*.

By the sixth century different Christian centers had developed their own liturgies. The main divisions were the Eastern and the Western. In the East were three major types of rites, known as the Alexandrian, the Syrian, and the Byzantine. The Byzantine liturgy became the adopted liturgy of the Orthodox Church in the East. In the West the primary classifications were the Gallican and the Roman liturgies.

During the early part of this period, Roman Catholic worship began to dominate the West. Baker delineates this development as follows: (1) Worship was centered in the observance of the Mass (the Lord's Supper), which was viewed as the "unbloody sacrifice" of Christ again. The symbolism was literal. The wine was not yet withheld from the people. The Supper was considered to be a sacrament. (2) An extensive system of mediating saints had developed. (3) The worship of the virgin Mary had also become more widespread. (4) Relics became an important part of the religious life. (5) The number of sacraments was increasing, although it was not yet fixed. Some contended for simply two, some for five, and others for more. (6) Auricular confession was already fairly well established. (7) The idea of merit from the sacraments and from external works was widespread.[8]

The Roman liturgy will serve as an example of the fixed order of worship which had developed by the Middle Ages. Sometime between the period of New Testament worship and A.D. 500 the order of worship had been divided into two parts, *The Liturgy of the Word* and *The Liturgy of the Upper Room*. All members of the congregation were invited to the Liturgy of the Word, but only the initiated or baptized Christians were invited to remain for the Liturgy of the Upper Room. All unbaptized persons were dismissed before this second part, which has been called "the liturgy of the faithful." According to Maxwell, the Roman Mass was the simplest of all rites. It was comparatively brief, austere, and rigid in the economy of words, structure, and ceremony.[9] A brief outline of this rite follows:

---

8. Robert A. Baker, *A Summary of Christian History*, rev. John M. Landers (Nashville: Broadman & Holman, 1994), 96.

9. Maxwell, *Outline*, 56ff.

Liturgy of the Word

Introit by two choirs as clergy enter

Kyries

Celebrant's salutation

Collect(s)

Prophecy or Old Testament lection

Antiphonal chant

Epistle

Gradual (Psalm sung originally by one voice)

Alleluia

Gospel, with lights, incense, responses

Dismissal of those not communicating (Greg. Dialog. I.ii.23)

Liturgy of the Upper Room

Offertory: Collection of elements, spreading of corporal on altar, preparation of elements for communion, offering of gifts, admixture, psalm sung meanwhile

Salutation and *Sursum corda*

Prayer of Consecration

Preface

Proper Preface

Sanctus

Canon

Kiss of Peace

Fraction

Lord's Prayer with protocol and embolism

Communion, celebrant first, then people (Psalm sung meanwhile)

Post-communion collect (Thanksgiving)

Dismissal by deacon

Maxwell describes details of the ceremony and indicates that there were many superstitious ideas connected with the Mass by the time of the Reformation.[10] There were several ways of celebrating the Mass. (1) The Pontifical High Mass was a sung Mass in which the celebrant had a bishop assisted by one or more priests. (2) The High Mass was a sung Mass celebrated by a priest assisted by deacons. The High Mass (*Missa Solemnis*) required a well-trained choir to sing choral parts. (3) The Low Mass was the popular Mass celebrated by a priest with neither choir nor assistant ministers. By the sixteenth century the Low Mass had become the popular service. (4) The *Missa Sicca* or Dry Mass was a low Mass said without consecration of the elements and without communion. Numerous Masses were said during the Middle Ages—for the dead in Purgatory, for safety on a journey, for recovery from sickness, for the capture of thieves, for the release of captives, for rain, and for fair weather. Maxwell says these "private masses became a cancer feeding upon the soul of the Church."[11]

By the sixteenth century the Roman Mass had attained uniformity. The doctrine of transubstantiation was complete, and the observance of the Lord's Supper was mixed with superstition. The people were urged to participate only once a year, at Easter. The worship service was conducted in Latin, which was unknown to the people. Passages from the lives and legends of the saints were substituted for Scripture passages. The Scriptures were not available in the vernacular. The practice of paid masses and indulgences became a source of exploitation. Reformation became an urgent necessity in the Church.

Certain defects are obvious in the Roman rite: (1) emphasis on the sacrificial character of the Mass led to all kinds of abuses; (2) members of the congregation became mere spectators rather than participants in the service; (3) the Mass became a patchwork of prayers taken from different sources which did not fit together and which were not intelligible; (4) there was an absence of prayer for the Holy Spirit to dedicate the worshipers and the elements; (5) the Mass became static because it was offered in a dead language. This encouraged superstition among uneducated people. Davies concludes that "because Roman worship is offered in a strange tongue, it lacks one of the essential marks of true worship: edification—the building up of the faith of the worshippers."[12]

The development of the liturgy during the Middle Ages has been described as the struggle of religion with art. The spiritual became subordinate to the artistic. There was an emphasis upon the visible church as the seat of

10. See appendix A for a copy of the Mass.
11. Maxwell, *Outline*, 68.
12. Horton Davies, *Christian Worship: Its History and Meaning* (New York: Abingdon Press, 1957), 39–40.

authority, upon buildings, set times for worship, set forms, and a certain way of celebrating the Mass. Artistic forms appealing to the five senses included vestments, bells, symbolic actions, frequent changes of posture, processions, prayers for the dead, and incense.

REFORMATION WORSHIP

During the medieval period the practice of worship became too objective, centering in symbols (verbal or otherwise) which became ends in themselves. This worship ceased to meet the deep needs of the people, and a restless spirit and a desire for reformation developed within the church.

Long before the sixteenth-century Reformation, there was wide dissent throughout Europe. The Reformation developed rapidly because, among other factors, Evangelical parties in Germany, Austria, Italy, and Bohemia had been in correspondence for three centuries.[13]

There was a growing desire for genuine religion among many people. Through the lives of outstanding Christian pietists and mystics, this desire was expressed in some of the monastic orders. Among the reformers who made outstanding contributions in the revision of worship were Luther, Zwingli, Calvin, and certain leaders in the Puritan and dissenting churches.

During the Reformation, worship took three main forms. The most conservative reform efforts were the Lutheran and Anglican. The second was more moderate and produced the Presbyterian or Reformed patterns. The third and most radical form came in the independent churches of the Puritan tradition, such as the Anabaptists and Quakers. These are the forebearers of the patterns of worship among Baptists, Congregationalists, and other Free Church groups.

The Lutheran service was considerably reduced when compared to the Roman Catholic liturgy. Luther did not intend to break with the Roman Catholic Church but meant only to reform it; therefore, he retained much of the structure of the liturgy. According to Maxwell, the following characteristics describe Lutheran worship:[14]

(1) Christians fellowshiped in and with the living Word. (2) The Lord's Supper was the central service. Luther believed the Lord's Supper ought to be celebrated daily throughout Christendom. (3) Luther believed in the real presence of Christ in the elements. This doctrine has been called the theory of consubstantiation. (4) The Mass is not a repetition of the death of Christ as the Catholics claim, but Christians enter into his sacrifice, offering themselves up together with Christ. (5) Luther urged a Mass conducted in the vernacular, first celebrated without the vestment at Wittenberg in 1521.

---

13. Baker, *Summary*, 185.
14. Maxwell, *Outline*, 72ff.

(6) Lutherans soon reverted to the old practice of the Roman Church, retaining the Latin, most of the ceremonial lights, incense, and vestments.

Luther gave the congregation a more intelligible role in worship, and there was greater use of hymns.[15] Liturgical uniformity was never a Lutheran ideal, for there were many variations and much creativity as seen in the Swedish, the Norwegian, and the American rites. Luther believed that all practices in the church should be patterned after the Scriptures. He proposed that whatever is not forbidden by the Scriptures is allowed if, in the judgment of the church, the practice is thought helpful.

Huldrych Zwingli exerted strong influence in the reformation of worship. His approach to religion was more rational than Luther's, and he sought more simplicity and more moral reality in worship. Zwingli's revision of the Mass was more radical. Unlike Luther, he did not consider the Mass the norm of worship. Zwingli believed that four times a year was sufficient for the celebration of the Lord's Supper. Moreover, he believed that the Lord's Supper should be stripped to its barest essentials. Zwingli rejected both the Roman Catholic doctrine of transubstantiation and Luther's doctrine of consubstantiation in favor of the memorial aspect of the Supper. He also rejected practically all symbols in worship, except those verbal symbols represented in the reading of the Word and in preaching; and he abolished all music from public worship, substituting instead antiphonal recitation of the psalms and canticles.

According to Thomas M. Lindsay, Zwingli broke free from the doctrines and practices of the medieval church, and his scheme of theology was wider and fuller than Luther's. Zwingli's position on indulgences and his manner of protesting against them was more radical than Luther's; yet even Zwingli did not see the underlying reason for indulgences as a cry for pardon of sins.[16]

John Calvin made the greatest contribution to the theology of the Reformation; therefore, he wielded the greatest influence in the formulation of non-Roman Catholic liturgies for generations to follow. Calvin was bolder than Luther in changing the liturgy, but he was less radical than Zwingli. Calvin did not think he was expounding a new theology or creating a new church. The theology of the Reformation, according to Calvin, was the doctrinal beliefs of the early Christians, founded on the Word of God and held by pious people.[17]

---

15. Luther was a hymn writer himself and his greatest hymn, "A Mighty Fortress Is Our God," is often credited as helping to spread the Reformation.

16. Thomas M. Lindsay, *A History of the Reformation*, vol. 2. (New York: Charles Scribner's Sons, 1916), 16.

17. Ibid., 100.

In Geneva in 1537, Calvin prepared a first draft of the reforms he wished to introduce. The first two of the four objectives are related to worship: (1) the holy Supper of our Lord, (2) singing in public worship, (3) the religious instruction of children, and (4) marriage. Calvin believed the Lord's Supper ought to be celebrated every Lord's Day in the apostolic church tradition and be well attended; however, rather than introduce radical change, Calvin suggested that the Supper be celebrated once each month.

Calvin took a mediating position between Luther and Zwingli concerning the theology of the Lord's Supper. He was unwilling to go as far as Zwingli in considering the Supper a mere memorial or symbol, but he did not agree with Luther that the real presence of Christ was in the bread and wine. He did believe in the spiritual presence of Christ, but related it to the receptivity of the believer.

Calvin felt that congregational singing of psalms ought to be a part of the public worship of the church. Since the people were not trained for congregational singing, Calvin suggested that children be selected and taught to sing in a clear voice. If the people would listen attentively, they might gradually learn to sing together as a congregation. Calvin was responsible for having the Psalms versified and he secured composers who wrote suitable tunes for them. His hymnbook, the *Genevan Psalter*, strongly influenced the development of congregational song.

In the development of the liturgy at Geneva, Calvin was influenced by other leaders in the Reformation. According to Ilion T. Jones, some of the most significant work pertaining to the reformation of the liturgy took place at Strasbourg. Actually, Calvin's liturgy was a modified form of the Strasbourg Rite.[18]

Calvin was greatly indebted to Martin Bucer of Strasbourg. Bucer rejected the title "Mass," preferring to call it the "Lord's Supper." He introduced the terms "minister" for "priest," and "table" for "altar." Special days for saints were abolished, and the vestments used in worship were discarded in favor of a black gown with cassock. Bucer insisted upon liberty in the formulation of the liturgy, and he believed in the inspiration of the Holy Spirit among those who worship and felt that everyone may worship and praise without restraint.

Calvin's *Genevan Service Book* has served as a model for most of the Reformed churches through the centuries; therefore, it seems appropriate to include the outline of worship used by Calvin in Geneva.

The Liturgy of the Word

Scripture Sentence: Psalm 124:8

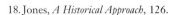

18. Jones, *A Historical Approach*, 126.

Confession of sins

Prayer for pardon

Metrical Psalm

Collect for Illumination

Lection

Sermon

The Liturgy of the Upper Room

Collection of alms

Intercessions

Lord's Prayer in long paraphrase

Preparation of elements while Apostle's Creed sung

Words of Institution

Exhortation

Consecration prayer

Fraction

Delivery

Communion, while psalm or Scriptures read

Post-communion collect

Aaronic Blessing.[19]

Calvin's rite became the norm of worship in Calvinist France, Switzerland, South Germany, Holland, Denmark, and elsewhere. Calvin's influence extended to Scotland, as seen in John Knox's *Book of Common Prayer* and in the "Directory of Public Worship" of the Presbyterian church of England. Calvin's order of worship has continued to influence the Reformed churches, including the Presbyterian churches in America.

John T. McNeill observed that these reformers insisted on simplicity in worship on the grounds that the "accumulation of rites in the church takes away Christian Liberty and substitutes ceremonies for faith."[20] The order of

19. Maxwell, *Outline*, 114–15.

20. John T. McNeill, *The History and Character of Calvinism* (New York: Oxford University Press, 1957), 89.

worship adopted in the different churches of the Reformation was in accord with their respective ideas of doctrine.

Calvin wanted to move further from the Roman liturgy than Luther. Calvin declared that whatever is not taught in the Scriptures is not allowable in worship, whereas Luther said that whatever is not forbidden in the Scriptures is acceptable. Calvin's principle called for the rejection of much ceremonialism of the medieval orders of worship; however, Calvin retained dignity and order and insisted upon a structured pattern of worship and a unity which was lacking in the extremes of Zwingli's pattern of worship. Calvin was not guilty of "barrenness and ugliness" in his liturgy.[21] Simplicity was Calvin's aim, for he abhorred unnecessary ornamentation. Calvin did not lack an appreciation for order and beauty, although later generations who claimed to be Calvinists were guilty of these extremes.

During the Reformation, a third group, known as the Radical Reformers, was more extreme in the reformation of worship. Some historians believe that twentieth-century Christianity reflects the theology and forms of worship of the radical groups more than any of the other reformers. Because of their efforts to restore the primitive New Testament order, these radical movements—uninhibited by the political and social commitments that limited Luther and Zwingli and Calvin—tossed aside many medieval practices in favor of an unstructured approach to Christianity.[22]

POST-REFORMATION WORSHIP

Since these Radical Reformers have influenced worship in the Free Churches for generations, it is appropriate that a brief study be made of their principles of worship. The nonconformist churches were loosed from all moorings of usage and ritual.

A religious awakening has always been accompanied by a revision of the liturgy. The Free Churches sought true worship by insisting on freedom from traditional rites and ceremonies. They were weary of the old, the habitual, the established—hungry for what was radically new and untried. The Radical Reformers discarded the fixed liturgies of the medieval church and insisted upon a simpler approach to worship emphasizing the spirit rather than the form.

The Christian groups known as the Radical Reformers were called by various names: Anabaptists, Puritans, Independents, Nonconformists, Separatists, and Dissenters. Prominent among these early reformers were the Anabaptists (literally, re-baptizers). Anabaptism, born January 21, 1527, in Grossmunster, Switzerland, was particularly strong between 1525 and

21. Phifer, Liturgical Renewal, 74.
22. Baker, Summary, 227.

1529.[23] The movement was based upon believer's baptism and the rejection of infant baptism. This earliest church of the Anabaptists was known as the Swiss Brethren. Their doctrinal conviction of the absolute necessity of personal commitment to Christ influenced the practice of Free Church worship.

Like other Free Church groups, the Anabaptists revolted against the Roman Catholic liturgies. In their worship, as well as in their living, they sought to return to primitive Christianity. Anabaptist worship followed several principles. (1) The preaching of the Word was central. (2) There was an emphasis upon congregational participation in the activities of worship. (3) The clergy and laity became practically indistinguishable, except for certain functions assigned by the church to the clergy. (4) There was an emphasis upon hymn singing by the congregation. The hymns which they sang were hymns of martyrdom telling the story of suffering at the hands of their persecutors.[24] For example, while George Blaurock was in prison in Switzerland, he wrote two hymns. The first sets forth the conditions of salvation, and the second is a hymn concerning Blaurock's personal faith in God.[25] (5) The Anabaptists adopted confessions of faith rather than creeds. The earliest of these was known as the *Schleitheim Confession*, written and adopted by the Swiss Brethren in February, 1527. It was composed of seven articles, two of which dealt with the way the ordinances were to be observed.[26] (6) Only two ordinances are to be observed by the church, namely baptism and the Lord's Supper. The Anabaptists rejected the sacraments of the Roman Church. Baptism was interpreted as a burial in water of those who had accepted Christ as Savior for themselves—this excluded infant baptism. All believers who had followed Christ in baptism were welcome to partake of the Lord's table, and some Anabaptists partook of the Lord's Supper as they sat about a round table in an attempt to return to the New Testament practice of the close fellowship of believers. (7) Latin was abolished, and the vernacular was introduced so that the common people understood the service.

Not all Free Church worship reforms were positive. Stephen F. Winward points out three problems: (1) There was the revival of clericalism as ministers continued to dominate the service of worship as had been done before

23. For an excellent treatment of the Anabaptists, see William R. Estep, *The Anabaptist Story* (Nashville: Broadman Press, 1963); Franklin H. Littell, *The Anabaptist View of the Church* (Boston: Star King Press, 1958); and George Huntston Williams, *The Radical Reformation* (Philadelphia: Westminster Press, 1962).

24. Martyr hymns are ballad-like, telling martyr stories in graphical detail. The longest hymn contains 445 lines; therefore, they have not remained in wide use. The Amish still sing from the *Ausbund*, the Anabaptist hymnal of approximately 1564.

25. Estep, op. cit. 34.

26. For a copy of this confession, see William L. Lumpkin, *Baptist Confessions of Faith* (Philadelphia: The Judson Press, 1959), 23ff.

the Reformation. Even to this day in many of the Free Churches, worship is dominated by the person in the pulpit, and the congregation is reduced to the role of listening. (2) They fell into the error of verbalism, which assumes that worship is almost entirely a matter of words and minimizes congregational participation. (3) Some churches failed to provide for vocal participation in public prayer. Worship should allow for the congregation to participate in prayers.[27]

Phifer observes a fourth weakness: Puritanism carried individualism and subjectivity to the extreme. The concept of the church at worship as a corporate unit was practically lost. The Puritan congregation was a collection of individuals at prayer; the service was more concerned with the individual than the corporate body. Because of the abuses of the medieval church, the reformers became suspicious of all objects appealing to the senses; therefore, there was a loss of symbolism in Puritan worship. Phifer says, "The rich liturgy of the Middle Ages was stripped away, and the simplicity of Christian worship revealed anew. However, the simplicity was prone to degenerate into barrenness."[28]

Among the Free Churches, Baptists have insisted upon certain guiding principles for worship. Perhaps more than others, Baptists have insisted on the centrality of the New Testament connection between baptism and personal faith as a symbolic act of surrender to God—on the realistic conversion of the whole life. Baptists have had a passion for spiritual liberty and have shown impatience with ecclesiastical control.

The history of Baptist worship is varied. Baptists owe a great debt to the reformers Luther, Zwingli, and Calvin, to the Puritans, to the Anabaptists, and to other Free Church leaders. Davies reminds us that in the whole range of Protestant worship—from the Quakers to the Anglicans, from the spontaneous to the formal, from the radical to the traditional—the worship of the Quakers and of the Baptists will be found furthest to the left in origin and development.[29] However, in the course of history the Baptists have been moving more to the center.

In England there were two streams in Baptist history, the General Baptists and the Particular Baptists. General Baptists practiced "general atonement," the doctrine that Christ died for all persons. They date to about 1609 in Amsterdam, Holland, under the leadership of John Smyth. The Particular or Calvinistic Baptists believed in limited atonement, that Christ died only for the elect. They date from 1638 when they were organized in London under the leadership of John Spillsbury.

27. Stephen F. Winward, *The Reformation of Our Worship* (Richmond: John Knox Press, 1965), 105.
28. Phifer, *Liturgical Renewal*, 83–86.
29. Horton Davies, *Worship and Theology in England: From Watts and Wesley to Maurice, 1690–1850* (Princeton, N.J.: Princeton University Press, 1961), 114.

The manner of worship in the General Baptist Church at Amsterdam was as follows:

> The order of the worship and government of our church is: (1) We begin with a prayer, (2) after read some one or two chapters of the Bible; (3) give the sense thereof and confer upon the same; (4) that done, we lay aside our books and after a solemn prayer made by the first speaker (5) he propoundeth some text out of the Scripture and prophesieth out of the same by the space of one hour or three quarters of an hour. (6) After him standeth up a second speaker and prophesieth out of the said text the like time and space, sometimes more, sometimes less. (7) After him, the third, the fourth, the fifth, etc., as the time will give leave. (8) Then the first speaker concludeth with prayer as he began with prayer, (9) with an exhortation to contribution to the poor, which (10) collection being made is also concluded with prayer. This morning exercise begins at eight of the clock and continueth unto twelve of the clock. The like course of exercise is observed in the afternoon from two of the clock unto five or six of the clock. Last of all the execution of the government of the Church is handled.[30]

It is surprising to find that these early Baptists rejected the singing of hymns by the congregation, since the Anabaptists had left a body of hymns. General Baptists decided that psalm singing was "so strangely foreign to the evangelical worship that it was not conceived any way safe to admit such carnal formalities."[31] A single voice might sing praise, but congregational singing was forbidden. Hymns were frowned upon even more as the singing of "men's compositions."

The Particular Baptists were closer to the Reformed tradition in worship. Many of them sang psalms and Scripture paraphrases but reluctantly sang compositions not directly from the Scriptures. For many years there was a controversy in Baptist churches over congregational singing.

The controversy began when Benjamin Keach, pastor of the Particular Baptist Church in Southwark, began, about 1673, to use hymns following the Lord's Supper. By 1691 hymn singing became a regular practice of the congregation. Most of the hymns were written by Keach. A small group of Keach's parishioners led by Isaac Marlow opposed this practice. Marlow and Keach engaged in a long and bitter controversy in which both issued series of pamphlets representing their views. Advocates of hymn singing eventually won, and by the year 1700 Particular Baptists accepted hymn singing as an established practice.[32]

Since then, the general pattern of Baptist worship in England has remained about the same to the present, consisting of Scripture reading,

30. See Ernest A. Payne, *The Fellowship of Believers: Baptist Thought and Practice Yesterday and Today* (London: The Carey Kingsgate Press, Ltd., 1952), 92.
31. Davies, *Worship and Theology in England*, 127.
32. William J. Reynolds and Milburn Price, *A Survey of Christian Hymnody* (Carol Stream, Ill.: Hope Publishing Co., 1987), 44.

prayers, and sermons, interspersed with hymns by the congregation and the choir. Payne mentions certain changes that have taken place: (1) the shortening of the sermons and prayers; (2) the occasional use of collects and set forms of prayer; (3) greater use of music by instruments (especially the organ) and choirs; (4) in some, the introduction of the children's sermon; and (5) a wider use of congregational singing, especially of hymns of original composition.[33]

Baptists were probably the first English Protestants to have a special collection of hymns for use at the Lord's Supper. In 1697 Joseph Stennett published "Hymns in Commemoration of the Sufferings of Our Blessed Saviour, Jesus Christ, Composed for the Celebration of the Holy Supper." Stennett was a Baptist minister with outstanding literary gifts and widely respected for his Christian character and learning.

Through Baptists the singing of English hymns of original composition became popular in America.

Worship in America

The influence of the radical reformers was carried by immigrants from England and Scotland to North America which accounts for the dislike, until recent times, of prepared forms of worship and ornate liturgy. However, certain Protestant communions were semiliturgical and continued to be bound by tradition. For example, in 1879 Charles Beard observed that in certain worship services, "The Apostle's Creed is recited without any recollection of the controversies which through six centuries have left their works upon clause after clause, and given them a meaning which present usage does little to suggest. The whole service belongs to the past; its newest word is three centuries old."[34]

The Frontier Period

Phifer describes the development of worship on the American frontier. The two denominations with a commanding position in American society were the Congregationalists and the Presbyterians, both Calvinistic in theology and Puritan in worship. In the American colonies, Congregationalists, Presbyterians, Baptists, and Methodists rejected any fixed order of worship. Freedom in worship was well-suited for early America, where people were enjoying their newly gained independence. The American frontier was characterized by individualism and revivalism; consequently, apart from the conversion of sinners, they did not take worship very seriously.

33. Payne, *Fellowship of Believers*, 96.
34. Charles Beard, "The Conditions of Common Worship in Free Churches," *Theological Review*, 16 (1879): 221.

Worship on the American frontier may be characterized by the following principles. (1) There were no set forms for worship. (2) The observance of the ordinances was infrequent because of the lack of ordained men to conduct them. (3) Frontier people were suspicious of educated ministers who to them represented an established church. (4) Preaching was the primary emphasis in worship services. (5) The prayers were spontaneous and were led by laypersons as well as ministers. (6) There was an informal enthusiasm on the part of the worshipers, often expressed in emotional ecstasy. (7) Worship services were characterized by exuberant singing. The songs were subjective and individualistic, yet buoyant and optimistic. (8) Frontier worship was characterized by a spirit of immediacy, and little attention was given to tradition. (9) Church buildings were plain and harsh and not intended to lend themselves to ritual.[35]

The early churches in America had no books of common worship to guide their ministers or to be used as prayer books by the worshipers. There were no fixed or standardized orders of service. The worship of the overwhelming majority of Christian churches in the United States was informal, spontaneous, and evangelistic.[36]

Roman Catholics, Lutherans, Anglicans, and Reformed and Puritan Protestants in their unique traditions felt the impoverishment of public worship from approximately 1650 to 1850. At least three factors affected the decline of worship in the Free Churches. First, there was an exaggerated hostility toward liturgical worship. Free Churches went to extremes to avoid any semblance of the formal worship of the liturgical churches. Second, the primitive circumstances of the American colonists and their cultural disabilities dulled their appreciation of the aesthetic aspects of worship. The low estate of musical culture and the shortage of hymnbooks added to this impoverishment. Third, the overemphasis upon revivalism caused a decline in attention to the basic elements of worship, especially among the Baptists and Disciples. This spirit of revivalism reduced all prayer and praise and reading of the Scriptures to "preliminary exercises" sacrificing other elements for the experienced or shared ecstasy of conversion.[37]

---

35. Phifer, *Liturgical Renewal*, 103.

36. For a more detailed description of worship in early American history, see William Warren Sweet, *Religion in the Development of American Culture, 1765–1840* (New York: Charles Scribner's Sons, 1952); also, Jerald C. Brauer, *Protestantism in America: A Narrative History* (Philadelphia: The Westminster Press, 1953).

37. James Hastings Nichols, "The Rediscovery of Puritan Worship," *The Christian Century* (April 25, 1951).

CHAPTER *4*

A Theology of Worship

*A*s we believe, so we worship. The doctrines we hold determine the nature of our worship. If we view God as only divine principle, we will seek to conform to the principle. If we view God as idea, we will seek to know God through intellectual understanding or reasoning. If we view God as a personal Being, we will seek to know God in personal relationship. If we conceive of God as Spirit, self-revealed in history, we will worship God in "spirit and truth."

Worship without theology is sentimental and weak; theology without worship is cold and dead. Worship and theology together combine to motivate a strong Christian faith and to empower a fruitful Christian life. Worship should be regulated and determined by doctrine.

Christian worship is first an experience, not an art. It is based upon a historical fact, the fact that God revealed himself in history. Evangelical worship is grounded in the great historical facts of God's creation, the Incarnation, the works of Jesus Christ, his atoning death, his Resurrection, and his abiding presence in the life of believers. The way we think about these historic facts is called theology. Worship that is not grounded in the knowledge and love of God is not true worship. Theology that does not lead to the worship of God in Christ is both false and harmful. A sound theology serves as a corrective to worship, and true worship serves as the dynamic of theology.

The basis of Christian worship is not utilitarian but theological.[1] Worship depends upon revelation, and Christian worship depends upon the revelation of God in Christ Jesus. Worship is therefore a revelation and a response which springs from the divine initiative in redemption. By faith we respond to grace as we find it in a face-to-face encounter with God.

Stauffer declared, "Theology is doxology or it is nothing at all."[2] We may further declare that unless worship is theologically sound, it becomes less than doxology. Worship and theology go together.

Actually, worship is the experience of conscious communion with God, and theology is the effort to describe the meaning of the experience. Worship is essential to religion. Creeds, however sound, can never be a substitute for worship. Those who seek refuge and safety in creeds soon lose the vitality which comes only from a living faith kept alive by worship.

GOD, WORTHY OF WORSHIP

No person is ever left alone without God. An individual may try to ignore God but peace cannot be found without God; he or she may deny or reject God but not without a consciousness of judgment. God claims every creature. Worship is the loving response of the creature to the Creator. There is no sovereign right but God's, no other totalitarian authority.

Christian worship is God-centered. God took the initiative in worship by creating humankind for fellowship with God. God is the source and sustainer of life. As sovereign ruler, God confronts humans. God comes to us as the one worthy of worship, and because he is worthy, God stands in judgment over us and makes demands upon us. As we respond in worship, he allows us to experience new manifestations of God's goodness and love.

A personal God. God is not an ideal or a philosophy of life or a metaphysical principle; God is a personal and spiritual Being who seeks personal relationships with individuals. Revelation is not acknowledged by a third-person proposition which says, "There is a God"; revelation is acknowledged in direct confession of the heart which says, "Thou art my God."[3] God is a personal presence continually pervading our lives. God comes to us not as sheer power, but as the living God seeking to commune with us. He is a thinking, purposing, and loving God, although God transcends all our understanding and experience.

1. Raymond Abba, *Principles of Christian Worship* (New York: Oxford University Press, 1957), 5.
2. Ethelbert Stauffer, *New Testament Theology*, trans. John Marsh (London: SCM Press, Ltd., 1955), 88.
3. H. Richard Niebuhr, *The Meaning of Revelation* (New York: The Macmillan Co., 1946), 153ff.

A transcendent God. When we worship, we do not worship an equal; we worship our Creator, the eternal, infinite God. God is the absolute source of being; the ultimate Being for which we seek. God's transcendence means that in his absoluteness, God is above us. "My thoughts are not your thoughts, neither are your ways my ways, says the LORD" (Isa. 55:8). God's holy character is a constant challenge to humankind's sinful condition. We stand in awe of the mystery of God's presence. In worship we experience a feeling of dependence upon God. When we experience the majesty of God, we respond with Isaiah, "Holy, holy, holy is the LORD of hosts; the whole earth is full of his glory" (Isa. 6:3).

Jonathan Edwards saw a qualitative difference between the rational joy of humankind and the experience of true worship: "The conceptions which the saints have of the loveliness of God and that kind of delight which they experience in it are quite peculiar and entirely different from anything which a natural man can possess or of which he can form any notion."[4] Efforts at worship without awe and adoration of God are empty and meaningless. To believe in God implies acknowledgment of God's infinite worth. The person who says in sincerity, "Thou art my God," will also have to say, "Worthy art thou, O Lord, to receive glory and honor and power."

An immanent God. God is constantly present in our lives. As giver of life, he is also the sustainer of life. In numerous ways God makes himself known to us. The most intimate and personal expression of God's revelation is his love in action. God continually offers abundant love and forgiveness; therefore, we are not left to speculate on the presence and purposes of God. God comes to us continually. To believe in God's absolute sovereignty is to believe in the sureness of God's love.

God's love is revealed to humankind through many God-ordained acts of revelation. His creative power, sustaining providence, special revelations to certain individuals who recorded God's words, and especially God's acts of sheer love in the Incarnation, the Cross, and the Resurrection all indicate the concern of a God who is eternally present with us. Paul said, "He is not far from each one of us, for 'In him we live and move and have our being'" (Acts 17:27–28). In true worship, we acknowledge total dependence on God's transcendent and immanent action.

Our knowledge of God is immediate, for we can stand in the presence of the living God. It is a "mediated immediacy" as God is revealed through his Word, through Jesus Christ, and through the Holy Spirit.[5]

A trustworthy God. The God who is worthy of worship is also trustworthy in response to our acts of worship. We are never disappointed when we lift

---

4. Quoted in William James, *The Varieties of Religious Experience* (New York: Modern Library, 1902) 229.

5. John Baillie, *Our Knowledge of God* (New York: Charles Scribner's Sons, 1959), 174.

our voices to God in praise or petition. The sovereign God is a God of purpose. By grace, God has elected persons to be saved. "Whom he did predestinate, them he also called: and whom he called, them he also justified: and whom he justified, them he also glorified. . . . If God be for us, who can be against us?" (Rom. 8:30–31, KJV). Belief in God's electing grace releases reserves of courage and energy.

People of faith will find God faithful and trustworthy when they approach God in worship. Because of God's faithfulness, nothing can separate us from the love of God in Christ. Of this Paul was firmly convinced (Rom. 8:37–39). We are confronted with God's invitation to intimate communion: "If any one hears my voice and opens the door, I will come in to him and eat with him, and he with me" (Rev. 3:20). Central in our religion is not our hold on God but God's hold on us, not our choosing God but God's choosing us, not that we should know God but that God should know us.

JESUS CHRIST, OBJECT OF FAITH

The church's worship is christologically based. Jesus' life is in some sense liturgical since his life was a "life of worship." In every act of worship the church experiences the fresh miracle of the coming of the risen Christ. In order to be redeemed by God, we must have an encounter with Jesus Christ. The worship of God is made possible in the person of God's Son. Christian worship is an experience of grace offered in Christ.[6] Jesus Christ is the object of our faith and of our worship. The primary distinction between Christianity and the other great religions of the world is found in the person of Jesus Christ. All true worship is Christocentric, for only in Christ can we find God.

Christ is the temple where God and persons meet. The divine presence which Israel once found in the tabernacle and in the temple, we now find in Christ. We encounter in the heart of history the glory and grace of God manifest in flesh. "And the Word became flesh and dwelt among us, full of grace and truth; we have beheld his glory, glory as of the only Son from the Father" (John 1:14). Worship may take place anywhere by a meeting with Christ.

Manifestation. "No one has ever seen God; the only Son, who is in the bosom of the Father, he has made him known" (John 1:18). A sound Christology is essential to a sound theology. The Incarnation, with all its mystery, is the only way in which the Christian conception of God becomes credible or even expressible.[7] All of Jesus' life, his teaching, his Cross, his Resurrection,

---

6. Jean-Jaques von Allmen, *Worship: Its Theology and Practice* (New York: Oxford University Press, 1965), 27.

7. Donald M. Baillie, *God Was in Christ* (New York: Charles Scribner's Sons, 1948), 65.

Ascension, and exaltation, is God's action in Jesus. In the worship experience Jesus comes to us as "God's own Word about himself."[8] Our vision of God comes through Jesus, "He that hath seen me hath seen the Father" (John 14:9, KJV).

Identification. In his humiliation Jesus identified with us in every area of our lives. To be reconciled to God in Christ is to be reconciled to life in all its concreteness. Jesus took the form of a servant, "being born in the likeness of men" (Phil. 2:7), to bring us into fellowship with God. We can worship a holy God because God came in lowly birth to our lowest condition. In Christ and in all the acts and manifestations of Christ, history and eternity meet. God has come to redeem us in history. That redemption is realized in worship. In worship we identify with Jesus Christ; we meet God through Christ.

Redemptive power. Atonement means that God came to meet our moral need in Christ. The New Testament does not speak of God's being reconciled to us, but of our being reconciled to God. God is the Reconciler taking the initiative in the Cross. "Therefore, if any one is in Christ, he is a new creation" (2 Cor. 5:17). In the Cross we see God's expressing concern in the act of suffering love. The Cross brings us to our knees with songs of adoration and praise in gratitude for God's matchless gift. The Cross is the only deed which releases a power sufficient to meet God at the depths of greatest need in worship, the need for forgiveness of sin.

Living lordship. Jesus Christ not only gave himself for the church in his death, but he also continues to give himself to his church in worship. Paul declared, "Therefore God has highly exalted him and bestowed on him the name which is above every name, that at the name of Jesus every knee should bow, in heaven and on earth and under the earth, and every tongue confess that Jesus Christ is Lord, to the glory of God the Father" (Phil. 2:9–11). The Resurrection is the eternal answer to the power of sin and death. In worship, the living Christ is present for every person. The earliest Christians acknowledged the presence and lordship of the risen Christ when they met for worship. Christian worship presupposes that people come together in the "name of Jesus." Worship as humankind's faith-event finds reality in the Christ-events—Incarnation, Cross, and Resurrection. The early Christians could proclaim their faith with the words "Christ is Lord."

HOLY SPIRIT, THE DYNAMIC OF WORSHIP

In worship, the Holy Spirit's presence and power are often neglected. All human aspiration and spiritual achievement are the work of the Holy Spirit.

---

8. Emil Brunner, *The Mediator: A Study of the Central Doctrine of the Christian Faith*, trans. Olive Wyon (Philadelphia: Westminster Press, 1947).

The Holy Spirit should be more prominent in sermons and hymns, and more attention should be given to the work of the Holy Spirit in worship.

God's personal presence. God appears to us as Holy Spirit. The Holy Spirit is personal. In worship, God is present in Spirit; the Holy Spirit is present as the manifestation of the Father and of the Son. Paul said, "You are in the Spirit, if the Spirit of God really dwells in you. Any one who does not have the Spirit of Christ does not belong to him" (Rom. 8:9). To ignore the Spirit is to ignore God. To quench the Spirit of God is to refuse the power of God in worship.

The transforming power. Salvation is made possible by the power of the Holy Spirit. The Holy Spirit comes to convince us of our guilt by making us aware of sin and righteousness and judgment (John 16:8). The Holy Spirit's work is to make Christ known and to make truth clear (John 16:14–15). The Spirit transforms us in God's work of grace. Jesus told Nicodemus, "Unless one is born of water and the Spirit, he cannot enter the kingdom of God. That which is born of the flesh is flesh, and that which is born of the Spirit is spirit" (John 3:5–6). Jesus again said, "It is the spirit that gives life" (John 6:63). God's saving acts can become personal to us only through the inward testimony of the Holy Spirit.

The Holy Spirit is the agency of moral transformation by which we are changed into the likeness of Christ from one degree of glory to another (2 Cor. 3:17–18). In the discovery of God through God's Spirit, the whole of our experience is gathered into the comprehensiveness of God's being and is given a new unity.[9] God's power coming into our lives brings a new quality of life which includes the transformation of our total being, including our rational, emotional, and volitional powers. Through the Spirit's power it is possible for us to live life in Christ (Gal. 2:20).

Life in the church. It is the Holy Spirit's function to inspire and guide the church in its worship and work. The Spirit created the church and continues to give life to the church. Without the Holy Spirit's power, the church cannot exist. The church cannot fulfill its mission without the Spirit's presence.

The Holy Spirit was central in the early church. After the Resurrection, the disciples were filled with inspiration, for the presence of the Spirit was felt everywhere. Jesus commanded his disciples to tarry until they were empowered by the Spirit (Acts 1:4–5). The disciples were not prepared for their work until they received the Spirit's power. The lordship of Christ could be understood and acknowledged only if the Spirit were present. The will of Christ could be accomplished only by the Spirit's living in the church and guiding it in all its worship and activity.

---

9. H. Wheeler Robinson, *The Christian Experience of the Holy Spirit* (London: Nisbet and Company, Ltd., 1952), 5.

Christian character is fortified by the work of the Spirit. All the virtues and fruits of the Christian life develop through the Spirit's living presence. Paul implied that the fruits of the Spirit—love, joy, peace, longsuffering, gentleness, goodness, faith, meekness, temperance—are possible only if we live and walk in the Spirit (Gal. 5:22–25). The fruits of the Spirit result when the Christian cooperates with the Holy Spirit in the discipline of life.

The early church was aware of God's presence in its worship through the manifestations of God's Spirit. They recognized that spiritual gifts were bestowed by the Spirit. By the Holy Spirit's power they sang and prayed and preached and prophesied and spoke in tongues (1 Cor. 12:8–11). All these diverse gifts were bestowed by the same Spirit (v. 4).

The Holy Spirit gives the church motivation for its ministry. The Holy Spirit inspires the singing, praying, teaching, preaching, and worship of the entire body (1 Cor. 14:36; Rom. 8:26–27; Acts 4:31; Eph. 5:18–20). Under the power of the Spirit, the early Christians had ecstatic experiences expressed by speaking in tongues. Paul did not oppose this phenomenon but insisted that it be guided by the principle of edification (1 Cor. 14:26). Inspiration in worship was bestowed for a higher purpose and not simply for the emotional experience. Paul urged that worship be carried out in an orderly manner (1 Cor. 14:40).

In worship God is known as Father, Son, and Holy Spirit. God the Father stresses the ultimacy and certainty of God's existence as expressed in creation. Jesus Christ defines the character of God expressed in Jesus' redemptive love. The Holy Spirit is the one who ultimately communicates God's presence to us in worship.

There may be a variety of forms in worship; however, the church is always dependent upon the Holy Spirit for the reality of its worship. The Spirit must release the desire for praise and prayer. The Holy Spirit must create in the minds of the congregation the consciousness of God. Genuine worship takes place only when God is worshiped for God's sake. This experience is made possible only by the creative work of the Holy Spirit in the hearts of individuals and in the entire body, the church.

THE BIBLE, THE ETERNAL WORD THROUGH WORDS

The Bible is the life book of the church. It provides objective content for worship. It points us to God, the source of truth and life. The worshiper waits for God to unfold the mystery of the Scriptures like a child who knows nothing and is waiting to be taught his ABC's. Scripture is dynamic, pointing to its center which is Jesus Christ. The Bible is a record of God's revelation of life-giving salvation to us.

Since the Bible is the church's source book of knowledge about its salvation, its guidebook for living, and the promise of its destiny, it must be kept central in the church's worship. The objective, intellectual content which guides worship is found in the Scriptures. As Emil Brunner has said, we turn backward to the Bible, but also forward to the living Word of God to which the Bible bears authoritative witness.[10] By the Holy Spirit we worship the living God, and the *living* Word witnesses to us by the *written* Word, the Bible.

The Bible is a necessary textbook in matters pertaining to the spiritual life—God's purpose for us, our relationship to God, and our relation to other persons. The Bible is concerned about life's ultimates—ultimate values, ultimate causes, ultimate objectives. The Bible is both trustworthy and authoritative for the worship of God.

The Bible should be acknowledged for what it claims to be, the message of God concerning humankind's redemption. The Bible claims to be a trustworthy guide in redemptive truth and in redemptive relationships. If we claim less for the Bible than it claims for itself, we deny God's power and purpose in our lives. If we claim more for the Bible than it claims for itself, we deny our faith in God and seek to build for ourselves a theological wooden house on the sands of bibliolatry, rather than a strong house on the rock of a dynamic faith in the Lord of the Bible.

A record of divine history. According to the Old Testament, Israel's history moves between promise and fulfillment. The New Testament testifies to the fulfillment of God's promises in history. A unity of purpose runs through the entire Bible.

The Bible is the story of God in history. The German word *Heilsgeschichte*, the "story of salvation," captures the story of a Savior, a saved people, and the means of salvation. History is seen as the process of divine revelation. All revelation is rooted in life. God was in history first, and all history has moved under God's sovereignty.

The Bible confirms that God has always sought creation. The Bible is a story of the acts of God—God's action in history. God's redemptive acts have value for the worshiper who reads the story in faith. Revelation is God revealing Himself, not merely imparting an idea. It is the opening of our nature to a new dimension of life, to life in God.

The Bible is the treasure in which God's Word is kept. The Word has been spoken, acted, lived, celebrated, and recorded. In worship, the written Word makes the living Word of God known to us. The Bible is a historic witness to God's continuous action in our lives.

A witness to Jesus Christ. Against the background of Old Testament history, the New Testament witnesses to the fulfillment of God's purpose in re-

---

10. Emil Brunner, *The Divine Imperative: A Study in Christian Ethics* (Philadelphia: Westminster Press, 1947), 565.

vealing himself through his Son. The writer of Hebrews says, "In many and various ways God spoke of old to our fathers by the prophets; but in these last days he has spoken to us by a Son, whom he appointed the heir of all things, through whom also he created the world" (1:1–2).

The Bible is a witness to the salvation that comes in Christ. God's redemptive purpose is seen in the incarnation, life, death, and resurrection of Jesus Christ. Through the Bible Christ can be known in history. The church's worship and ministry are based on what we know through the Bible. The Bible is a revelation concerning redemption that comes by actions rather than by words, by deeds rather than by doctrines. Goethe said, "The highest cannot be spoken; it can only be acted."

The Bible is more than a book of teachings; it is a witness to a life. It requires more than formal belief in its teachings; it requires union with Christ. The purpose of the Bible is to lead the soul to living contact with the Redeemer, and thus to an awakening of the whole nature—emotional, intellectual, volitional. To bow down to the mere letter of the Scriptures apart from vital faith would be a defeat of all for which the Bible stands.

The Scriptures do not speak in a vacuum but in relation to Jesus Christ. The pattern of authority in Christian worship is found in Christ, the living, personal Word of God; in the Holy Spirit, who conveys revelation and witness to its divinity; and in the sacred Scriptures, the document of revelation, the Spirit's instrument in effecting illumination.[11]

A record of human experience. The Bible is relevant in worship. It is a record of divine or revelation history; and a record of human experience in the worship of God. It is a story of humankind's response to the God who controls history. The historic Christ presented in the Bible is verified by the living Christ which is given in the experience of Christians. The Bible story presents persons in all the stark realism. As sinners, we stand in need of redemption. In our rebellion we defy God and attempt to carve out a life for ourselves without God. Made in the image of God, we can hear and respond to the voice of God. We have been created with the power to choose, and our redemption is dependent upon our decision to follow the call of God in Christ. The Bible appeals to every human condition, reminding us of the grace of God revealed in Jesus Christ.

The glory of the Bible is found in its portrayal of persons as they are and its offer of hope of what they may become in Christ. The Scriptures present the message of grace and what it can do for the person "in Christ."

The Word of the Spirit. The Bible has rightly been called the "Book of the Spirit." If Scripture is to be heard and received as the Word of life, there

---

11. See Bernard Ramm, *The Pattern of Religious Authority* (Grand Rapids: Wm. B. Eerdmans Publishing Co., 1959), 36–37.

must be inspiration not only in the Scriptures themselves but also in the reader and interpreter of the Scriptures. We understand the Scriptures when we are possessed by the same Spirit who possessed their writers.

Christian worship depends on the Bible for truth concerning redemption and Christian living. Personal piety is not possible without the testimony to truth provided by the Bible. The Bible as the living Word of God must revitalize and guide our hearing. We need to hear the fresh Word of God. We need the Bible as a discipline for our ideas about God. The text we read retains the power to speak more loudly than our distortions of it. When we read the Bible, we always risk that God may speak to correct our errors of judgment. The Scriptures, then, should determine the content of the church's worship. God's Spirit lives and works in the fellowship of Christians, including corporate worship as guided by the truth recorded in the Bible.

THE CHURCH, THE PEOPLE OF GOD

Our doctrine of the church will to a great extent determine the type of worship we follow. The hierarchical or institutional church tends to follow the liturgical pattern adopted by the "established church," whereas the congregational or "gathered church" tends to insist on freedom to plan its own patterns of worship. Christian worship must be understood in the context of the church.

The church as the people of God is as universal as the action of God. Our estrangement and loneliness can be overcome only when we participate in the worship of God and become aware that we belong to an eternal people. The church is formed in worship, and its vitality is sustained in proportion to the genuineness of its continuing worship. Christian worship occurs only as the people of God respond to God's claims upon them.

A local church is a part of the entire body of Christ, a living unit in the kingdom of God's redeemed people. Christ prayed that believers "may all be one" as the Father and the Son are one (John 17:21). If a true ecumenicism is ever realized, it must begin in an ecumenical spirit in worship based upon New Testament principles.[12] The church as a living fellowship precedes the church as a functioning institution. Paul included both ideas in his use of the term *ekklesia*.

A redemptive fellowship. The church is different from any other unit of society. It is more than a humanitarian institution concerned with human sentiment and service. It is a redeemed fellowship (*koinonia*) of persons created by the Holy Spirit and united under the lordship of Jesus Christ. As a re-

---

12. See William R. Estep, *Baptists and Christian Unity* (Nashville: Broadman Press, 1967).

deemed fellowship, the church must worship. Without worship it is not the church.

God's purpose for the church is redemptive. The church does not exist for its own sake, but for the kingdom of God. The church is a part of God's plan in holy history. As a redeemed fellowship, it is also a redeeming fellowship; it exists for witness. The church can fulfill its mission only as it is continually renewed in its relationship to God. Renewal can take place only in worship.

The fellowship of the church is inclusive. It embraces all strata of society. There is no place for snobbishness in the church of Christ. The rich and the poor, the cultured and the uncultured, the elite and the outcast—all are included in the fellowship of Jesus Christ. Persons of every station and condition may sit down together in the worship of God through Jesus Christ, who has broken down every wall of partition (Eph. 2:14).

Religious faith is social as well as individual and finds its full expression only in corporate worship. In the fellowship of the church's worship, the individual faith affirms itself and educates itself. Worship begins with the priesthood of each believer, but it comes to its full and richest realization in the collective priesthood of the church as one.

A living organism. The church is more than an institution: it is a living organism. The church is a sort of reenactment of divine incarnation. When Jesus Christ comes into the life of believers, his life becomes incarnate in their life. The church, as the "body of Christ" at worship, is not merely a reminder that he once lived but also a witness to the living presence of the risen Lord. It is a continuation of the life of Christ as he lives in and through the life of his people. The church as a community of the Resurrection is the vital, vibrant, and victorious body of the reigning Christ.

Every congregation is a representative part of the living body of Christ. Congregational worship insures vitality to the entire body and to individuals.

As a worshiping organism, the church must always be subject to change. As it was created, its life must be in the process of constant renewal and re-creation. Through meaningful worship, the church can be saved from becoming a dead branch. In vital communion the church continues to receive its essential life from the vine whose life is eternal (John 15). It is possible for the church to be "reshaped" in Christ. "For my children you are, and I am in travail with you over again until you take the shape of Christ" (Gal. 4:19, NEB).

A worshiping congregation. Every church must recognize itself as a historic, human institution as well as a divinely created organism. It is involved with truth as well as with spirit. The forms of doctrine which the church embraces directly affect its understanding of worship. The church as an institution must adopt what it considers to be its best means for expressing its beliefs and its worship.

A church can remain alive only as it continually comes to God in worship. In worship the congregation comes under the judgment of God. Unless the church repeatedly confesses, it cannot remain the witness to God's saving grace: "For the time has come for judgment to begin with the household of God" (1 Pet. 4:17). A church without judgment is a church without power. The church must always see itself as a "congregation of sinners" dependent upon the grace of God. Jesus taught his church to pray, "Forgive us our sins; for we also forgive every one that is indebted to us. And . . . deliver us from evil" (Luke 11:4, KJV). As an institution, the church has not inherited goodness; its essential righteousness is personal and can only be created in humble worship.

The church must always be what the early church was after the Ascension—a group of redeemed people, gathered together to pray and to wait for the coming of the Holy Spirit. The church cannot command or possess the Holy Spirit; it can only wait for the Spirit and live by the Spirit's power. The church is born today, as it was in the beginning, by a miracle of grace in the hearts of believers. In the midst of all its activities, the church is primarily a worshiping congregation.

A holy priesthood. In the worshiping congregation, Christians find their highest value. As Dargan affirmed, congregational worship quickens our interest, develops our Christian intelligence, and deepens our spiritual discernment.[13] Furthermore, dynamic worship is the safest and most enduring attraction of the church to those persons outside the church. The worshiping church is a self-transcending community.

The New Testament presents the church as a "holy priesthood." Peter exhorts us to come to the "living stone," Jesus Christ, that we may like living stones be built into a spiritual house, a "holy priesthood, to offer spiritual sacrifices acceptable to God through Jesus Christ" (1 Pet. 2:5; cf. Rev. 1:6).

The doctrine of the priesthood of believers, suggested by the "holy priesthood" of the church, implies that every member of Christ's body is responsible to worship Christ by offering spiritual sacrifices. This doctrine requires participation by the entire congregation. Since all are priests, Christians have the privilege and obligation to worship God for themselves and to serve as priests unto God for others.

The doctrine of the priesthood of all believers implies that salvation comes by the faith of the individual presenting himself or herself as an offering to God. The church's worship is personal participation by acts of faith and not by the offering of material sacrifices. Only the active faith of

---

13. Dargan, *Ecclesiology*, 560.

the worshiper can activate actions and deeds so that they become a means of God's grace.

God's grace may be recognized in various ways in our experience of worship. The manner in which grace operates in worship depends upon the human situation, the state of the soul. From the human point of view, communion with God and the reception of God's grace depends upon our faith. Our positive response to God's grace is faith. Paul declared, "By grace you have been saved through faith" (Eph. 2:8). God has acted by grace; we must respond by faith in worship.

Faith is the commitment of the self to God. It includes openness toward God, decision to accept what God gives, the opening of our whole being to the incoming of God as the Savior of life, an attitude of submission and trust in God, and a definite commitment to the will of God in adventurous living.

The priesthood of believers stresses the preeminent importance of personality. However, the doctrine does not imply extreme individualism. An individual can know God in the truest sense only in relation to other worshipers in the church. We can worship God only as we are rightly related to others.

CHAPTER 5

A PSYCHOLOGY OF WORSHIP

W hat happens when we worship? What kind of experience do we have in worship? What are our attitudes when we come to worship? What are our basic needs that need to be satisfied? How can the worship experience help to satisfy these needs? These are some of the questions which psychology may help us to answer. Psychology can also aid in validating religious experience and in suggesting more effective means of enriching religious experience.

A PERSONAL EXPERIENCE

Worship is basically a personal experience. It is a communion between persons. Worship involves the whole person and not a mere segment of his or her personhood. The biblical concept of humankind presents each individual as a unitary person. "Blessed are those . . . who seek him with their whole heart" (Ps. 119:2). "With my whole heart I seek thee" (Ps. 119:10).

Paul prayed, "May the God of peace himself sanctify you wholly; and may your spirit and soul and body be kept sound and blameless" (1 Thess. 5:23). The first and most important commandment implies that we express our love toward God with our total beings: "You shall love the Lord your

God with all your heart, and with all your soul, and with all your mind, and with all your strength" (Mark 12:30).

The biblical terms used to designate the various aspects of our personality are not to be considered independently of one another. *Nous* (the mind), *psyche* (the soul), *pneuma* (the spirit), *soma* (the body), and *kardia* (the heart) all speak of the various aspects of our total personality. These terms present a unitary concept of humankind. Worship is experienced by the total person.

Worship is a conscious act in which the worshiper understands God's revelation toward him or her and in which the worshiper knowingly turns toward God. The worship of God affects the unconscious as well as the conscious aspects of personality; however, communion with God is a conscious experience that demands response. Faith comes as a conscious understanding of God as God appears in Christ. Our communion with God intensifies as we exercise conscious faith.

We respond to God with various aspects of our total being. Psychologists primarily regard three modes of conscious activity—feeling attitude, knowing attitude, and willing attitude. All are present in the religious experience, and they function as a living unity. They are affected by various symbols and actions in worship. The act of worship involves knowledge, recognition of an object with which the worshiper is in relation. The worship experience involves certain emotions such as fear, love, and trust. Genuine worship also involves the will, concrete acts and commitment such as sacrifice or service. According to H. R. Mackintosh, all these actions are combined in one vital experience. They are not necessarily successive but are simultaneous and interdependent.[1]

We respond with our *senses*. The physical body with its sensory aspects must be considered in worship. We are reached through our physical senses—sight, hearing, smell, taste, touch. Visually the worshiper enjoys the beauty of the world, and especially the sanctuary, its architecture, its decorations, and its symbols. The sense of hearing enables us to enjoy the musical sounds of voices and instruments. Some churches appeal in their worship to the sense of smell by means of pleasant aromas from burning incense. With our hands we touch the Bible, the hymnbook, and the offering which we bring. The sense of taste is part of our experience in worship through partaking of the bread and the cup of the Lord's Supper. Since different people perceive their world through different sensory avenues, every worship experience should be consciously planned to include experiences which appeal to all senses. Whenever possible, worship should appeal to many senses at once.

---

1. H. R. Mackintosh, *The Christian Apprehension of God* (New York: Harper & Bros., 1929), 26.

We respond with our *minds*. God created us as thinking beings, capable of understanding the truth of God's revelation. Knowledge of God is not possible except through mental activity; therefore, the various actions in worship should "make sense" to the worshiper. Karl Heim in *Spirit and Truth* says that worship is a transaction between God and the human conscience, accomplished "in the light of clear thinking." Paul urged his followers to have the "mind" of Christ Jesus (Phil. 2:5), to "think" on the graces of the Christian life (Phil. 4:8), and to become transformed by the renewing of their "minds" in worship (Rom. 12:1–2). Jesus declared that we should worship "in spirit and truth" (John 4:24).

We respond with our *emotions*. In the Bible the "heart" is synonymous with the emotions. "God is love" (1 John 4:8). We were created with the capacity to love. "You shall love the Lord your God with all your heart, and with all your soul, and with all your mind" (Matt. 22:37; see also Deut. 6:5).

David Roberts suggests that objectivity has become a fetish in certain religious circles, and the validity of belief is thought to be directly proportional to its dispassionateness. He says that this is as bad as the opposite view of equating intensity of feeling with certainty.[2] Actions in public worship occur somewhere between the extremes of abject passivity and unbridled enthusiasm.

David Roberts further observes that we do not have to choose between cold objectivity and blind feeling. Neither rational detachment nor fanatical emotionalism will lead to reality. Our emotions can either prevent or implement our search for truth and our willingness to act. We must acknowledge that our feelings and unconscious motives, as well as our intellectual processes, play a part in forming our religious beliefs.

Our emotional attitudes may be conditioned by the atmosphere surrounding us. We are capable of hating as well as loving. We may be led into a mood of hope or a mood of despair. Our emotions may be kindled into enthusiasm or lulled into lethargy.

There should be a balance between the intellectual and the emotional. In worship we may need to intellectualize our emotions and to emotionalize our intellect. Emotions may be given direction and discipline by intelligent worship, and intellect can be kindled by fervor and compassion. Worshipers should avoid equating their own emotions with the power of the Holy Spirit. Inner motivation should be tested by the teachings of the Bible, by reason, and by prayer.

We respond with our *wills*. In confronting God, worshipers must make a choice. We must choose to commit ourselves to God's will. God does not

---

2. David Roberts, *Psychotherapy and a Christian View of Man* (New York: Charles Scribner's Sons, 1951), 59.

have our allegiance of the whole person until our will is combined with God's mind and God's emotions in total commitment. The Bible implies that we are free to choose God or to reject God. We can respond in submission and dedication or in rebellion. God presents the invitation, "Come," and leaves us free to decide. Willing discipleship is costly and will tolerate no "cheap grace."

We respond on a *superconscious level*. Music, art, drama, and other symbolic actions in worship add a dimension to our worship experience. In the superconscious, God's power provides spiritual awareness and new insights and inspirations.

Persons often say, "I just *felt* the presence of God"; however, this awareness may be experienced as the "still small voice," or it may come in cataclysmic force such as Paul's Damascus road experience. This aspect of worship cannot be formalized nor carefully defined theologically. Indeed, we should acknowledge mystery in worship which is accepted by faith and needs no explanation. We yield to God's moving power in our willingness to explore new dimensions of being, which may in turn reveal new dimensions of ministry in God's ever-expanding universe. Mystery appeals to our imagination and often fires creativity.

AN OBJECTIVE-SUBJECTIVE EXPERIENCE

Worship is an objective-subjective experience—objective because we think about God, subjective because we think about ourselves. A balance of the two is realized in genuine communion with God.[3]

Subjectivity has been the critique of much Free Church worship. Some Free Church worship may lack the objectivity that can lift the worshipers out of themselves and reveal to them a better existence beyond themselves.

Worship involves *objective experience*—it has objective content. In worship, we do not give primary concern to our own inner feelings and desires for our attention is focused first upon God.

God is objective in holiness, transcendence, and absoluteness. God does not depend upon us for his being. In worship our minds and hearts must be directed toward God. Our worship is more than sentiment or emotion. It finds objective reality in God. P. T. Forsyth declared that unless there is within us that which is above us, we shall soon yield to that which is around us. Objectivity can be assured only if we begin to worship for God's glory and not for our own. The objective worth of God is the basis of true worship.

Our faith rests in Christ, not in our own desires. Worship is a creative encounter and a redemptive act. Subjectivity is indispensable to a sense of guilt

3. A. W. Blackwood, "Public Worship," *Twentieth Century Encyclopedia of Religious Knowledge*, 2:1190.

and the need for purification. Objectivity is indispensable to a sense of forgiveness and healing.[4]

In its objectivity, worship is directed away from us and toward God. The acts of God in history are primary in our worship. We are concerned about the historical facts, the revealed truths, and the person of God as manifested in Jesus Christ. These facts are objective to us. Without objective foundations in history, worship can become too subjective. Christianity must be more than religious sensibility. It must balance objective revelation with subjective experience.

Worship involves *subjective experience*. In worship the consciousness of God's presence becomes a subjective experience. Worship is a dialogue in which we hold personal communion with God. God's revelation is a personal and individual experience.

Worship takes place within us. In our self-examination, we are concerned with our finiteness, our weakness, our guilt, our grief, our brokenness. It is legitimate for us to be concerned about ourselves so long as this is secondary to our concern about the glorification of God.

Worship is communion, a dialogue between God and humanity. It is an experience in which God confronts humankind. It is dialogue in which God and a person consciously commune with one another. We know ourselves in relation to God.

We can never treat God as a mere object of worship. There is danger in speaking of the objectivity of God as a synonym for the reality of God.

God is not a part of our subjectivity. In a secondary sense, God is the object of our knowledge. God is the knower who confronts us. We know God as the "wholly other." In worship, our knowledge *about* God must become knowledge *of* God. The New Testament has two words for knowledge. *Ginosko* means knowledge about a fact, or objective knowledge. *Epiginosko* is the knowledge of experience such as one exercises in coming to know God. God takes the initiative, and we respond. It is always a personal experience.

Our Creator respects our personhood. As we respond in faith to God's loving call, our nature is transformed. When we submit to the lordship of Christ in worship, we become Christlike. Christ became human in order that we may become like God. Worship is a dynamic experience in which we are re-created by God's power. As Paul said, "It is the Spirit himself bearing witness with our spirit that we are children of God" (Rom. 8:16).

God meets us, not as one among the many objects of our knowledge, but as another knower by whom both these objects and we ourselves are known. A balance between the objective and the subjective is the ideal. "If objective

---

4. Franklin Segler, "Worship," *Encyclopedia of Southern Baptists*, ed. Norman W. Cox (Nashville: Broadman Press, 1958), 2:1547.

worship is likely to seem cold, subjective worship is almost sure to be weak."[5] In the combination of the objective source and the subjective experience, certainty and assurance are found.

OUR BASIC NEEDS FOR WORSHIP

We have basic needs which can be met in worship. Augustine said, "Thou hast made us for thyself, O God, and our souls are restless until they find their rest in thee."[6] In the depths of our nature we have certain conscious needs which must be met. There are hungers of the human heart to be satisfied. These psychological necessities have been approached in various ways. The following categories are another effort at expressing our conscious needs for worship.

1. The sense of finiteness seeks the infinite. In worship we seek completion, communion with God. Sensing our limitations, we go in search for the rest of ourselves. The psalmist said,

   > O LORD, our Lord, how majestic is thy name in all the earth! . . . When I look at thy heavens, the work of thy fingers, the moon and the stars which thou hast established; what is man that thou art mindful of him, and the son of man that thou dost care for him? Yet thou hast made him little less than God, and dost crown him with glory and honor (Ps. 8:1–5).

2. The sense of mystery seeks understanding. We stand in need of knowledge. We approach God as the source of all knowledge. Paul exclaimed, "O the depth of the riches and wisdom and knowledge of God! How unsearchable are his judgments and how inscrutable his ways!" (Rom. 11:33). Paul prayed that his fellow Christians might "have power to comprehend with all the saints what is the breadth and length and height and depth, and to know the love of Christ which surpasses knowledge, that you may be filled with all the fulness of God" (Eph. 3:18–19).

3. The sense of insecurity seeks refuge. In an age of uprootedness, we realize our need for refuge and stability. With the psalmist we find ourselves saying, "God is our refuge and strength, a very present help in trouble" (Ps. 46:1).

4. The sense of loneliness seeks companionship with God. In our estrangement and our lostness, we feel the need to be loved. Worship is the search for this love which can satisfy our loneliness. Job cried, "Oh, that I knew where I might find him, that I might come even to his

---

5. Andrew W. Blackwood, *The Fine Art of Public Worship* (Nashville: Abingdon Press, 1939), 19.
6. Augustine, *Confessions*, trans. R. S. Pine-Coffin (New York: Penquin Books, 1961), 1:1.

seat!" (Job 23:3). In genuine worship we come ultimately to experience personal companionship with God. "I had heard of thee by the hearing of the ear, but now my eye sees thee" (Job 42:5).

5. The sense of human belongingness seeks mutual fellowship with other worshipers. The children of Israel sang a song of ascent going up to the temple, "I was glad when they said to me, 'Let us go to the house of the LORD!'" (Ps. 122:1–2). In worship the early church felt itself to be one body in Christ. Joined and knit together in Christ, each one worked to contribute his or her part in building up the body in the love of Christ (Eph. 4:1, 4–6, 16). It is by the grace of God that a congregation is permitted to gather visibly for fellowship in worship.[7]

6. The sense of guilt seeks forgiveness and absolution. In worship our soul is laid bare before God. We acknowledge our guilt, and we plead for cleansing. David cried out, "Have mercy on me, O God, according to thy steadfast love; according to thy abundant mercy blot out my transgressions . . . . Against thee, thee only, have I sinned, and done that which is evil in thy sight. . . . Create in me a clean heart, O God, and put a new and right spirit within me" (Ps. 51:1, 4, 10). The more real our sense of guilt, the more necessity there is for confession and dependence upon the atoning grace of God.

7. The sense of anxiety seeks peace. Anxiety is a normal experience of human finiteness.[8] In this deep threat of non-being, we seek in worship the courage to become our true selves. As emotional tensions build up, we seek peace from them in the deepest of all emotional experiences—worship. This emotional experience can reach to the depths of our need for rest and peace. In great distress the psalmist prayed, "As the hart panteth after the water brooks, so panteth my soul after thee, O God" (Ps. 42:1, KJV). "Why are you cast down, O my soul, and why are you disquieted within me? Hope in God; for I shall again praise him, my help and my God" (Ps. 42:11).

8. The sense of meaninglessness seeks purpose and fulfillment. The search for meaning is perhaps our deepest need. In the depths of our soul we realize that we were created for a purpose. In the midst of life's harassment we affirm, "We know that in everything God works for good with those who love him, who are called according to his purpose" (see Rom. 8:28–30). The search for meaning finds its deepest significance in worship.

7. Dietrich Bonhoeffer, *Life Together* (London: SCM Press, 1954), 8.
8. Wayne Oates, *Anxiety in Christian Experience* (Philadelphia: Westminster Press, 1955), 42.

9. The sense of brokenness seeks healing. We cannot grapple with the enemies of righteousness in a realistic world without becoming broken and bruised. In a broken world we seek to be made whole, and as Tournier says, this can happen only as God becomes incarnate in us through the Holy Spirit.[9] Isaiah wrote, "A bruised reed he will not break, and a dimly burning wick he will not quench" (Isa. 42:3).

10. A sense of grief seeks comfort. Our innumerable losses leave us with a feeling of emptiness. We grieve over our losses. "Comfort ye . . . my people" (Isa. 40:1, KJV). In the worship of the living Lord who overcame all such grief and loss, we hear the words, "Let not your hearts be troubled; believe in God, believe also in me. . . . Peace I leave with you; my peace I give to you; not as the world gives do I give to you. Let not your hearts be troubled, neither let them be afraid" (John 14:1, 27).

ATTITUDES EXPRESSING WORSHIP

There are certain general psychological attitudes expressed in worship referred to as emotions or moods. However, an attitude is more than an emotion or sentiment or mood, although all of these are involved. An attitude includes emotion or feeling, thought or idea, and will or deliberate commitment in the total act of personal consciousness.

According to W. E. Sangster, the most appropriate word to use in defining the centrality of personal thought and action is *attitude*.[10] Attitude implies motivation and purpose and determines decision and action. Sangster says attitude is prompted by religious and moral motivation and is inclusive of thinking, feeling, and willing. It is similar to Paul's use of the term *mind*, when he said, "Let this mind be in you, which was also in Christ Jesus" (see Phil. 2:1–5, KJV). Another kindred word is the word *heart*. "As he thinketh in his heart, so is he" (Prov. 23:7, KJV). "With the heart man believeth unto righteousness" (Rom. 10:10, KJV).

Not only do we come to worship with certain attitudes, but worship is also a way of changing our basic attitudes so that the quality of the experience becomes different and richer. "Of all voluntary acts which shape the attitude of the psycho-physical organism, none can go so deep and none are so effective as worship."[11]

The first attitude of worship is *adoration* expressed in praise. Adoration, a spirit of reverence and awe, is the starting point for all genuine worship. We

---

9. Paul Tournier, *The Whole Person in a Broken World*, trans. John and Hellen Roberstein (New York: Harper & Row, 1964), 168.

10. W. E. Sangster, *The Secret of the Radiant Life* (New York: Abingdon Press, 1957).

11. Henry Nelson Wieman and Walter Marshall Horton, *The Growth of Religion* (New York: Willet-Clark and Co., 1938), 391.

do not praise God if we do not adore God. To adore is to worship with profound reverence.

The Westminster Catechism declared that "the chief end of man is to glorify God and to enjoy him forever." Our most fundamental need and duty are to glorify God. Worship should begin and end in adoration of God. We stand in awe of God's beauty and splendor and mystery. His ways are past tracing out. Although we cannot completely fathom the nature of God, we can respond in adoration to the God who can answer all our needs.

Adoration is expressed in praise. The true language of praise is found in the Bible in such passages as Psalm 103:1, "Bless the LORD, O my soul; and all that is within me, bless his holy name!" Isaiah's vision of God in the temple, and the closing chapters of the book of Job, the prologue to the Gospel according to John, and the lofty passages in the book of Revelation give examples of our most worthy effort to express our adoration for God. In the early church, worship was proclaimed in the act of adoration: "Worthy art thou, our Lord and God, to receive glory and honor and power, for thou didst create all things, and by thy will they existed and were created" (Rev. 4:11). In worship we stand before God to receive and to acknowledge what God has already provided.

A second attitude in our worship is *gratitude* expressed in thanksgiving. This is similar to adoration and perhaps grows from thanksgiving. Thanksgiving is made possible by God's gracious movement toward us. God's grace expressed through his benevolences creates within us a spirit of gratitude that results in thanksgiving, a joyful acceptance of life, a celebration of the gospel. Every Lord's Day is a festival of joyful worship, the thanksgiving (*eucharistia*) of the church.

Bowing in the presence of God, we call to mind the blessings we have received. We acknowledge God as the source of our blessings, and our hearts rise in praise and thanksgiving. The Old Testament contains many songs of worship. "Praise the LORD! O give thanks to the LORD, for he is good; for his steadfast love endures for ever!" (Ps. 106:1). Psalm 107:1–2 repeats the phrase, "O give thanks to the LORD, for he is good; for his steadfast love endures for ever!" and then adds, "Let the redeemed of the LORD say so." Again the people sing, "Praise the LORD. I will give thanks to the LORD with my whole heart, in the company of the upright, in the congregation" (Ps. 111:1).

In counting our blessings, we are brought to the heights of genuine worship. We cannot remain in sorrow and despair when we realize God's great blessings. Thanksgiving is a celebration of life itself as a gift from God.

At the heart of Christian worship is thanksgiving for God's redemptive love. In Paul's exhortation to the Corinthian Christians to express their gratitude to God, Paul rises to the heights of worship with the words, "Thanks be to God for his inexpressible gift" (2 Cor. 9:15).

Confession expresses the attitudes of humility and *repentance*. In the presence of the holy God, we recognize ourselves as sinners in need of repentance. C. S. Lewis observed that repentance is not fun at all, for it is harder than just eating humble pie; it means undergoing a kind of death of the self.[12] True confession is Godward, for we learn genuine humility only in the worship of God in Christ, who experienced the ultimate humiliation in the Cross.

True confession includes the acceptance of God's forgiveness. The richness of confession is realized in the assurance of forgiveness. Through John's witness God affirmed this reality: "If we confess our sins, he is faithful and just, and will forgive our sins and cleanse us from all unrighteousness" (1 John 1:9). The worshiper's hunger for restoration to fellowship with God is satisfied in God's assurance of forgiveness.

In the presence of an infinite God, we realize that we are needy creatures, and we acknowledge our *dependence*. Dependence is the act of asking God for what we need. Petition is asking God to supply the needs of prayer. Jesus taught us to pray, "Give us this day our daily bread; and forgive us our debts" (Matt. 6:11–12).

Dependence also includes asking for God's blessings on others—intercession. Jesus' high priestly prayer is the best example of intercession (John 17). Paul urged that "supplications, prayers, intercessions, and thanksgivings be made for all men" (1 Tim. 2:1).

Asking is an act worthy of being included in worship, for God delights to give good things to God's children (Luke 11:13). To ask for God to enter fresh into the life of the worshiper is an ultimate experience.

Worship involves also the attitude of *submission* or surrender. In his struggle with his destined role, Jesus himself prayed, "Abba, Father, all things are possible to thee; remove this cup from me; yet not what I will, but what thou wilt" (Mark 14:36). Again at Calvary Jesus worshiped God in the agony of death: "Father, into thy hands I commit my spirit!" (Luke 23:46).

Every significant worship experience calls for submission and surrender to the will of God. Genuine surrender is never reluctant but always joyful. Jesus' agony on the cross resulted in unreserved surrender. As George Buttrick observed, there was no rebellion in Paul as he was approaching martyrdom.[13] As he was being "poured out as a libation on the altar," he saw as his reward a "crown of righteousness" awarded to "all who have loved his appearing" (2 Tim. 4:8). Paul's final act was an act of worship.

---

12. C. S. Lewis, *The Case for Christianity* (New York: Macmillan, 1944), 49. Cf. Simone Weil, *Gravity and Grace* (New York: G. P. Putnam's Sons, 1952).

13. George Buttrick, *God, Pain, and Evil* (Nashville: Abingdon Press, 1966), 166.

Worship climaxes in *commitment*. Though the worshiper is acted upon by the sovereign power of God, commitment involves the willful dedication of oneself to God.

Isaiah's worship began in adoration with his vision of God's holiness and glory, proceeded into dialogue with God, and climaxed in his commitment, "Here am I! Send me" (see Isa. 6:1–8). Worship includes commitment that knowingly becomes involved in the redemptive work of God. God prefers to incline the will rather than the intellect, for a commitment in faith is total humility.

THE EFFECT OF LEARNING STYLES ON WORSHIP

Educators are becoming increasingly aware of the effect of preferred learning styles on the ability of students in the classroom to learn at their best. This information has great relevance for worship as well. People receive three types of input from their environment: (1) Visual input—seeing, using mental images; (2) Auditory input—hearing sounds; (3) Kinesthetic input—touching, feelings. Although people use all of these channels to receive information about their environments, they tend to have preferences for channels which, through their particular personalities, have become effective ways of learning.

These preferences have a marked effect on the way worshipers perceive the worship in which they participate, and these preferences directly affect the way worship ministers and committees plan for their congregations. People tend to expect other worshipers to worship best through the channels in which they also worship best. Hence, a worship planner who prefers auditory channels may plan worship that virtually excludes visual and kinesthetic experiences. A worshiper who prefers visual channels may see as meaningless auditory and kinesthetic experiences in worship. Because persons are conditioned by their experiences and successes in using and preferring various channels, worship experiences must be planned where, as much as possible, all three channels are used.

Visual. Persons who prefer visual channels will respond well to visual symbols, will appreciate visually attractive rooms and bulletins, and will prefer that other worshipers are attractively dressed and well-groomed. These persons will respond well to video, overhead transparencies, and other visual media. They will appreciate maps, outlines, and diagrams when learning. Visual persons may not want physical closeness in conversation and may not easily remember conversations filled with auditory signals. However, these individuals will keep steady eye contact and will closely observe visual communication such as body language.

Auditory. Persons who prefer auditory channels will respond particularly well to spoken language and music. These persons are sensitive to changes in voice inflection and changes in rate of delivery. In conversation, they may turn their ear to the speaker instead of making eye contact. In conversation and in worship, they may change seats or physical postures in order to place themselves in a better position for hearing. They are sensitive to subtle changes in acoustics, such as air conditioner noise during worship and the effectiveness of the sound system. These persons will enjoy lecture presentations and will be less likely to complain about long sermons.

Kinesthetic. Persons who prefer this channel are affected most when they have the opportunity to touch or feel. In worship, these persons may be particularly sensitive to the texture of paper, the feel of the hymnal or Bible, the handshake or hug of another worshiper, and the feel of the bread and cup during communion. Kinesthetic persons desire physical closeness in conversation and worship, and they learn best from relaxed, comfortable, non-threatening situations. They appreciate hands-on learning; the act of writing down information may be important for them. They respond well to real-life experiences which relate to feeling, and they appreciate practical application. Kinesthetic persons are likely to touch a person as they speak, and they tend to be affectionate and feel that persons who show their feelings are physically genuine.

Smell and taste. Churches are becoming increasingly aware of the need to plan worship experiences which allow each person to respond in ways that he or she finds most meaningful. In addition to the above, worship should also attempt to involve the senses of smell and taste. While these senses are more difficult to involve, they nevertheless have unique contributions to the total worship experience. Studies show that moods are strongly affected by the sense of smell. Many times when one is overcome with a sense of intense emotion by a previous life experience (the person feels as if she has been in a place or circumstance before or feels as if he has met a person before), the individual may be responding to the sense of smell, which is the most emotional of all senses and has a direct relationship to the ability to recall feelings. The sense of taste is closely identified with smell. Many persons associate the smell of evergreens and candles with Advent worship, the smell of Easter lilies with Easter, and the smell of bread and juice with communion. Creative worship leaders can formulate new ways to involve these senses in congregational worship.

THE EFFECT OF BRAIN HEMISPHERE ON WORSHIP

Scientists and behaviorists have documented that the two hemispheres of the brain have distinct functions. Most people use one side of their brain more than the other; therefore, they tend to perceive their world accordingly. *Right-brained* people are more visual, have a higher appreciation for humor and emotion, appreciate story and contemporary application, and have higher appreciation for fine arts. *Left-brained* people are more analytical, appreciate verbal communication, derive meaning from written language, and appreciate well-documented rational presentations. For these people, the impact of emotion on meaning and action is less profound. Recognizing these differences can help worship planners and leaders design and lead in worship experiences that allow all persons to find ultimate meaning in worship and can help to explain why, in a given worship service, one person may respond positively to an act of worship while another responds negatively to the same act.

CHAPTER 6

WORSHIP AND CHURCH RENEWAL

T he church stands always in need of renewal and revitalization. It must be forever building, for it is forever decaying within and being attacked without. People inside and outside the church are calling for church renewal.

Church and society are in crucial tension. The church faces the challenges of secularization, cultural and religious diversity, high technology, information explosion, declining Western culture, ethnic and gender struggles, and others. The church must take account of this reality and seek new ways to communicate with the contemporary world. It must not, however, turn to the world for its norms of basic life and character. In its response to secularization, the church has sometimes been guilty of drawing its norms from the world and feeding them back to the world.

Genuine worship in the church is the secret of renewal. If renewal does not take place in the church, genuine renewal does not take place anywhere. Renewal is not an end in itself but a result of sincere worship. Worship is certainly the source of the church's power, but the summit is reached in the life and ministry of the church for which worship prepares the faithful. Life and ministry are an extension of worship.

Church renewal and worship renewal should be interrelated since corporate worship is the culminating expression of the individual member's private encounters with God. The current emphasis on spiritual disciplines by writers such as Richard Foster and Henry Blackaby should parallel an increase in the power and renewal that occurs in worship.[1] When individual church members begin to have meaningful personal encounters with God through prayer, Bible reading, and other acts of personal devotion, renewal in the church's corporate worship will be a natural result. When churches focus on worshiping God as an end in their search for meaning instead of focusing on worship as a means to boost attendance, reach the unchurched, and build a sense of excitement; then worship renewal can occur. Ultimately, corporate worship renewal cannot be orchestrated by changing the music, the sermon, the structure of the service or any other external dimension, although these may be important. True worship renewal is an affair of the individual as he or she relates to God and the gathered body of individual worshipers (the church) as they come together to meet God in corporate worship.

True worship will bring new life in the church. As branches must be vitally connected with the vine, so must the church itself be vitally related to the source of its life, the living Christ.

Worship is the fountainhead of all the ministries of the church—indeed, the "life of the church." If this fountain grows stale from disuse or becomes clogged from foreign pollutions, the life of the church will ebb and its ministries diminish or cease altogether. This is why there must be a revival of worship before there can be church renewal. What is needed is an authentic encounter in fellowship with God. It may be true that many churches are seeking to escape this genuine encounter by taking refuge in the liturgy. True worship renewal will occur when theologically based form is combined with genuine Christian spirit and zeal. "The church lives, not on ideas about God, but on God's grace itself, mediated by his spirit in corporate worship."[2]

A CONSCIOUS RELATIONSHIP WITH GOD

The first step toward renewal in the church is the consciousness of a personal relationship with God which can come about only in worship. If our first duty is to glorify God, then our first privilege is to learn to enjoy God in personal communion. Worship is not primarily utilitarian—God is

---

1. Richard J. Foster, *Celebration of Discipline: The Path to Spiritual Growth* (San Francisco: Harper & Row, 1978); *Prayer: Finding the Heart's True Home* (San Francisco: Harper & Row, 1992); and Henry Blackaby, "Experiencing God: Knowing and Doing the Will of God," Videorecording (Nashville: Baptist Sunday School Board, 1990).

2. John Sheldon Whale, *Christian Doctrine* (Cambridge: The Cambridge University Press, 1952), 152.

worshiped for God's own sake, and true worship results in the glory of God. God is always seeking our fellowship. Augustine realized this as he prayed,

> For late loved I thee, O thou beauty of ancient days, Yet ever new! For late loved I thee! And behold, Thou wert within, and I abroad and there I searched for thee; deformed I, plunging amid those fair forms, which thou hast made. Thou wert with me, but I was not with thee . . . thou touchest me, and I burned thy peace.

A new awareness of the transcendent holiness of God and the acceptance of God's cleansing grace will bring renewal. The church needs to recall Isaiah's deep consciousness of God in the commanding vision in the temple; Paul's Damascus road experience as he heard the voice of the Lord and was blinded by the light of the Lord's outshining holiness; or the early church assembled in the breaking of bread and in prayers, waiting for God, as they suddenly became aware of his presence manifested in the tongues of fire. New experiences in worship bring new revelations of God and God's kingdom and new perspectives on life.

Confrontation with the holy God brings judgment. It is impossible for us to confront Calvary or the Resurrection without being challenged to the depth of our personhood. The honest person goes to worship because he or she is guilty, but God's judgment also brings cleansing and forgiveness. "The blood of Jesus his Son cleanses us from all sin" (1 John 1:7). God's judgment and forgiveness are creative, prompting in us positive cooperation with God. "True forgiveness is not the remission of a penalty; it is the restoration of a relationship."[3] Forgiveness brings renewal—it produces holiness of character. To receive God's cleansing power is to obtain the likeness of God's character.

BUILDING UP THE CHURCH

The church is built up and unified in worship—where there is no worship, there is no unity. We seek fellowship with others in one way or another. The common worship of one Lord assures fellowship and unity. Paul said, "There is one body and one Spirit, . . . one Lord, one faith, one baptism, one God and Father of us all, who is above all and through all and in all" (Eph. 4:4–6). Unity in worship builds up the body of Christ.

Building up the church does not necessarily mean the church will grow numerically. Many times church leaders assume that spiritual renewal will equal numerical growth and numerical growth should result in spiritual growth. A large, growing congregation may not be very mature spiritually

---

3. James Stuart Stewart, *A Faith to Proclaim* (New York: Charles Scribner's Sons, 1953), 63.

while a small, plateaued church may be quite spiritually mature but not growing numerically.

Individual Christians strengthen one another in worship. Even the physical presence of other Christians is a source of joy and strength to the believer. The church is composed of persons who acknowledge their dependence upon one another. Each worshiper contributes to other worshipers, for worship is cumulative.

In worship the church experiences forgiveness and thus becomes a forgiving community. Confession of one's sins in the presence of other Christians is the profoundest kind of humiliation. Worship is costly just as discipleship is costly. Bonhoeffer observed, "In the presence of a psychiatrist I can only be a sick man; in the presence of a Christian brother I can dare to be a sinner."[4] Worship is a part of discipleship. There is no place in worship for "cheap grace."

CHRISTIAN NURTURE FOR THE INDIVIDUAL

One of the purposes of worship is the edification of the individual. It is wrong to base the necessity of worship on its usefulness, but it is equally wrong not to keep in mind the usefulness of worship for the individual worshiper. The key to the building up of the body of Christ is the building up of the individual Christian. Church renewal can come only through personal renewal.

Christian nurture has its foundation in public worship. Other ministries of the church find their inspiration in worship.

Edification means the building up of the individual—the mind through instruction, perception, and discernment; the emotions through the energizing of interpersonal relationships; the conscience through the sensitizing power of God's Spirit; and the will in its motivation to action. To grow in grace does not mean that we progressively root out sin in our lives. It means that we are progressively more aware of sin's subtleties, progressively more conscious of God's love and forgiveness, progressively bolder and less apprehensive as we live more fully by God's power and grace.

Worship has healing power for the individual worshiper. We find our wholeness in proper relationship to God. In his healing miracles, Jesus showed the importance of becoming a new creature. The psalmist prayed, "Create in me a clean heart, O God; and renew a right spirit within me" (Ps. 51:10, KJV). We find peace and assurance in proportion to our wholeness in Christ. In worship, our physical and psychological needs find a creative dynamic which produces wholeness in our relationships.

---

4. Dietrich Bonhoeffer, *The Cost of Discipleship* (New York: Macmillan Co., 1959).

We are seeking to be a free people, but we feel bound by our finiteness and our weaknesses. In worship our true selves are handed back to us. We mature only as we find edification in the worship of God. Paul said that Christ frees us in order that we may be free to grow in the life of the Spirit. The fruits of the spirit—love, joy, peace, patience, kindness, goodness, faithfulness, gentleness, self-control—are realized only when we walk with Christ. We find our highest achievement in public worship. William Temple said, "Throughout our growth as Christians, worship is a duty; as we advance, it becomes a delight; and at all times a true act of worship is the fulfillment—for a moment—of the true destiny of our being."[5]

Personal edification involves ethical and moral responsibility. Worship results in the commitment of our self, which includes our abilities, possessions, and opportunities.

The doctrine of Paul's union with Christ was basic to his ethics. According to Paul, to seek the mind of Christ is God's gift of power for living. Paul said, "I am ready for anything through the strength of the one who lives within me" (Phil. 4:13, Phillips).[6]

THE CHURCH IN THE WORLD

The church that finds God in regular worship will also take God into life. In the broadest sense, worship is glorifying God in everyday life. In too many instances, worship has been used as escapism. As we discover our personhood in Christ, we accept the challenge for the church at worship to become the church in the world.

The Christian life is not the following of a set of rules; it is a dynamic engagement—a way of buying and selling, of paying taxes, of relating to sexual behavior, of treating our neighbor, of sharing with the poor, of relating to the moral outcast, of giving support to political leaders. The worship of the church is the stimulus to the Christian life in the world.

Church renewal comes when the church makes itself relevant to the world. Many of the elements of worship—the body, the voice, the ear, the eye, the hands, food, water, song, prayer, and the affirmation of belief—are also the "materials of social and cultural action."[7] Although the primary object of worship is God and the primary object of social and cultural action is humankind, the two find their common goal in the unified action of a genuine dialogue between God and persons. The practical denial of God's claim in our lives is perhaps more serious than our intellectual doubts and

5. *William Temple's Teachings*, ed. A. E. Baker (Philadelphia: Westminster Press, 1951), 107.

6. From *The New Testament in Modern English* [Copyrighted], J. B. Phillips, 1958. Used with permission of The Macmillan Company.

7. See Richard M. Speilmann, *History of Christian Worship* (New York: Seabury Press, 1966), 162.

denials. By denying God in our deeds we come nearer to obliterating the recognition of God that exists in the bottom of our hearts than we can by denying God with the top of our minds. When we sincerely worship God with our mouths, we will also serve God with our hands.

Worship is related to Christian vocation. For the church there can be no dichotomy of worship and work. As Luther said, to pray is to work, and to work is to pray. Every revelation of God is a call to vocation.

The God who forgives people as they worship in the church demands that they carry this same spirit of justice into the world. For the Christian the whole world becomes a temple, and in every part of the earth—shoe shop, factory, mines, and scientist's laboratory—time flows into eternity. The church that seeks to do its duty toward God will also perform its duties toward the world. The world may be unholy anywhere, inside or outside the church, and at any place it may be the throne of grace where God meets creation and finds it responsive to God's will.

In worship the church sees itself as a unique form of human society. Fellowship with Christ produces in the church a new solidarity with all other communities—the nations, races, tongues, and peoples who constitute the world.[8] The church in serious dialogue with God will also seek relevant dialogue with the world. To worship with the primary purpose of building up the institution is idolatry, but for the church to be preoccupied and satisfied with its own esoteric experiences in worship is worse than idolatry: it is hypocrisy.

The church at worship remembers Jesus Christ as present in the "world of the flesh." A new meeting with the incarnate, living Christ will bring a new awareness of the church's involvement in the world.

The restoration of meaning in contemporary life can come only if the church carries meaning into the world. Whatever glory may be ours must be encountered in the place where we find ourselves now in the world. If the conscience of the world is to be affected, it must come through the God-consciousness of the church in the world. Business and politics and production and communication will become righteous only as the people of God live righteously in these various areas of everyday life.

MOTIVATION FOR SERVICE

The church's motivation for service will be found in the inspiration of its worship. There is a certain rhythm in the Christian life which moves from the experience of worship to the life of service. "One must rise to the mount of transfiguration and then return to the valley of everyday living . . . to

---

8. Paul S. Minear, *Horizons of Christian Community* (St. Louis: Bethany Press, 1959), 125.

remain on the mountain top is to become sterile. To stay too long in the valley is to become exhausted of the spiritual."[9]

The biblical word *leitourgia*, translated "worship," actually means service. We speak of worship as going to church and service as going out into action in the world. Actually, our worship of God is part of God's service, and our service a part of God's worship.

The church finds its ministry by sharing the ministry of Christ which it discovers in its worship. Jesus said, "Whoever would be great among you must be your servant . . . even as the Son of man came not to be served but to serve, and to give his life as a ransom for many" (Matt. 20:26, 28). The church does not exist for its own comfortable enjoyment of worship: it is redeemed for ministry. It does not exist as a pure fellowship in a vacuum. It is created within an empirical context for a concrete purpose. In worship we come to feel the same compassion and desire to serve that Christ feels. The church has a concern for people in their current conditions, not in the ideal or the abstract but in the raw, concrete situations.

The church is motivated to minister not only to its own members but also to those on the outside. One of God's ministers who understands worship in its deeper implications has stated it perceptively:

While there is a lower class
I am in it.
While there is a criminal element
I am of it.
While there is a man in jail
I am not free.[10]

In the context of worship the church becomes a ministering fellowship. Its people serve as a healing community in the world. The care of souls is the responsibility of the entire church. All the laity find renewal for ministry in worship.[11]

The church is compelled to find new ways of ministering to a new world condition. Worship brings new and fresh experiences of the Holy Spirit, making the church aware of new opportunities for sharing the good news of Jesus Christ. The church must not become static with no place for creative deviation.

---

9. J. S. Arlen, *Reality in Worship* (Nashville: Convention Press, 1965), 112.

10. Howard Thurman, *The Inward Journey* (New York: Harper & Bros., 1961), 101f.

11. For a more thorough discussion see C. W. Brister, *Pastoral Care in the Church* (New York: Harper and Row, 1964), chap. 4.

EVANGELISM AND MISSIONS

Evangelism must find its source in worship if it is to be genuine evangelism. Separating worship from evangelism is heresy. Organizations and campaigns and human activities are essential in God's work, but they alone cannot bring a revival of evangelism. It is the week-by-week experience of worship which keeps the church renewed for sharing the gospel. The burning heart is a result of fellowship in the presence of the living Christ. Because of what had happened in her own life as she had talked with Jesus, the woman of Sychar rushed eagerly to others with the invitation, "Come see a man who told me about my life and who brought new life into my existence." Her motive was sharing the good news. This should always be the motive for evangelism.

Salvation does not come through pastors, or through evangelists, or through the priesthood of believers, but through God's grace. Grace is a free gift and cannot be earned by ecclesiastical form or action. Attempting to guarantee grace through our efforts is humanism and presumption.

The common experience of God's power felt in worship can attract lost persons to church services. In the fellowship of God's church, the presence of God is felt as judgment for the sinner which brings about a spirit of repentance; therefore, in worship the unbeliever is encouraged to acknowledge Christ as Savior and Lord in public commitment. Worship also encourages the new Christian to enter into the fellowship of the church. As Arthur C. Archibald says, "The New Testament knows nothing of evangelism apart from the church. Everything goes out from the churches and draws back into the churches."[12]

Worship is tridimensional. It brings the worshipers close to Christ in the context of congregational fellowship; it extends into all the activities of the life of the community; and it carries the good news of Christ from one person to another to the boundaries of the world. When the church truly worships, it will become missionary and evangelistic. A missionary of Christ is one who lets his or her own convictions be known, approaches other faiths as systems of conviction held by honored friends, and depends upon God (not upon personal power in any form) for any conversions that may take place. There is no better means of preparing the church for life in this horizontal dimension than honest, open-souled, sensitively responsive, corporate Christian worship; for in that fellowship, one develops towards one's neighbor the same depth of concern expressed in the love of Christ for the world.[13]

---

12. Arthur C. Archibald, *New Testament Evangelism* (Philadelphia: Judson Press, 1946), 40, 49.
13. Douglas Horton, *The Meaning of Worship* (New York: Harper & Bros., 1959), 75.

Seeking Christian Unity

True worship in the church will move toward the goal of Christian unity among the people of God. The conscious worship of the living Christ tends to unite all people who worship him and to elicit the yearning for all to be one as Christ and the Father are one. True ecumenicism can be realized in true worship. Christian unity may be realized only in a spirit of humility and worship. It is possible to achieve a spirit of unity within a diversity of institutions if Christ is worshiped and served as the head of the church. This spirit of unity is first realized in the local congregation and then is extended to embrace all who acknowledge Christ as Savior and Lord. All Christians should be willing to join all other Christians in worshiping our Lord, regardless of their church or organizational affiliation. Where the Spirit of the Lord is, there is liberty; where there is liberty, there is unity.

Many encouraging signs point toward a growing spirit of unity among God's people. Churches are sharing and borrowing worship practices. Liturgical groups are finding freshness in charismatic elements, and charismatics are finding renewal in liturgy. The Holy Spirit is working boldly among all Christians to bring about a true unity within the church universal. Ministers and local congregations in various churches share pulpits with those of different denominational affiliation.

Convocations on world missions and evangelism are being held in various parts of the world. Into these meetings come people from various churches—Orthodox, Anglican, Roman Catholic, Lutheran, Baptist, Methodist, Presbyterian, Disciples, Pentecostal, and other Free Church groups. Whereas people with differing theological positions cannot agree thoroughly, they can join in a spirit of worship when Christ is acknowledged as head of his church.

In every service of worship, whatever and wherever the congregation, hymns of praise and prayer point to the fulfillment of God's kingdom. Every new encounter with God foreshadows the triumphant appearance of the risen Christ. This hope is portrayed in John's worship experience:

> Then I saw a new heaven and a new earth; for the first heaven and the first earth had passed away, and the sea was no more . . . and I heard a loud voice from the throne saying, "Behold, the dwelling of God is with men. He will dwell with them, and they shall be his people, and God himself will be with them; he will wipe away every tear from their eyes, and death shall be no more, neither shall there be mourning nor crying nor pain any more, for the former things have passed away. . . . I am the Alpha and the Omega, the first and the last, the beginning and the end." . . . He who testifies to these things says, "Surely I am coming soon." Amen. Come, Lord Jesus! (Rev. 21:1, 3–4; 22:13, 20).

PART TWO:

THE MEANS OF
EXPRESSING WORSHIP

CHAPTER 7

MUSIC IN WORSHIP

Music is generally accepted as the most universal means for expressing human emotions; therefore, it should play an important role in public worship. Even from Old Testament times, the people of God have given music a major role in their worship. In the primitive Song of Moses (Exod. 15), as well as in the relatively sophisticated music of the temple, music was sung and frequently accompanied by musical instruments. The music of Israel consisted of songs of praise, thanksgiving, instruction, personal experience, and historical celebration. There were choirs, singers, instrumentalists, teachers, directors, and composers. The book of Psalms constituted the early hymnbook of the Jewish people. David appointed Levites to provide music for the liturgical services (1 Chron. 16:4–7). A later chapter in 1 Chronicles lists the number of offices of the musicians.

At the dedication of Solomon's temple, worship and music were blended in magnificence: "It was the duty of the trumpeters and singers to make themselves heard in unison in praise and thanksgiving to the LORD, and when the song was raised, with trumpets and cymbals and other musical instruments, in praise to the LORD, 'For he is good, for his steadfast love endures for ever,' the house, the house of the LORD, was filled with a cloud, so that the priests could not stand to minister because of the cloud; for the glory of the LORD filled the house of God" (2 Chron. 5:13–14). It is implied that this music brought to the people a sense of the presence of God.

According to Erik Routley, Old Testament music had three outstanding characteristics. First, it expressed emotion. The psalmist could rejoice in the "singing" of the hills and valleys, and the author of Job rejoiced that the morning stars "sang" at the creation. Second, the music was liturgical. Third, the music had not only power to speak, but also power to act. The influence of music is seen in the story of David as he charmed away Saul's madness by playing on his harp.[1]

Although not a great deal is said in the New Testament about music in worship, it is clear that Jewish psalmody became the inheritance of the Christian church. At the birth of Christ, the angels broke forth into song. Luke records this song and also the *Magnificat* (Luke 1:46ff.), the *Benedictus* (Luke 1:68ff.), and the *Nunc Dimittis* (Luke 2:29–32).

The singing of a hymn followed the institution of the Lord's Supper (Matt. 26:26–30). Paul and Silas sang praises to God in prison at Philippi. Paul instructed the Christians at Ephesus and Colossae to teach and admonish one another in psalms and hymns and spiritual songs (Eph. 5:19; Col. 3:16). There are many passages in the New Testament regarded as fragments of Christian hymns, such as Ephesians 5:14, 1 Timothy 3:16, Titus 3:4–7, and Revelation 15:3–4.

Dale Moody suggests that the majestic hymn included in John 1:1–5, 10–11, 14, 18 may have been sung by early Christians in the second century. There are many hymns in 1 Corinthians. Romans 5:12–21, 6:3–11, 8:31–39, and 13:11–14 may be completed hymns, according to Moody. Certainly Philippians 2:5–11, 1 Peter 3:18–22, 1 Timothy 3:16 and 6:1–2, 2 Timothy 1:9–10 and 2:11–13, Titus 2:11–14 and 3:4–7 are all hymns.[2]

The book of Revelation speaks of the singing of the heavenly hosts. In John's vision it was fitting for the people to worship through music: "And they fell on their faces before the throne and worshiped God, saying, 'Amen! Blessing and glory and wisdom and thanksgiving and honor and power and might be to our God for ever and ever! Amen'" (Rev. 7:11–12).

CHURCH MUSIC IN HISTORY

History presents a convincing witness to the power of music in worship. R. W. Dale said, "Let me write the hymns and the music of the church, and I care very little who writes the theology."[3] In the third century Basil said,

---

1. Erik Routley, *The Church and Music* (London: Gerald Duckworth & Co., 1950), 15–17.
2. Dale Moody, *Christ and the Church* (Grand Rapids: Wm. B. Eerdmans Publishing Co., 1963), 113.
3. R. W. Dale, *Nine Lectures on Preaching Delivered at Yale, New Haven, Connecticut* (London: Hodder & Stoughton, 1952), 271.

"Psalmody is the calm of the soul, the response of the spirit, the arbiter of peace." In the fourth century, Augustine wrote, "When I remember the tears I shed at the psalmody of thy church, in the beginning of my faith; and how, at this time I am moved not with the singing, but with the things sung, when they are sung with a clear voice and modulation most suitable, I acknowledge the great use of the institution." The opponents of the Reformation were accurate when they said, "Luther has done us more harm by his songs than by his sermons."[4]

During the early Middle Ages, "A highly organized body of chant, codified during the papacy of Gregory the Great (590–604), was almost the only worship music of the church for a thousand years."[5]

The practice of singing in parts began around 1100. This movement, which led to a number of later musical developments, reached maturity in the polyphonic music of Josquin (c. 1440–1521) and Palestrina (1525–1594). The music of Palestrina and his contemporaries consisted of independent vocal lines which were melodically conceived. Around 1600 operatic and instrumental music began to develop which produced harmonically oriented music.

During the Reformation Luther sought to restore congregational singing, which he saw as a means of indoctrination as well as a source of joy. Luther declared,

> Music is a fair and lovely gift of God which has often wakened and moved me to the joy of preaching. . . . Music is a gift of God. Music drives away the devil. . . . Next after theology I give to music the highest place and the greatest honor. . . . Experience proves that next to the Word of God only music deserves to be extolled as the mistress and governess of the feelings of the human heart. We know that to the devil music is distasteful and sufferable. My heart bubbles up and overflows in response to music, which has so often refreshed me and delivered me from dire plagues.[6]

Luther, Calvin, and Zwingli were all well-trained musicians; however, their views on music's place in worship differ widely. Luther had the highest regard for music and approved of the organ as an accompaniment for congregational singing as long as it did not drown out the voices. Zwingli felt that music had no part in Christian worship, and he even burned church organs. Calvin on the other hand believed in the unison singing of psalms without using instruments.

Metrical versions of the Psalms were sung in English congregations in the sixteenth and seventeenth centuries. "Although Queen Elizabeth detested

4. T. Harwood Pattison, *Public Worship* (Philadelphia: American Baptist Publication Society, 1900), 161.

5. W. Hines Sims, "Church Music," *Encyclopedia of Southern Baptists*, 2:934.

6. Roland Bainton, *Here I Stand* (New York: Abingdon Press, 1950), 341.

these public songs which she called 'Geneva jigs,' singing in her reign became almost a passion . . . and the Psalms were 'roared aloud' not only in church but in every street."[7] Johann Sebastian Bach (1685–1750) and George Frederick Handel (1685–1759) greatly influenced the music of the seventeenth century and beyond. This period marked the beginning of such outstanding hymn writers as Isaac Watts (1674–1748), Charles Wesley (1708–1788), John Newton (1725–1807), and John Neal (1818–1866). It was the Wesley brothers who popularized Watts's hymns. Among Watts's hymns are "O God, Our Help in Ages Past" and "When I Survey the Wondrous Cross." He has affectionately been called the father of English hymnody.

Churches in America patterned their worship services after those in England. From the beginning, psalms were sung in the Free Churches. The standard psalm tunes and Americanized English folk tunes were the sources for most of the music in the early churches. The Wesley revivals with the music of Charles Wesley and other English hymn writers gradually replaced the tradition of psalm singing in most Free Churches.

America has contributed to music in worship in several ways. Among them are the following: (1) The Puritans and the Pilgrims brought metrical psalters from England and Holland and used them until they published the *Bay Psalm Book* in 1640. (2) American composer Lowell Mason, who led the movement against the exclusive use of the psalms in New England, published many hymns and conducted great choruses in the presentation of oratorios.[8] (3) Gospel songs of the nineteenth century are an exclusive American contribution. These hymns of personal experience are a by-product of the era's revivalism, and they have become a recognized part of standard hymnic literature.

Music has made great strides in America during the twentieth century. Choral and oratorio societies have come into being. The American Guild of Organists was organized in 1896 and throughout its history has encouraged high standards in the preparation and presentation of church music. The Choristers Guild has encouraged music education in churches of all denominations, and the Hymn Society of the United States and Canada has fostered hymn singing through its hymn festivals, its commissioning of new works, and its many publications which enhance the congregation's worship repertoire.

Churches are continually examining the meaning of worship and the value of music in worship, and universities and theological seminaries offer degrees for church musicians. Many hymnals have been compiled by various

---

7. Albert Edward Bailey, *The Gospel and the Hymns* (New York: Charles Scribner's Sons, 1950), 12–13.
8. See Luther D. Reed, *A Study of Corporate Devotion* (Philadelphia: Muhlenberg Press, 1959), 175.

denominations during this century. Students continue to give attention to the relationship of theology and music in worship.

Hymns have brought all of us closer together in a spirit of Christian unity. Catholic churches now sing hymns written by Free Church authors, and people in the Free Churches now sing hymns composed by Catholic writers. Throughout the twentieth century, a universal body of worship music has continued to develop. This body of music contains historic Catholic hymns, hymns by Reformation writers, metrical psalms, hymns by Watts and Wesley, hymns of the Oxford movement, worldwide folk hymns, American gospel songs, hymns of the English hymn renaissance of the late twentieth century, and contemporary expressions of praise. Every major denomination in America published a hymnal in the late twentieth century, and each of these hymnbooks shares an increasingly large common repertoire.

BAPTIST HYMNALS

Among the other Free Churches, Baptists began to feel the need for a hymnal in their services of worship. In 1850 the *Baptist Psalmody* was compiled by Basil Manly, Sr., and Basil Manley, Jr. It contained 1,295 hymns and was a selection of excellent quality. The publications of other hymnals soon followed. Between the years 1923 and 1956, the Southern Baptist Convention published eight hymnals.

The first hymnal which brought a degree of unanimity in Southern Baptist congregational singing was the *Broadman Hymnal* (1940). It was edited by B. B. McKinney and published by the Baptist Sunday School Board. Within a decade there was need for a new hymnal. Through the combined work of a committee of thirty-seven, including ministers, musicians, and other denominational leaders, the *Baptist Hymnal* was published in 1956. The general editor was W. Hines Sims, secretary of the Church Music Department. This hymnal, used in most of the churches of the Southern Baptist Convention, included both classical hymns and gospel songs. It contained a greater number of historical hymns than any other hymnal Southern Baptists had previously published.

In 1975 under the leadership of editor William J. Reynolds, Southern Baptists published the *Baptist Hymnal* which was yet broader in scope than its predecessors and included more historical hymns while embracing the popular youth-folk culture of its era. The *Baptist Hymnal*, 1991, is the first hymnal by Baptists to include a large body of international ethnic hymns and is the first Baptist hymnal to embrace "Praise and Worship" musical elements. Edited by Wesley Forbis, this hymnal utilized more people in its planning and has been widely accepted by Southern Baptist churches.

MUSICAL EXPRESSION IN WORSHIP

Music in itself is neither religious nor sacrilegious; however, some of its various musical forms may be more appropriate for worship than others. Even the Old Testament writers had an acute sense of the moral force of music.

The purposes of music in worship are to create an awareness of God and a mood for worship, to enhance the inner life of worshipers, to unite the congregation for a worship experience, and to express the convictions of the congregation. Music may bridge our convictions with our feelings and attitudes.

Music is related to worship in at least three ways. First, music points to the aim or spirit of worship. Music is not an end in itself, but it provides an avenue through which various worship needs can be expressed. Second, music serves as an aid to worship, as we recall fundamental truths and experiences of text and music writers and share these experiences with others. Third, music may also be an act of worship, for when voices are lifted in praise, the music produced is actually an act of worship.

The traditional importance of hymns in the Free Churches was emphasized in Bernard L. Manning's *The Hymns of Wesley and Watts*: "Hymns are for us dissenters what the liturgy is for the Anglican. They are the framework, the setting, the conventional, the traditional part of divine service as we use it. They are, to adopt the language of the liturgiologists, the dissenting use. . . .We mark times and seasons, celebrate festivals . . . and expound doctrines by hymns."[9]

From the beginning of worship, God's people have expressed their praise in music through the human voice and through instruments. The voice and instruments are complementary. The church should make the best use of both.

INSTRUMENTAL MUSIC

The organ has traditionally been the primary instrument for accompaniment in worship; however, pianos, synthesizers, and orchestral instruments are used effectively in churches around the globe. While the organ, piano, and orchestra are used primarily for accompanying congregational singing and choral singing, there are other ways in which these instruments may be used as an aid in worship.

The prelude. Prelude music should create an atmosphere and provide an introduction to the worship service. A brief period prior to the beginning of the worship may help create a worshipful attitude for those who come early

---

9. Quoted in Davies, *Christian Worship*, 96.

to the service. The prelude should call people to attention as they prepare to meet God in worship. It should not be background music for congregational conversation—small talk does not need accompaniment. The prelude is a genuine worship gift on the part of the presenter, and the congregation should join with the presenter in offering this gift to God. Unless a gathering period is held prior to the congregation's entering the worship room, the congregation will probably talk as they gather. For this reason, the prelude should be included within the body of the service—after some verbal worship has occurred or a worship leader has guided the congregation toward God.

The offertory. Music played during the time when people are dedicating their offerings to God should be appropriate to worship. The selections should suggest to people themes of dedication and commitment and may range in mood from meditation to celebration.

The interlude. Music can do much to unite the various elements of a worship service.

The postlude. At the close of worship, the postlude should inspire the congregation as they leave the sanctuary.

CHORAL AND ENSEMBLE MUSIC

The primary function of the choir is to lead the congregation in worship. Music by the choir may be used throughout the service. The choir may sing the call to worship, prayer responses, stanzas of hymns, or any other worship music. Choral music can significantly enrich the worship experience.

Many churches have a graded choir program in which children's and youth choirs participate in some of the services. Children's and youth choirs should always contribute to worship by singing worthy texts well. As with any musical element, if the text is not well-chosen and well-presented, it may hinder rather than aid worship. Graded choirs are extremely valuable in giving children and youth a repertoire of worship music and in teaching the importance of worship.

Other ensemble music and solos often make genuine contributions to worship. Whatever the musical presentation, music should be presented as an act of worship and never as a display of the musician's ability. Only music that contributes genuinely to worship should be used.

CONGREGATIONAL SINGING

Congregational singing is the primary musical expression in worship. It is an error to think of the choir and the instruments as being primary. Worship planning should adequately provide for the congregation to express itself through singing. All members of the congregation ought to be encouraged to join in song. The singing church is a victorious church.

THE CHOICE OF CONGREGATIONAL MUSIC

In the Free Churches two books have always been considered handbooks of worship, the Bible and the hymnbook. Both should be seriously studied in worship planning. The careless choice of hymns may limit the worship experience of a congregation. Several principles should guide in the selection of hymns: (1) The worship leader should know the hymnal well and know how to select the appropriate hymns for a given service. (2) The pastor should assist the music minister in the selection of hymns. (3) Every hymn should have a definite objective and a specific purpose. (4) The hymns in a service of worship should provide a well-rounded worship experience. There should be hymns of adoration and praise, hymns of devotion and prayer, hymns of affirmation and proclamation, and hymns of dedication and commitment. The hymn preceding the sermon might be selected on a theme related to the sermon, but the other hymns should be chosen to express particular attitudes in worship. Except for special occasions, all the hymns should not be selected on one theme. This is not psychologically sound because comprehensiveness and variety in the expression of worship are essential. (5) It is good to keep a balance between objective hymns and subjective hymns. To use only objective hymns is to starve the emotions, to use only subjective gospel songs is to deprive the intellect. Objective hymns point to God, while subjective hymns speak of our experience in personal worship. There is a place for both, and a balance between the two is preferable. (6) Hymn choices should also include hymns with various keys, meters, and tempos. When consecutive hymns have identical meters, tempos, and/or key signatures, worship may develop a sameness. (Worship may seem a bit dull and routine although no one really seems to know why.) (7) Hymns with higher pitches should be sung in later services or later in the service. Most people do not come to church with their voices warmed up. If they sing a lower-pitched hymn first, their voices will then be ready for higher pitches. (8) When a hymn text fits the service well but the tune is unknown, choose another tune that has the same meter (see hymnal metrical index), and sing the new text with a familiar tune.

Tests for hymns. Every hymn ought to meet certain tests if it is to be used in worship. The following tests will help in selecting usable hymns: (1) Is the content Christian? In other words, is the theology sound? Hymns and other texts that violate sound Christian theology ought to be forbidden. Texts may be theologically incorrect in fact as well as tone or point of view. Careful examination of texts is mandatory for the worship leader. (2) Is the text worshipful? Does it express Christian feeling? Does it express Christian experience? (3) Is the style lyrical? Does it appeal to the imagination? Can it be followed easily? Does it measure up to good literary form?[10] (4) Is it singable? Can the congregation sing it? A hymn that is appropriate for one congregation may not be suitable for another.

Purpose. Hymns should be chosen for a particular purpose. Every hymn should make a specific contribution to the experience of worship. A worship service should begin with hymns of adoration and praise, hymns whose objective content points to God. As the service progresses, hymns of dedication, Christian service, and didactic themes may be used. The hymn of response or commitment should come at the end of the service.

It may help worshipers if hymns are designated by a modifier, such as adoration, devotion, or commitment. The following suggestions may be helpful in the selection of hymns according to purpose: (1) Some hymns of adoration, praise, and thanksgiving are "Holy, Holy, Holy," "Come, Thou Almighty King," "O for a Thousand Tongues to Sing," "Great Redeemer, We Adore Thee," "Crown Him with Many Crowns," "O God, Our Help in Ages Past," and "All Hail the Power of Jesus' Name." (2) Hymns of devotion, fellowship, concern, and faith include "Oh, for a Closer Walk," "O Master, Let Me Walk with Thee," "Take Time to Be Holy," "Savior, Like a Shepherd Lead Us," "My Jesus, I Love Thee," and "Sweet Hour of Prayer." (3) Hymns of affirmation, confession, and instruction may be called thematic hymns, hymns chosen according to a particular theme. This type of hymn is usually sung closer to the sermon and may be related to the theme of the sermon. Some examples are "The Church's One Foundation," "Love Divine, All Loves Excelling," "When I Survey the Wondrous Cross," and "Jesus Shall Reign Where'er the Sun." (4) Hymns of dedication, response, commitment, and invitation are usually sung at the conclusion of the worship service. Some examples are "O Jesus, I Have Promised," "Have Thine Own Way, Lord," "Just As I Am," "Lord, Here Am I," and "Take My Life, and Let It Be." When modifiers are used, they must accurately reflect the content of the hymn.

INTRODUCING NEW WORSHIP MUSIC

New hymns and other worship music should not be presented for the first time in the church's main worship service. New music should be introduced gradually so that, over time, people become familiar with either the tune or the text. If the tune or the text is well known, the congregation will probably sing with relative ease; however, when both are new a congregation will have difficulty. It is possible for a congregation to struggle through a new

---

10. For a study of literary form, see Austin C. Lovelace, *The Anatomy of Hymnody* (Nashville: Abingdon Press, 1965).

hymn and have a bad experience which can taint this new music forever. New music should be introduced gradually. The following suggestions are helpful: (1) Introduce the new music through Sunday School department assemblies and other smaller-group gatherings. (2) Have the choir or a soloist sing the new music in several services before the congregation is asked to join in. (3) Use the new music as a prelude, offertory, or postlude. Many arrangements are available for most tunes. (4) Use the text of the new music in a call to worship, response, prayer, or other reading. (5) Use the church newsletter or other publication to highlight interesting information about the new musical expression. (5) Use Sunday evening, Wednesday evening or other smaller worship services to gain familiarity with new music.

When you finally use new music in a worship service, avoid the norm of announcing the hymn, playing an introduction, and singing the hymn. Use creativity such as having a soloist sing the first stanza, the choir the second, and the congregation the others. Ask the organist to play the entire hymn (melody only) for the introduction. Reinforce the melody for the first several stanzas with piano and organ or with other instruments. Untrained musicians have a difficult time choosing which note is the melody when four or more notes are being played by a keyboard instrument. Whenever possible, allow the congregation to see the words and the music while they learn. This allows for more senses to be involved in the learning process. While most people in the congregation do not read music well, they are capable of and accustomed to watching the direction of the melody.

Once you have introduced new music, repeat it often over the next few weeks and months. A congregation must hear a musical element many times before they consider it theirs.

MUSIC LEADERSHIP

Depending on the church's size and organization, musical leadership may be organized in different ways. Many churches have ministers of music whose primary responsibility is to plan and lead worship; other churches have volunteer music leaders while the pastor is responsible for planning the music. Whatever the structure, every attempt should be made to correlate the entire worship life of the church by giving proper emphasis to the music. Pastors should have a knowledge of worship music and should lead the congregation to give its best musical gift in worship. The pastor is not required to be a trained musician, but the pastor should have a general knowledge of music.

Every minister can be a student of hymnology and other worship music, which includes not only the history of hymns and hymn writers but also a theology of hymnody. Some ministers have the literary gift and training to write hymns.

The pastor should be acquainted with the graded music program of the church, since he or she may need to provide leadership and direction. The pastor ought to be a student of the hymnal. He or she should understand what the church's denomination is projecting in the area of music. The pastor should always set a good example by singing hymns with the congregation at worship. It is probably true that the level of church music can rise no higher than the pastor's estimation of its importance in the life of the church.

The minister of music is directly responsible for the church's music program. He or she is a specialist in church music and at the same time a minister of the gospel. Responsibilities fall in four general areas: performer, teacher, administrator, and spiritual leader.[11] The minister of music's performance skills include conducting, keyboard, and voice. He or she will serve as a teacher of voice, speech, theory, and conducting. As administrator of the music program, the minister of music will share skills, methods, and materials for the various age groups in the church. Qualifications include acquaintance with organizational planning, budgets, promotion, keeping of records, the securing of equipment, and other practical matters. A spiritual leader must have a knowledge of the Bible, of Christian doctrine, and of the total program of the denomination.

The pastor and the music minister should respect each other's different training and should seek to affirm their differences. Both should be aware of their tendencies toward individualism. They are fellow ministers of the gospel and are responsible to know something about the relationship between theology and music and should seek to work in harmony as they plan and conduct worship for the glory of God. The pastor and music minister should focus on their many common goals and should build a shared vision by attending conferences together, reading the same books, and spending time discussing the church's worship.

The keyboard musician also has a vital place in the church's ministry. He or she must be a well-trained musician, capable of performing effectively. The effective accompanist will understand the relationship between that function and the entire worship service. The accompanist's primary task is to accompany and support the other leaders of church worship. A sense of timing is essential in unifying all the elements of a worship service. Making transitions between various elements and providing good preludes, offertories, and postludes can enrich and strengthen a worship service.

The church choir has two tasks in worship. First, it should lead the congregation in expressing worship through the singing of hymns. Second, it should provide choral music which will inspire and enrich the worship experience of the entire congregation.

---

11. James McKinney, "Developing Musical Leadership for the Church," chapel message given at Southwestern Baptist Theological Seminary, Fort Worth, Texas, September 13, 1962, 2–4.

Many contemporary churches have a graded choir program which provides musical training and participation for all age groups. The music ministry includes organized choir groups for the purpose of study and development in the knowledge and performance of music for all areas of the church. It is concerned with all age groups; an effective graded choir program ensures the strength of the church's music program for the future. Graded choirs offer children the opportunity to prepare for a lifetime of effective worship; therefore, they are crucial to a church's role as the worshiping church.

The music committee of the local church can contribute immeasurably to the success of the church's music program. The music committee is primarily an advisory group working with the minister and the director of music. The committee should select good leadership and then support the program that is projected. The committee should realize its limitations and not attempt to advise where it is not competent. By assisting the music minister in recruiting new singers and accompanists, handling business matters, and educating the congregation, this committee guides the music program of the church.

God deserves only the best music in worship. It is imperative that the leadership of the church seek the highest possible standards for church music, even in smaller churches. All music selected for worship should contribute to a particular purpose for which the congregation is assembled—to turn hearts and lives toward God.

The level of appreciation for music's role in worship can be raised in any congregation. Congregations can be led to understand the primary purpose of church music. Their knowledge concerning congregational music can be increased. A congregation should not be willing to settle for its present level of church music.

The level of appreciation for music will vary among congregations and even among individuals within a given congregation. Worship leaders must be responsible in their selection of hymns to fit the needs of a particular congregation. When selecting music for public worship, three factors must be kept in mind: first, music must enable members of the congregation to express themselves in an idiom with which they are familiar; second, music must be the best which the congregation is capable of appreciating; third, music must assist in turning their minds Godward. William J. Reynolds concludes that church musicians must continue to work for the day when every individual in the congregation, with full awareness of the Person he or she is approaching, stands to sing:

> Praise God, from whom all blessings flow;
> Praise Him all creatures here below;
> Praise Him above, ye heav'nly host;
> Praise Father, Son, and Holy Ghost.[12]

---

12. Ibid., xxxi.

CHAPTER 8

PRAYER IN WORSHIP

P rayer is the soul of worship. Many believe that prayers form the most important part of public worship. Throughout history, people have worshiped God by calling upon God's name in praise and petition. The Bible is filled with examples of private and public prayers. David's prayer as recorded in Psalm 51 is an outstanding example of individual confession. Many of the psalms mingle praise and petition, showing a concern for the individual as well as for the nation (Pss. 60, 79, and 80). One outstanding example of public prayer is Solomon's prayer at the dedication of the temple. This prayer is an eloquent recitation of God's glory and an earnest plea for God's continuing favor upon the people (2 Chron. 6).

Jesus considered prayer so important that he gave the following as a model prayer for his disciples:

Our Father who art in heaven,
Hallowed be thy name.
Thy kingdom come,
Thy will be done,
On earth as it is in heaven.
Give us this day our daily bread;
And forgive us our debts,

As we also have forgiven our debtors;
And lead us not into temptation,
But deliver us from evil.[1]

The Lord's Prayer includes various attitudes essential for worship—adoration, submission, confession, petition, and dedication.

There is a definite pattern in this model prayer: (1) God's name—who God is, including the essence of God's person; (2) God's kingdom—God's realm of life, including all God's relationships with God's people; (3) God's will—what God desires and purposes, including plans, procedures, and methods; (4) our material needs—petitions for God to supply those needs; (5) our need for confession of sins—prayer for guidance in paths of right living and deliverance from evil; (6) our commitment of all things to God—acknowledgment of God's sovereign lordship over all of life. The prayer begins in adoration, as God's name is hallowed, and concludes in doxology, as all things are committed to God's purpose and glory.

One of the dynamic characteristics of the early congregation of Christians in Jerusalem was its practice of continuing steadfastly in prayers (Acts 2:42). The Christians may have prayed at stated hours replacing the Jewish synagogue tradition in much the way that the apostles' teaching had replaced that of the scribes.[2]

Their prayers may have included both new and old elements as seen in Ephesians 5:19, Colossians 3:16, and James 5:13. The story of the church in Acts indicates the people joined as a congregation in the practice of common prayer. When Peter and John returned from prison, the congregation lifted up their voices together to God and said,

> "Sovereign Lord, who didst make the heaven and the earth and the sea and everything in them, who by the mouth of our father David, thy servant, didst say by the Holy Spirit, 'Why did the Gentiles rage, and the peoples imagine vain things?'" . . . And when they had prayed, the place in which they were gathered together was shaken; and they were all filled with the Holy Spirit and spoke the word of God with boldness (Acts 4:24–25, 31).

George A. Buttrick observes that corporate prayer is the heart of corporate worship. "The heart of religion is in prayer—the uplifting of human hands, the speaking of human lips, the expectant waiting of human silence—in direct communion with the Eternal."[3] Buttrick adds significantly that prayer must go *through* the order of worship, Scripture, symbolism, and sermon, as "light through a window."

---

1. Matt. 6:9–13.
2. *The Expositor's Greek Testament*, ed. W. Robertson Nicoll (New York: Hodder & Stoughton, 1917), 2:95.
3. George A. Buttrick, *Prayer* (Nashville: Abingdon-Cokesbury Press, 1942), 283.

Although prayer is an intensely personal matter, it is not individualistic, especially when the Christian joins with the congregation in worship. Prayer then becomes an expression of community, of human solidarity, and of spiritual fellowship within the body of Christ. The church incorporates the community of prayer as a contemporary, worldwide fellowship, for in the church we pray for all kinds of people in every part of the world; and when we pray as members of the body of Christ, we bear witness to our faith that God loves all people and will hear our petitions for all humankind.

There are generally three kinds of prayers used in public worship: (1) fixed or liturgical prayers in which all of the prayers are read in public worship; (2) spontaneous or extemporaneous prayers, which are prayed without planning; and (3) prayers given extemporaneously after preparation. In this third method of praying there is both discipline and freedom, both planning and spontaneity. This balanced approach to public prayer is accepted by most Free Churches as a good model.

In liturgical prayers everything is written and there may be no room left for spontaneous promptings of the Holy Spirit. Planned prayer with freedom avoids this particular pitfall. Planned prayer that includes both discipline and freedom enables the prayer leader to gather and express the desires of the people, but free prayer does not mean freedom to license. In unprepared, spontaneous prayer there is always the danger that the prayer leader may lack discipline in his or her thoughts; the prayer may be spoiled by unsuitable expressions; it may involve too much repetition; or the prayer leader may inflict a personal agenda upon the congregation.

Carelessness in leading public prayers has often bordered on the ludicrous. A pastor who had forgotten to make an announcement included in the benediction, "Lord, kindly remind the deacons that their meeting set for Monday night has been canceled." Another error is often made by informing God of what God already knows. One minister began his petition for people who lost their possessions in a flood: "Lord, as thou hast probably heard, many people lost their homes in the recent flood." Using public prayer to retaliate or to condemn other people is a horrible error sometimes practiced by persons. These instances are proof that more serious attention should be given to leading public prayer.

GUIDING PRINCIPLES CONCERNING PUBLIC PRAYERS

Public prayers demand sincerity and intelligence. Zeal with intelligibility will inspire a congregation to join the leader in prayer. If public prayers are to be most meaningful to a congregation, certain principles should be followed:

1. Every prayer should have a specific purpose of its own. A prayer should not deal in vague generalities, but it should speak specifically; for example, a prayer for forgiveness of sins should specify which sins. When a prayer expresses gratitude for blessings, it should name the blessings. The petition should be concrete and definite. Fosdick said, "Some prayers are a confused jumble of all sorts of requests, meditations, aspirations, and even homilies, which occur to the extempore pray-er."[4] A well-organized prayer can be followed and participated in by each member of the congregation.

2. Every prayer should have good style. The style should be simple, clear, direct, pleasing, and of good literary construction. Prayers should not be limited to biblical style, but the prayer leaders should immerse their minds in the Scriptures, especially those passages which are prayers themselves.

3. Every prayer should be addressed *to* God. It is not a discourse *about* God. For example, it is inconsistent to pray, "Our Father, we know that God is concerned about us and will hear our petitions." Here the address is directly to God, and the remainder of the statement is a preachment about God.

4. Generally Old English pronouns "Thee, Thou, Thine," etc., should be avoided. It is preferable to use language that is understood by the majority of worshipers who are being led in prayer.

5. The delivery of the prayer is important if the congregation is to follow the leader. It should be delivered in a clear voice so that the congregation may hear distinctly. One should avoid a monotone or a so-called preacher voice in public prayers.

6. Public prayers should not be too long. A few brief prayers are probably better than one or two long prayers. George Whitfield once said of a certain preacher, "He prayed me into a good frame of mind, but he prayed me out of it again by keeping on."[5]

7. Some planning of public prayers seems to be essential if prayers are to be most effective in leading people to worship. Some may object to planning prayers in advance. "Is not prayer a matter of the heart?. . . Yes, prayer is a matter of the heart. But public prayer is a matter of

---

4. Harry Emerson Fosdick, *A Book of Public Prayers* (New York: Harper & Bros., 1959), 8.
5. Charles H. Spurgeon, *Lectures to His Students*, ed. David Otis Fuller (Grand Rapids: Zondervan Publishing House, 1945), 53.

many hearts . . . and involves the mind of the church."[6] Planning and spontaneity, discipline and freedom should be kept in balance.

8. All corporate worship prayer leaders should be notified in advance. Prayer leaders need to study the principles of leading in public prayer. Each prayer should have a distinct purpose in worship; therefore, no two prayers should repeat the same phrases.

TYPES OF PRAYERS

Every prayer should have a definite purpose. Unless this principle is followed, there is danger of violating Jesus' command, "Use not vain repetitions, as the heathen do" (Matt. 6:7, KJV). One man asked, "Doesn't God know what we have already prayed earlier in the service without our repeating it to him?" Without definite purpose it is easy for prayers to become mere verbal formalities. Well-worn clichés soon lose their significance and their interest. The following classification of prayers may be helpful.

The call to prayer. A prayer may well be introduced by a call to prayer. The leader may simply say, "Let us pray." He or she should never begin, "Shall we pray?" or "May we pray?" as if asking the congregation's permission. A prayer promise from the Scriptures may be quoted, such as, "Ask, and it will be given you; seek, and you will find; knock, and it will be opened to you" (Luke 11:9); or a call to worship may be printed for congregational participation, such as:

> Minister: God is our refuge and strength, a very present help in trouble.
>
> Congregation: Therefore we will not fear, though the earth should change, though the mountains shake in the heart of the sea.
>
> Unison: The Lord of hosts is with us; the God of Jacob is our refuge.

The invocation. The invocation is the opening prayer in which adoration and praise offered to God are prominent. This type of prayer is often called a collect. The purpose is to lead the people to become conscious of God's presence and to open their hearts to receive God's blessings. The invocation should be more objective (focusing upon God) than subjective (focusing upon the feelings of the people).

The invocation has five parts: (1) address to God; (2) a relative clause giving an attribute of God—who God is or some of God's promises; (3) a petition, or simple statement of desire; (4) the purpose or objective of the petition; and (5) the conclusion.

The pastoral prayer. This prayer has sometimes been called the main prayer, the morning or evening prayer, or the long prayer of the service.

---

6. Robert L. Williamson, *Effective Public Prayer* (Nashville: Broadman Press, 1960), 9.

The main prayer usually consists of the following parts: (1) Adoration and thanksgiving may be expressed, unless this has been done already in the invocation. Even then, as God is addressed, there should be the spirit of adoration. (2) Confession follows naturally when people have entered into the presence of God and acknowledged God's being worthy of worship. The purpose of this prayer is to lead the congregation to confess their sins to God. (3) Petition is asking God for the things desired. It concerns those who are present in the congregation. (4) Intercession is prayer offered for those beyond the assembled group: absent members of families, community and national leaders, people of other nations, missionaries and other servants who are serving God in other areas of the world, and other concerns of the congregation. (5) The climax of prayer is reached in submission to the will of God and willful commitment of our lives to God and God's service. (6) Ordinarily, prayers conclude with an ascription to the Trinity or to some member of the Godhead. For example, prayers may conclude "in Jesus' name," "through Jesus Christ our Lord," "for the sake of him who brought redemption and victory to all who believe in his name," or other appropriate ascriptions.

It may be preferable to break this prayer up into several parts, the leader indicating each brief prayer which is to be prayed by the congregation. For example, after having addressed God and expressed a spirit of adoration and praise, the leader may pause briefly and say, "Let us now offer our thanks to God for his blessings," and, after a brief pause, lead the congregation in specific thanksgiving. The leader would proceed to say, "Let us individually confess our sins to God," and, after a brief pause, lead the congregation in confession. By following this procedure the congregation is enlisted to participate more readily than if the leader simply leads a long prayer without a break.

The silent prayer. The silent prayer may be a part of another prayer. Before beginning a prayer, the leader may simply suggest that the congregation pause for a brief period of meditation and prayer, and then proceed to lead the congregation in prayer; or sometimes it is preferable to have the silent prayer at a different place in the order of worship. It is usually preferred that complete silence reign and that not even soft organ music be played during the silent prayer. The length of silence should be determined by the leader. Generally when the leader has prayed what he or she has asked the congregation to pray, enough time will have lasped. The worship leaders must always be a participant.

The bidding prayer. The leader may mention specific concerns and then bid the people to pray for them one at a time. This may be included in the period of silent prayer. It is not necessarily used in every worship service. Many feel that it is an excellent practice for the midweek prayer service.

The litany. The litany is a form of prayer in which fixed and frequent responses are made by the congregation to brief petitions said by the leader. It is an effective way to encourage congregational participation. The following is an example of a litany. The litany may be as brief or lengthy as is needed. The response is taken from Psalm 123:3.

> Minister: Gracious God, we have neglected to worship You regularly.
>
> Congregation: Have mercy upon us, O Lord.
>
> Minister: We have been guilty of prejudice toward others.
>
> Congregation: Have mercy upon us, O Lord.

The prayer before the offering. The prayer before the offering is specifically for the dedication of gifts. It may include a brief sentence of thanksgiving for God's gifts to us, a reference to the use of our gifts, and other matters of stewardship. The dedication of self along with the gift is important. This offertory prayer should be specifically related to the offering. It is better not to call this prayer the offertory prayer because, technically, the offertory is the music played while the offering is collected; therefore, the term offertory prayer would be for the music, not the gifts.

The benediction. The benediction commends us to God's care and announces God's blessings upon us. It is an important climax to worship. Andrew W. Blackwood has said that it ought to be like the period at the end of a sentence. It should gather up the attitudes expressed in the worship service, and it should be offered to God as a commitment of the congregation to go forth into the world to carry out God's will. Scriptural benedictions are excellent. The Aaronic blessing is often used: "The LORD bless you and keep you: the LORD make his face to shine upon you, and be gracious to you: the LORD lift up his countenance upon you, and give you peace" (Num. 6:24–26).

Paul's conclusion to his Second Epistle to the Corinthians contains another favorite benediction: "The grace of the Lord Jesus Christ and the love of God and the fellowship of the Holy Spirit be with you all" (2 Cor. 13:14). Other excellent benedictions are found in the following Scripture passages: Ephesians 3:20–21; Hebrews 13:20–21; 1 Peter 5:10–11; Jude 24–25; and Revelation 22:21.

PREPARATION FOR LEADING IN PRAYER

Most Free Churches do not use fixed forms of prayer for public worship. On the other hand, it must not be assumed that one can be most effective in leading a congregation in worship without some kind of preparation. Without preparation the leader may pray meaningless terms or even nonsense syllables. Just as the preacher draws from every resource in the preparation of sermons, the prayer leader should utilize various resources in preparation for leading in public prayer.

Henry Sloane Coffin has suggested the following qualities should characterize public prayers: comprehensiveness, orderliness, concreteness, objectivity, freshness or relevance, and variety.[7]

Prayer must be absolutely forthright, honest. It demands mental, moral, and religious integrity. Genuine prayer that links humanity with the purposes of God deserves the best preparation. The following suggestions are offered for leaders in their preparation.

1. *Pray in private.* No person is prepared to lead other people in worship until he or she has first worshiped God in private. Spurgeon declared that private prayer is the drill ground for public prayer. Jesus taught his disciples to enter into the secret place and talk with God alone. The leader has no right to lead people in public prayer unless he or she has a private prayer life also. The prayers to be led in public should first of all be prayed in private.

2. *Consider the needs.* The prayer leader should survey the needs of the congregation as he or she prepares for prayer. Ultimately the contents of prayer are more important than the techniques or types of prayer. The desires of the leader must be joined with the desires of the congregation to enable all worshipers to be fully engaged in corporate prayer. This calls for deep and sympathetic insight into human need, for sensitive awareness of both individual and social problems, and for faith in God's grace and mercy. Perhaps it demands as much dedicated and careful preparation as does the preaching of a sermon. If public prayers are to be helpful in worship, they must be relevant to the needs of the people.

3. *Study the prayers of the Bible.* The Bible contains a treasury of prayer. The book of Psalms through the centuries has been the book of devotion which best expresses the universal spirit of prayer. A pastor in a prominent church testifies that the Psalms have meant more to him in preparing to lead people in public worship than perhaps any other piece of literature. The prayers of Jesus exemplify the honesty and intensity with which one must come into the presence of God. The prayers of Paul are also excellent examples for public worship.

4. *Study other prayers.* Prayer leaders are enriched when they study the classical prayers which others have formulated. The leader should

---

7. Coffin, *Public Worship*, 72f.

become familiar with manuals of public prayer so that he or she may have the benefit of what others throughout history have learned about leading in public prayer. There are classics in liturgical literature as well as in secular literature. *The Episcopal Book of Common Prayer* is one of the outstanding examples of prayers for public services, both from the viewpoint of the purposes set forth in the prayers and from the viewpoint of their literary form. Many resources are available to guide the prayer leader.

5. *Outline and write out prayers.* Whether the prayer leader reads the prayer or not, written prayers will give concreteness and purpose. There should be no more objection to writing prayers than there is to writing sermons. Writing prayers can improve public worship and can also enhance the devotional life of the leader.

6. *Memorize portions of prayers.* It is particularly good to memorize the beginning of a prayer. Well-chosen introductory phrases may mean the difference between a helpful prayer and one which distracts in worship. Also consider incorporating phrases from hymns into public prayers.

7. *Depend upon the Holy Spirit.* All who worship should depend upon the Holy Spirit in both private and public praying. Paul exhorted the people to pray with the spirit and with the mind also (1 Cor. 14:15). When prayers are planned, the Holy Spirit has more with which to work in leading the congregation in prayer. This will not hinder the spirit of spontaneity in prayer any more than preparation for preaching will hinder spontaneity in the delivery of the sermon. As H. E. Dana affirmed, "Preparation is as wings, not as weights, to freedom and spirit."[8]

8. *Connect the prayer to its surrounding elements.* The prayer should be tied closely to other elements that surround it. When preparing to pray be aware of a hymn that precedes it or a Scripture that follows. Pay careful attention to the theme for the day or season and the mood of the service.

---

8. H. E. Dana, *A Manual of Ecclesiology* (Kansas City, Kans.: Central Seminary Press, 1944), 339.

CHAPTER 9

COMMUNICATING
THE WORD OF GOD

T he Bible is central in worship. God communicates his Word to us
through our words. Since the Bible is a record of the acts of God
in history as revealed to us by the Holy Spirit, it is the primary
source of the objective content in worship. The Bible presents Jesus Christ
as the object of faith in worship.

The writers of the Old Testament story were conscious that God spoke
to them. Moses received the Law by the Spirit of God through faith, and
the prophets heard God speaking to them. Jeremiah said, "The word of
the LORD came to me" (Jer. 1:4). The author of Hebrews testified that "in
many and various ways God spoke of old to our fathers by the prophets"
(Heb. 1:1). He goes on to imply that the appearance of the living Word in
the person of God's Son verifies the trustworthiness of God's written
record.

Many elements in the order of worship are filled with biblical content.
The music, particularly the hymns, communicates biblical truth. Public
prayers are often saturated with the spirit and terminology of the Bible. The
sermon proclaims the gospel as recorded in the Bible. The public reading of
the Bible allows God's Word to speak for itself.

THE READING OF THE SCRIPTURES

The Free Churches boast, "We are a people of the Book," and yet there is great neglect of the Bible. People fail to read it regularly in private; in many homes the Scriptures are rarely read. Even in public worship services the reading of the Bible is often neglected. When it is read, it is often read carelessly and hurriedly.

The reading of the Scriptures in public worship is highly significant. H. E. Dana cites two biblical models. One is found in Ezra as recorded in Nehemiah 8:5–8: "And Ezra opened the book in the sight of all the people, for he was above all the people; and when he opened it all the people stood. And Ezra blessed the LORD, the great God; and all the people answered, 'Amen, Amen,' lifting up their hands; and they bowed their heads and worshiped the LORD with their faces to the ground." After the Babylonian exile Aramaic was the common language of the day, since many Jews did not understand Hebrew. Ezra would read the Scripture, then explain its meaning.[1]

The other example is recorded in the fourth chapter of Luke where Jesus is "reading in the synagogue the prophetic witness concerning himself while the eyes of all were fastened on him, and men marveled at the gracious words." Dana further states, "These two model examples not only exalt the reading of the Bible as a channel of the Spirit's power, but demonstrate the supreme value of the content of the portions read and the manner of the reading."[2]

Bible reading is in itself an act of worship—not the worship of the written word but the worship of the living Word to whom the written word gives witness. The influence of the Bible in worship is direct. Usually some portion of the Scriptures is read aloud, frequently two portions (one from the Old Testament and one from the New Testament) and in some churches three passages are read (one from the Old Testament, one from the Epistles, and one from the Gospels). In the Puritan and nonconformist churches there was always a lengthy reading.

SELECTING THE SCRIPTURE PASSAGE

Careful attention should be given to the selection of Scripture passages. Some churches have a lectionary suggesting appropriate passages for particular seasons according to the Christian year. However, many churches do not use the lectionary; therefore, serious attention must be given to the selections. Most hymnals contain selections for responsive readings. The following suggestions may aid in selecting Scripture passages:

1. *Holman Bible Handbook*, ed. David Dockery (Nashville: Holman Bible Publishers, 1992), 845.
2. Dana, *Ecclesiology*, 337f.

1. For the public reading of God's Word, select a passage other than the passage upon which the sermon is based. The Bible should be allowed to speak for itself in the worship service.

2. The selection should be relatively devotional. The passage should not only instruct, but also it should encourage commitment. Passages from the Psalms, certain passages from Isaiah and other prophets, the Gospels, the Epistles, and Revelation are particularly appropriate.

3. The passage should be comparatively simple in style, language, and imagery. Poetic and rhythmical passages which appeal to the emotions and the imagination are particularly good for congregational reading.

4. Familiar passages that are universally loved comfort worshipers and call them to remember past associations; however, the choice should not be limited to familiar passages. Lesser-known passages also are appropriate for congregational reading.

5. Passages should vary between the Old Testament and the New Testament. Some leaders feel that if the sermon is to be from a New Testament passage, the passage for public reading may well be selected from the Old Testament.

6. Use various versions of the Bible in public worship. Not every passage reads equally well from every version. Consult different translations before each public reading in order to find the best version for the particular passage.

7. The passage for public reading should be comparatively brief; it should not be so long as to lose the attention of the congregation. The following are examples of good passages for reading in public worship: Psalms 1; 8; 23; 27; 46; 84; 90:1–12; 91; 103:1–17; 104:1–15; Isaiah 40:1–5, 9-11; Matthew 5:1–12; John 1:1–14; Romans 8:28–30, 35–39; 12; 1 Corinthians 13; 15:51–58; Hebrews 11 (certain portions); Revelation 5:11–14.

8. Consider having pew Bibles available so that the congregation can read from a common translation.

THE ART OF READING THE SCRIPTURES

Truth, not eloquence, is to be sought in reading the Holy Scriptures, and every passage must be read in the spirit in which it was written. To read the Bible well is a rare accomplishment. Good preachers are more numerous than good readers of the Scriptures. R. W. Dale suggests that the Scripture reader should, by a vigorous imaginative effort, stand by the very side of those who wrote the Bible to see what they saw and feel what they felt.

S. S. Curry reminds us that expression grows naturally and inevitably out of the reader's own grasp of the meaning of what he or she communicates to others. Curry affirms that the reading of the Scriptures is a peculiar, serious, and difficult function which demands special study and earnest preparation. The Bible is written in different literary forms which express a variety of spirits, such as the narrative spirit, the didactic spirit, the lyric spirit, the dramatic spirit, and the epic spirit.[3]

The following suggestions for reading the Scriptures may be helpful:

1. Handle the Bible reverently. Convey the feeling that it is God's Word. It is a symbol of the living Word speaking to the hearer.

2. Announce the passage intelligently and distinctly. One may say, "Let us hear God's Word as recorded in the Gospel according to Matthew, chapter five, verses one through sixteen."

3. Read the passage interpretively. Emphasize the important words, especially the verbs and the nouns. Imagine the setting and attempt to capture the spirit of the writer's experience. Good reading is in itself exposition.

4. Read clearly and distinctly to be understood. For good enunciation one must read slowly and deliberately. Much of the Bible is written in poetic form and cannot be properly interpreted without an understanding of poetic rhythm and Hebrew parallelism. For example, Psalm 24 begins, "The earth is the LORD'S and the fullness thereof, the world and those who dwell therein."

5. Let the Bible speak for itself. Read, ordinarily, without interruptions or comment. If some explanation is needed for a proper understanding of the passage, give the explanation before you begin reading. Do not preach and exhort in the middle of reading.

6. Practice reading aloud to yourself. Become thoroughly acquainted with the passage, and then read it aloud until you feel that you thoroughly understand how to communicate its message.

A Scripture lesson must be read intelligently and reverently if it is to be a means of worship. Scripture reading demands careful preparation.

---

3. S. S. Curry, *Vocal and Literary Interpretation of the Bible* (Boston: The Expression Co., 1923), 3. See also: Thomas Edward McComiskey, *Reading Scripture in Public: A Guide for Preachers and Lay Readers* (Grand Rapids: Baker Book House, 1991).

There are various ways of reading the Scriptures in public worship: (1) One person may read the passage. (2) The passage may be read in various combinations: leader, congregation; two leaders; leader, choir; choir, congregation; and other ways. Most hymnbooks have a section of Scripture passages appropriate for responsive reading. (3) The leader may invite the congregation to join in a unison reading of the entire passage.

The congregation should be encouraged to listen to God's Word and to participate in responsive or unison reading. The leader's attitude and actions can enhance congregational participation and listening. H. Grady Davis has observed, "When we listen properly, our listening also is worship."

THE PREACHING OF THE WORD

Through the centuries thousands of pastors have been preaching the gospel week in and week out, "constantly reminding the farmer and the shopkeeper of charity and humility, persuading them to think for a moment about the great issues of life, inducing them to confess their sins." Historian Herbert Butterfield continues, "This has been a phenomenon calculated greatly to alter the quality of life and the very texture of human history; and it has been the standing work of the church throughout the ages."[4]

Primitive Christianity depended almost exclusively on the preaching of the gospel. The preaching of the gospel at Pentecost was an innovation: the pre-Christian world had known nothing like it. Following in this New Testament tradition, Free Churches have made preaching central in the worship service.

There have been two extreme attitudes toward preaching in worship. The sacramentalists have often rejected the place of preaching in favor of the sacraments. Martin Luther deplored the lack of preaching in the churches of his time, and he declared that the Christian congregation should never assemble except the Word of God be preached. The other extreme view is observed in those who have consumed the prayer, praise, and Bible reading as the "hors d'oeuvres," prior to the meat of the Scriptures in the sermon. So much emphasis has been placed on the sermon that the significance of other parts of worship has been obscured. Some people in the Free Churches think of the other elements of a worship service as mere "preliminaries" to the sermon. A sermon must never be considered alone—the prayer and the praise will have their influence.

Preaching should take its place with the other elements of a worship service. The sermon is important, but it is not the only important part of worship. In the past, people have referred to Sunday worship as the "preaching

---

4. Quoted in Davies, *Worship and Theology in England*, 3–4.

service." The Six Point Record System once used in Southern Baptist Sunday Schools read, "Attending Preaching, 20%." A clear understanding of the relationship between preaching and the entire worship service is important. Hays and Steely believe that the strength of many Baptist churches is directly related to the strength of the preaching they have heard. They warn, however, of the danger that people will think of the worship service as simply a time for "listening" to a sermon.[5] So much stress has been given to preaching in many churches that the sanctuary has been designated the "auditorium."[6]

Contemporary preaching using inductive and narrative approaches views preaching as a participatory event. In this approach the sermon engages the congregation and elicits their participation in the gospel narrative. This method of preaching shifts part of the responsibility of the sermon to the congregation.

P. T. Forsyth believed so strongly in preaching that he declared that nothing in the service goes to the root of the gospel like the preaching; therefore, he believed preaching to be the chief part of our evangelical liturgy. Forsyth believed preaching gave credence to all worship, since the message is what stirs worship and makes it possible.[7] The Baptist tradition of magnifying the importance of preaching in worship is based on Romans 10:17 (KJV), "So then faith cometh by hearing, and hearing by the word of God."

In order to emphasize the unity of other elements and the sermon in the service of worship, the following propositions are offered:

1. All biblical preaching is contemporary dialogue. The sermon is an offering to God, while at the same time the sermon is God's Word to the congregation. Preaching is an event in which God acts. All preaching should open the Scriptures and find in them God's Word to us which has its focus in the person of Jesus Christ. Only preaching that brings the Scriptures to focus on concrete historical life situations can be called biblical preaching.

   Since all worship is encounter with God, it is the purpose of preaching to bring us into a conscious confrontation with our Maker. The preacher speaks to believers to build them up as a Christian community, and the preacher speaks to the world to build it into a Christian community. Pronouncing the good news may be designated both as

---

5. Brooks Hays and John E. Steely, *The Baptist Way of Life* (Englewood Cliffs, N.J.: Prentice-Hall Inc., 1963), 103.

6. The term *auditorium* is derived from the root *audit*, "to hear." Since worship includes more than listening, another term for the place of worship must be found.

7. P. T. Forsyth, *Positive Preaching and the Modern Mind* (London: Hodder & Stoughton, 1907), 88.

prophetic preaching and pastoral preaching.[8] Many effective teachers of preaching indicate that the sermon should meet certain specific objectives as related to the text and the life of the congregation, such as the ethical objective—the point at which the converted person touches the life of another person; the consecrative objective—which calls people to dedicate to God all the resources under their control, including time, talent, and personality; and the supportive objective—which is designed to meet the needs of the people who are enduring great burdens and suffering.[9] We may also compare Roy Pearson's fourfold objective for preaching: "to celebrate the wonderful works of God; to contend for the faith delivered to the saints; to fill the hungry with good things; and to speak to the children of Israel, that they go forward."[10]

One object of preaching is to present the gospel of God's redeeming grace to unbelieving persons who will respond in faith and commit their lives to God as their Savior and Lord. To preach is to become a part of a dynamic event wherein the living, redeeming God reproduces acts of redemption in a living encounter with humankind through the preacher.[11]

2. Preaching is the witness of the church to the world. Preaching belongs to the church before it belongs to the individual preacher. It is a part of the commission which the Lord delivered to the church; therefore, preaching is a confession of the church's faith.

The church is the caretaker of preaching. Christ founded a community, a church, whose first charge was the preaching of the gospel. Forsyth calls the preaching of the gospel, the central work of the church going forward, the "organized hallelujah of an ordered community."[12]

Preaching the gospel is the business of the church. The preacher's voice is a representative voice of the entire church. The preacher speaks *for* the church and *with* the church *to* the world. The story of the early church tells us that all the followers of Christ were scattered,

---

8. For a helpful discussion of pastoral preaching and worship, see C. W. Brister, *Pastoral Care in the Church* (San Francisco: Harper & Row, 1992); J. Randall Nichols, *The Restoring Word: Preaching as Pastoral Communication* (San Francisco: Harper & Row, 1987); and William H. Willimon, *Peculiar Speech: Preaching to the Baptized* (Grand Rapids: Eerdmans, 1992).

9. See H. C. Brown, Jr., H. G. Clinard, J. J. Northcutt, and Al Fasol, *Steps to the Sermon*, rev. ed. (Nashville: Broadman & Holman, 1996).

10. Roy Pearson, *The Preacher, His Purpose and Practice* (Philadelphia: Westminster Press, 1963), 278.

11. See William H. Willimon, *The Intrusive Word: Preaching to the Unbaptized* (Grand Rapids: Eerdmans, 1994).

12. Forsyth, *Positive Preaching*, 88, 105.

except the apostles, and they went everywhere "preaching the word" (Acts 8:1, 4).

3. Preaching is also the personal witness of the preacher. In the individual preacher the everlasting gospel is contemporized, individualized, and actualized. The preacher, redeemed by the grace of God and energized by the Holy Spirit, speaks the things he or she has seen and heard and experienced. The preacher actually becomes the instrument of Jesus Christ to present Christ's claim to humanity. Unless the preacher feels the gospel within his or her own being, it is not likely that others will feel its impact as they hear. We are reminded of Phillips Brooks's much-quoted definition of preaching as the communication of the truth of God to humanity through personal witness. It is truth presented effectively through dedicated personality.

If preaching is to be worshipful and is to contribute to worship, thorough preparation of heart and mind is required of the preacher. Such preparation is not confined to the development of a particular sermon but involves the whole personality of the preacher during the whole of life. Direct preparation goes on in the study while the minister consults commentaries and lexicons on next Sunday's sermon text. The real quality of the sermon depends upon a disciplined spirit and a well-stored mind, a deep knowledge of the people, and a vital experience of the saving power of God in the life of the preacher. The continual cultivation of the minister's own spiritual life requires time for devotional reading of the Bible, the reading of great devotional literature and theology, periods of prayer and meditation, and a sensitivity to the presence of God in the lives of others.

The test of worshipful preaching is the effect it has upon those who hear. There is a close interrelationship between preaching and pastoral work. The preacher must be able to relate theology to life. The primary purpose of preaching is to build up the church, not to glorify the preacher. Effective preaching creates a church in which the people no longer center their attention on the preacher but have their faith grounded in the revelation of the Scriptures. The sermon should guide all worshipers to their calling to be servants of the Word.

The minister both as leader in worship and as preacher should be willing to become submerged in the gospel and be content to be a representative of the Spirit of God. The time of worship is not a time for cleverness or excessive levity or the display of oratory for the sake of exalting the vanity of the preacher. As James Denny long ago said, "No man can give at one and the same time the impression that he himself is clever and that Jesus Christ is mighty to save."

Perhaps another suggestion from the eighteenth century may be helpful. Strickland Gough of the Established Church once wrote to the Dissenters, "I think there are two faults in your manner of worship, that your prayers are too short and your sermons too long. The one has too little reverence toward God and the other is too tedious toward ourselves." He added that God was worshiped for twenty minutes and the reason of humanity was titillated for sixty minutes in the sermon.[13]

In summary, the sermon should point toward worship, not toward the preacher.

4. Preaching and the other elements of worship mutually support each other. They are at their best in a complementary relationship. Preaching makes a positive contribution to all other acts of worship. All liturgical elements are important in worship. The worshiper in the congregation needs to understand the liturgy. Preaching translates all the other elements of worship into the language of the common person. Preaching helps the worshipers relate worship to their life experiences. Preaching is worship's interpreter, the instrument whereby the heart that has "dwelt awhile in heaven is connected with the hands and feet that now must dwell on earth."[14]

Preaching may be regarded as the most highly creative aspect of the minister. The emotions and the imagination of the preacher stimulate a like response on the part of the hearer. Inspired preaching can make all the other elements of worship come alive for the congregation.

The sermon is particularly fitted to climax the service. It may recapitulate the various moods and movements of the service and draw them together as the minds and judgments and wills of the hearers are focused upon the gospel. Commitment, which is the climax of worship, may be challenged by the sermon as it presses for decisions and actions as a proof that the person means what he or she says and is changed by what he or she feels.

Preaching is dependent upon the response of the people. The congregation is not simply an audience which remains passive while it is being preached to. The worshiping people are the source of the sermon, for their lives and their needs mold and make the preacher. The preacher

13. Davies, *Worship and Theology in England*, 97.
14. Pearson, *Preacher*, 137.

realizes that the church is a body of worshipers with whom to share insights revealed in study and prayer. Actually, the preacher acknowledges the need to allow the congregation the last word after the sermon. The preacher always hopes that the emotions and purposes of the congregation will be expressed in commitment as a result of the appeal made by the sermon. Good worship and good preaching go together. The reverse is also true. Poor preaching and bare worship usually go together.

Ideally, worship will contribute to better preaching and preaching to better worship. Participation in the preaching of the gospel and in the other elements of worship provides a shared experience for the minister and the congregation. God has been at work in the lives of the entire congregation, and the gospel finds witness in the hearts of all present. They recognize and give assent to the gospel when it is preached. The Holy Spirit can work in the common worship experience of the entire congregation. Preachers should trust the Word to produce its own message in the minds of the hearers.

5. Preaching is an act of worship. If worship is two-way communication between God and humanity, preaching that brings humanity into the presence of God surely must be considered an act of worship. Preachers who do not worship while preaching deny their calling; churches that do not worship while hearing the sermon deny their commission. Preaching that does not express worship is not really preaching; it is only a form of oratory or religious public speech. Worship is a sort of congregational sermon by way of testimony and witnessing, and preaching is but another form of God's part in the dialogue with his people in worship.

Preaching and the other elements of worship belong together. Worship gives preaching its reason for being, and preaching helps to make worship relevant.

THE WORDS WE CHOOSE

Much worship communication is verbal, and the words that we choose portray the person within us. Words reflect thought and define action and must be carefully and intentionally chosen if they are to communicate effectively. The words we speak are not only owned by the person speaking, but in corporate worship, they become the shared property of all worshipers. The words which we choose for worship must (1) demonstrate acceptable grammar and syntax, (2) speak truthfully about God's nature, (3) affirm all worshipers, and (4) clearly portray the speaker's intent.

Archaic language is not understood by modern worshipers and should be avoided in worship. There is little rationale for using language in worship that has no consistent use in society. Use of terms such as "thee," "thou," "wouldst," while very popular in the past because of their association with the King James Version of the Bible, are no longer preferred by most worshipers.

Insensitive racist and ethnic language is no longer acceptable. No longer are references to internationals as "foreigners" appropriate. Persons from other countries should be identified according to their origin, "She is from Kazakhstan." When it is necessary to refer to people as groups, they should always be referred to as they wish to be referred to, (e.g., Native Americans rather than Indians) not as the speaker wishes. Language is in transition, and speakers must make every attempt to make appropriate references according to current terms.

Stereotypical language invariably is false language, for there are always exceptions. To refer to the pianist as she or the minister of education as he invariably is misleading and results in offense. Language that stereotypes a person as handicapped or disabled should be avoided. When necessary to refer to a person's difference, say "He is blind," not "He is handicapped." Rarely is it necessary to pit an individual or group against the "norm" by giving them a stereotyped label.

Non-inclusive gender language, while the norm in the past, is no longer acceptable by many persons and is increasingly misunderstood by younger persons not steeped in this tradition. To use male language (man, men, mankind, he, his, him, father, son, brethren, brotherhood) when intending to address persons of both genders is to fail to speak clearly and to risk miscommunication. Consider the following: (1) Instead of masculine words use masculine and feminine pronouns; all people; humankind, one, and similar terms. (2) Use "fine person" instead of "fine man" or "fine woman" to communicate a high status among all persons. (3) Use terms that are gender neutral such as chairperson and laypersons.

Language that names is preferable to language that labels. When referring to a married couple refer to them as "John and Ann" not "John and his wife." Identifying persons by their names is preferred to identify them by role positions, such as pastor, brother, teacher, president, wife, or husband.

Language order often shows how our minds have been conditioned and how they operate. Always referring respectively to "men, women, and children," shows both conditioning and thought. When listing or naming persons, always alphabetize to avoid openly admitting the order in which you thought of the names, thereby reflecting the priority of the person in your mind.

Unequal reference to males and females can diminish a person's uniqueness in the group and has poor grammatical agreement. "Men and Women,"

"Girls and Boys," "Ladies and Gentlemen" are in agreement, whereas, "Men and Ladies" gives the expectation that the behavior of the females is to be refined whereas the males can be men in the generic sense.[15]

---

15. For more information see: Carolyn Jennings, "Why Are You Walking Away?" *Creator Magazine*, November/December 1991.

CHAPTER 10

CHILDREN IN WORSHIP

*T*he worship of God should be experienced by the entire congregation; therefore, the children should certainly be included. Too often worship services are planned with adults in mind, and children are neglected. Among the earliest instructions which God revealed to his people was the command to love God and keep his words in the heart. This particular passage in Deuteronomy continues, "You shall teach them diligently to your children, and shall talk of them when you sit in your house" (Deut. 6:7). Later in Deuteronomy 6, parents are instructed when the children ask, "What is the meaning of the testimonies and the statutes and the ordinances that the LORD our God has commanded you?" to reply, "We were Pharaoh's slaves in Egypt; and the LORD brought us out of Egypt with a mighty hand" (Deut. 6:20–21). The church is to tell God's story to each succeeding generation of children, for without this retelling, how will the story continue?

Jesus himself included the children in his ministry. He said "'Let the children come to me, and do not hinder them; for to such belongs the kingdom of heaven.' And he laid his hands on them and went away" (Matt. 19:14–15).

Churches vary widely in the ways in which they include children in worship: churches may have no nursery or preschool care and everyone (including babies) is included in worship; children at age four may go to big church; four- and five-year-old children may leave before the sermon; or children may be excluded from adult worship and segregated for "children's church."

Albert Schweitzer once commented about his being brought to church as a child:

> From the services in which I joined as a child, I have taken with me into life a feeling for what is solemn, and a need for quiet and self-reflection, without which I cannot realize the meaning of my life. I cannot, therefore, support the opinion of those who would not let children take part in grownup people's services until they, to some extent, understand, but that they shall feel something of what is serious and solemn. The fact that the child sees his elders full of devotion, and has to feel something of their devotion himself—that is what gives the services meaning for him.

Children's educators are quick to point out the importance of mood when teaching children. Children in worship are strongly affected by the moods of adults around them even if they are aware of all the cognitive content. Since worship is an inclusive event, children should be included in the corporate worship experience of the church. While positive aspects may be realized from children's church where children sit in a children's room in small furniture, children are ever aware that they are participating in "pseudo-church" and that "real church" is going on somewhere else. A sensitive minister once said, "For years I was bothered by the noise and occasional disruptions by children in church until I found myself serving in a congregation made up exclusively of older adults. I find myself longing for the sounds of children—a baby's cry, a preschooler's loud whisper, an exit at an odd time—for these are the sounds of life in a church."

There are times when children's needs are best served in separate worship experiences. When many children are brought to church in busses or vans without their parents and these children have no previous worship participation experience, a children's church is recommended; however, these children should be integrated into the church's main worship service as soon as possible. Enlisting adults to serve as "church parents" or "sponsors" for these children can help this system to progress smoothly.

WORSHIP IS INCLUSIVE OF ALL PEOPLE

The level of acceptance of children by the congregation is apparent to a child and his or her parents and ultimately has an effect on the child's acceptance of herself and how he may view God's acceptance. The church's goal is to be God's people on earth; therefore, the church becomes, even for the small child, a microcosm of how he or she ultimately views God. If a church is truly dedicated to carrying out the mandate of the gospel, then the church must be inclusive of God's people of all ages, races, and social status. Gobbel and Huber respond appropriately. The question of "What can we do *for* the children during worship is much better approached as what can we do *along with* the children in worship so that all of us together may do the proper work of the community."[1] Worship should never be an exclusive act. Therefore, worship leaders must do all within their power to ensure that corporate worship experiences represent at least some unique aspect of all of its members, children, youth, young adults, median adults, and older adults.

Ng and Thomas offer the following as guidelines for the church's worship: (1) that no one should be bored, (2) that all of our senses should be involved, (3) that all participants should have the opportunity to contribute, (4) that persons should be able to receive gifts from each other, (5) that signs and imagery should be developed corporately and shared so that worshipers may grow in faith, (6) that faith should be transmitted through rituals and the input of previous generations, (7) that elements of worship such as prayer and praise are essential parts of the daily life of all Christians, and (8) that attention should be given to the level of understanding of each member of the worshiping community.[2]

CHILDREN LEARN BY EXAMPLE

Children learn more by example than by words; therefore, adult worshipers must model full participation. If verbal communication does not match nonverbal communication, the nonverbal will be believed. If a Sunday school teacher teaches about the importance of worship and leaves after Sunday school, the message is lost. If a parent talks of God's valuing worship and fails to sing hymns, the lesson is lost. If the minister talks with children about appropriate worship conduct and later whispers to the minister of music, the lesson is lost. Recent studies in reading point out that children who observe their parents reading are more likely to become lovers of reading than children whose parents read to them but rarely read themselves. Although all worship content may not be understood, children will learn the behavior and attitude that are modeled.

CHILDREN RESPOND WITH ALL SENSES

Children are more likely than adults to perceive their world through multiple senses; therefore, worship designed for meaningful child participation should include all senses. Hazel Morris cites ways in which children can be involved in worship:

> *Sounds invite children to worship:* Reverently listening during the prelude reminds children of the Bible verse "Be still, and know that I am God" (Ps. 46:10). A brass ensemble. A guitar. Psalm 150 read as a litany from different parts of the

---

1. A. Roger Gobbel and Phillip C. Huber, *Creative Designs with Children at Worship* (Atlanta: John Knox Press, 1981), 3.
2. Daniel Ng and Virginia Thomas, *Children in the Worshiping Community* (Atlanta: John Knox Press, 1981), 120.

sanctuary. "Jesus Loves Me" sung in Korean. The familiar words of the "Doxology" set to the tune of "Edelweiss." Nickels and quarters clinking into the offering plate. The choir processing to the choir lift, their voices growing stronger and louder as they reach the front. A familiar verse of Scripture. The splash of water in the baptistery. The cry of a new baby being dedicated.

Sights invite children to worship: Clusters of daisies at the end of each pew on Easter Sunday. The stacks of trays on the communion table. The familiar face of the Sunday School teacher reading the Old Testament passage. Rainbows shattered and recast in stained glass windows. The names of worship leaders in the bulletin. A nativity scene. The flickering light of the Advent candles. A banner created by the fourth-graders in Sunday School celebrating Pentecost. The Bible at a central place of worship.

Touches invite children to worship: Hands blessing at ordination. The smooth wood of the pews and the soft velvet of their cushions. The hand of a friend passing "the peace of Christ." Leaning against a parent during the sermon. One student says her first memory of church is that of going to sleep in her mother's arms. When she sang "Leaning on the Everlasting Arms" as an adult, that imagery came forth, for in that place she had felt most "safe and secure from all alarms."

Smells and tastes invite children to worship: An evergreen decorated with Chrismons, symbols of Christ, during Advent. A loaf of fresh baked bread broken for the Lord's Supper. A pitcher of grape juice. Tulips, irises, and daisies brought by family members to fill a wire cross on Easter Sunday.

Movement invites children to worship: The echoing motion of the bodies of worshipers as they stand and sit to read a litany or sing a hymn. The procession of women and men, boys and girls to the Lord's Supper table as they place their milk carton banks for world hunger upon it. Turning to greet fellow worshipers with words of welcome and peace. Standing to sing the "Hallelujah Chorus" at the end of Handel's *Messiah*.

Silence invites children to worship: The words "The Lord is in his holy temple; let all the earth keep silence before him!"[3] Leaving the church in darkness after Good Friday services. Quietly watching while the Advent candles are lighted. Praying silently for concerns voiced by the pastor. The silence surrounding as people are led into a lake, pond, or baptistery for baptism.[4]

EXPLAINING DIFFICULT CONCEPTS TO CHILDREN

Many concepts with which worship deals are difficult for adults to understand; therefore, they are difficult to explain to children. However, children do not have to understand all aspects of a subject or experience in order to participate meaningfully in worship. It is not necessary to explain all aspects of intricate theological concepts to children but, when dealing exclusively

---

3. Hab. 2:20.

4. Hazel M. Morris, "Children and Worship," *Southwestern Journal of Theology* 33, no. 3 (Summer 1991): 19–20. Used by permission.

with children, it is important to make statements and respond to questions with simple and direct language. Admitting your difficulty in understanding a subject can be helpful to children and to other adults.

"Children's use of language far outstrips their understanding of that language."[5] Children often use many words of which they do not understand the full meaning. The fact that children may not understand the full content of worship does not mean that children should not sing the songs and hear the stories of their faith. Faith is developmental and children, through their worship experience, must be given opportunity to experience a complete faith. No stage of development can be fully recovered during a later stage. Morris summarizes,

> Understanding starts at the level of impression and awareness. If interest is created on the basic level, then understanding will follow. While children need to learn their vocabulary of worship from a young age, developmental psychologists tell us that they use words before they fully comprehend them. Because they are motivated by language at the level just above where they are, worship designed to involve children should not be condescending but challenging.[6]

INCORPORATING CHILDREN INTO CORPORATE WORSHIP

Children can be incorporated into corporate worship in ways that are not exclusively childlike. "Worship can have the depth of content and the integrity that reflect the highest biblical and traditional standards and at the same time have appeal to children."[7]

The following suggestions are helpful for the worship leader who seeks to incorporate children's needs in worship:

1. Know children by their names and seek opportunities to dialogue with children other than on Sunday morning as they exit.

2. Pace the service, varying physical postures and acts of worship which appeal to different senses.

3. Include as much congregational participation as possible.

4. Be flexible with room arrangement whenever possible and encourage children to sit close to the front so they feel a part of the action.

5. When needed, explain worship terms that may not be understood by the children.

6. Use lay leadership often. Children need to see their teachers, parents, and peers in leadership roles.

---

5. Morris, 20.
6. Ibid., 22.
7. Ng and Thomas, *Children*, 24.

7. Utilize children's literature for sermon illustrations.

8. Balance traditional worship language with simpler, easier to understand language.

9. Set the Scripture in context simply and briefly: "These are the words of Jesus speaking to the disciples." "David wrote this song when he was a shepherd boy."

10. Include children's concerns in the prayers of worship (important events such as school starting should receive corporate prayer).

11. Use music in worship that is familiar to children. Work with Sunday School, missions leaders, and choir leaders to include their music in the congregation's worship.

12. Remind ushers to give each child a bulletin and other worship materials and to recognize and honor the presence of children.

13. Use drama in worship to capture the attention and imagination of children.

14. Plan occasional children's times within worship.

15. As you plan worship keep the needs of children before you.

16. Allow children the privilege of leading in worship. With appropriate preparation, children can lead almost any act of worship as well as adults.[8]

Hazel Morris and Paul Oakley offer the following potential worship leadership opportunities for children:

1. Children and their families can be greeters and ushers.

2. Children and their parents can prepare the sanctuary for worship by distributing envelopes, hymnals, pew Bibles, and visitors' cards. Some churches use families to clean the church rather than a janitorial staff. In these churches, children can pick up left over bulletins, set up folding chairs, dust, sweep, and vacuum.

3. Children can help with communion by baking bread, filling the cups with grape juice, and preparing the table.

4. Children's choirs and handbell choirs can provide music for worship. Such times should not be seen as performance or entertainment for adults but rather as the children's offering to God.

---

8. Morris, "Children and Worship," 22–23.

5. Children can be included in services signifying special events in the life of the church such as the Lord's Supper, baptisms, ordinations, family life dedications, teacher and church leader dedication, funerals, Bible presentation, and welcoming a new minister.

6. Children can read the Scripture lessons. Be sure the child wants to participate and has been adequately prepared for the experience by practicing reading from the pulpit.

7. Children can lead in prayer. They can write prayers and litanies in Sunday School, Vacation Bible School, family worship, or private worship that can contribute to the theme of worship.

8. Children can design worship bulletin covers for special occasions.

9. Children's choirs can be interspersed with the adult choir occasionally so that both generations can sing and serve together.

10. Children can participate in special services of the church year by lighting the candles on the Advent wreath, waving palm branches on Palm Sunday, and sharing flowers.

11. Children can lead the congregation in litanies and responsive readings.

12. Children can assist in taking up the offering.[9]

13. A child (or children) can provide interpretive movement to a hymn or another spoken or sung part of the service.

14. Have a child and an adult read a passage of Scripture or a Psalm in antiphonal dialogue.

15. Have the children dramatize one of the Scripture lessons, or teach individual children to mime the lesson.

16. Ask the children to write sentence prayers to be used at one of the service's prayer times.

17. Have the children dramatize the story of the writing of a favorite hymn, and use the dramatization as an introduction to the hymn.

18. Ask the children to make small banners covered with all types of inexpensive bells to carry in procession.

19. Have children lead in dedication and commitment readings for unique or seasonal Sundays.

9. Morris, 23–24.

20. Have the children illustrate the Scripture lesson, or a hymn text, and show it on an overhead projector during the service.

21. Have a child sing an a capella hymn text during one of the more sensitive portions of the service such as before or after a prayer, or during a time of confession.[10]

INTEGRATING CHILDREN INTO CORPORATE WORSHIP FOR THE FIRST TIME

When a child has been in extended session (preschool care) for the first three years of life, the first experience in "Big Church" can be traumatic for the child and the parent. Churches should help parents to prepare for the experience by offering training sessions for new parents and by publishing helpful articles and inserts in church publications. The following can serve as a guide for parents bringing a preschooler into corporate worship for the first time:

(1) Remember that children sense the attitude of worship and follow their parent's example. (2) Take the child to the worship center at a time when services are not in session. (3) Explain to the child that he or she will not be able to talk very much during the worship service. (4) Arrange for the child to meet the pastor or other church staff members. (5) Talk with the child about what takes place in the worship service. (6) Remember that the observance of baptism and the Lord's Supper may seem unusual to the preschooler unless someone takes the time to explain and answer questions. (7) Never make statements in front of your child that imply that you do not really want the child to attend worship with you. (8) Consider sitting closer to the front where the child can see what is going on. (9) Share a Bible or hymnal with the child and point to the words. (10) Encourage the child to think about God or say thank you to God during prayer times. (11) Let the child look at books or draw quietly with a crayon and pad of paper. (12) Take the child to the bathroom before the service begins. (13) Practice using a quiet voice or whisper at home. (14) Allow the children to place an offering in the offering plate.

PREPARING CHILDREN'S WORSHIP GUIDES

Many churches provide separate worship guides, booklets, bags, and other items for child-worshipers. These items are prepared specifically for children and are available from ushers when adults receive their bulletins.

Worship guides. A children's worship guide may have children's art on the front and back with regular contents on the inside. It may have a completely different design and contain questions or pictures to relate to various wor-

10. Paul E. Oakley, "Why Wait? Creatively Using Children in Worship," *Creator Magazine* (May/June 1986).

ship elements. Most churches expect children to participate in singing and other activities but realize that sermon participation may be limited; therefore, the worship guide may directly enhance the sermon. Children's worship guides can be targeted for various age groups.

Worship workbooks. Workbooks with materials to enhance a special service of worship such as Advent or Lent, or a season of the year (spring, fall), or ongoing workbooks are often utilized. The workbooks (geared for various age levels) contain activities to enhance the service. These workbooks can be taken home by the children, and parents are given instruction for helping their child reflect on last week's worship and for preparing their child for next week's anticipated worship. Communication with parents helps this process to be effective. If "home work" is not a goal, then the workbooks may be obtained each week from a specific location. Coordinating this project with Christian education teachers is encouraged.

Worship bags or boxes. As they enter worship, children may receive a specially decorated cloth bag or wooden box which contains materials designed to enhance the children's worship experience. It may include a bulletin (child's or adult's), pictures related to the theme of the day, markers or crayons, a special message or memento from the pastor or worship leader, a take-home copy of a song or hymn used in worship, suggestions for homework, puzzles—the possibilities are endless! The bag or box is returned to an usher after worship and a church committee refills the bags or boxes with appropriate material for the upcoming week.

THE CHILDREN'S SERMON

One way to include the children in a worship service is to provide a children's sermon. Some denominations have regularly included the children's sermon in the order of worship, while others have not made it a regular practice.

Values in the children's sermon. There are certain values in providing the children's sermon as a part of the order of worship. (1) It makes the children aware that they are included in the fellowship of the congregation. They are assured of their importance as persons. (2) It ensures that the children will have at least one part designed specifically for them. Certain parts of the worship service may be beyond the understanding of the smaller children. (3) It is a means of instruction, and it also becomes a means of teaching children to participate in the general worship service. (4) It may create interest among the children, teaching them to listen to other sermons. (5) It emphasizes family unity by encouraging families to attend public worship service together. Parents may take a more vital interest in the church when they realize that the church is personally interested in their children.

Some guiding principles. Not all congregations feel that the children's sermon should be included in their worship service. The decision to include it will depend upon several important factors.

1. The church should consider who will present the children's sermon. Will this be a pastoral responsibility or one done by other church members?

2. The church may choose to have occasional children's sermons instead of every Sunday.

3. There should be a large enough group of children in the congregation to justify the practice.

4. The children's sermon should be periodically evaluated to determine its effectiveness.

5. The children's sermon should be blended in as a part of the entire order of worship to avoid distracting from the spirit of worship. Whatever aids in worship is worthy of being a part of the order of worship, and whatever distracts from worship should be deleted.

6. The children's sermon should be doctrinally sound. Children must always be dealt with truthfully. Under no circumstances should a children's leader justify telling a child a half truth by the intention of correcting the lie once he or she feels the child is old enough to understand.

7. The children's sermon should be based on Scripture. All worship should be scripturally based.

8. A children's sermon should seek to communicate a major truth. One idea is enough for a children's message.

9. The leader should speak on the child's level. It is abusive to children to intentionally speak to them on one level when you are really aiming the message to adults. Avoid humor that is not understood by the children. Children will laugh as if they understand, when inside they realize that the leader is not really loyal to them. Under no circumstance should the leader say to children, in the presence of adults, what the leader would like to say to the adults if courage allowed.

10. Preparation is necessary. The leader must plan what to say, carefully crafting each statement in order to communicate clearly and concisely, and he or she must always be prepared for serendipitous teaching moments that may go beyond the prepared script.

Sources for sermon ideas. The children's sermon will demand creative imagination, study, and detailed planning in advance. Sources for sermons are almost limitless. Historical incidents and epochs, the biographies of outstanding leaders, Bible stories, fables, literature, art, science, nature, school activities, and sports are among the many resources available.

While object lessons are often the staple of children's sermons, they are often the least effective because of their use of symbolism. Since children are unable to think abstractly until approximately twelve or thirteen, a highly symbolic message is not understandable. Object lessons may be used but only when the object stands for itself—not when it represents an abstract idea. The following examples illustrate correct and incorrect use of objects: (1) If fruit is the object, a presenter could show fruit to the children and proceed to discuss God's generous provision in giving fruit for us to enjoy—the object stands for itself. (2) If the presenter shows fruit and then tells the children how the fruits of the spirit are different yet similar as bananas and apples are different yet similar; the child may conclude, "The fruits of the spirit are bananas and apples."

Adults enjoy and communicate well through symbolism; however, they must not assume that children also think in their way. It must also be pointed out that, although a child can mimic back to an adult an abstract idea, this parroting does not assure that the child understands the idea in the way in which the adult perceives that he or she understands.

PREPARING THE CHILDREN'S SERMON

Sara Covin Juengst offers the following suggestions for preparing the children's sermon:

When using biblical material—

1. Be faithful to the text. Do not alter the text so that it makes your point.

2. Remember the purpose: not to teach Bible trivia but to draw attention to God.

3. Use your creative imagination—see the passage through the eyes of a child.

4. Be dramatic with voice and gestures without being trite.

5. Use repetition and action words.

6. Keep your main idea in mind. Limit the story to a single episode and a minimum of characters.

7. Simplify your vocabulary. Use familiar language and explain unfamiliar language in concrete terms.

8. Make stories personal.

9. Use visuals to bring your story to life—pictures, flannel boards, and puppets are excellent.

When presenting stories about everyday life, consider the following:

1. Stories about the children themselves.

2. Stories about children of similar ages doing familiar things.

3. Episodes from children's fiction.

4. Stories about special occasions.[11]

Procedural suggestions. The following suggestions may be helpful to leaders in planning and presenting a children's sermon. (1) The presenter must never approach the sermon without careful, advance preparation. (2) The children's sermon should be placed at an appropriate point in the order of worship. (3) Participation should be voluntary on the part of all the children and their parents. As children feel too old to participate in the children's sermon, they will gradually stop coming forward. (4) Give instructions ahead of time as to the procedure which will be followed and what is expected of the children and the parents. Suggest that children sit with their parents toward the front part of the sanctuary but not necessarily on the front rows. (5) The leader may come forward and direct the children to assemble immediately and quietly near the front and call for them to listen carefully. (6) The leader should firmly and kindly insist upon attention before beginning. He or she should begin with an interesting statement and lead immediately into a story or illustration. (7) The entire period should take only about three or four minutes. As the leader moves to the climax say, "Let us pray." Pray a brief prayer pertaining to the lesson. (8) The children will then return and sit with their parents. (9) Consider having a helper if large numbers of children participate.

Children like to identify with adults and will learn to do so as they are accepted as a part of the congregation. Some characteristics of children that we must keep in mind in preparing our services and our sermons for them are spontaneity, enthusiasm, optimism, a challenge to action, and emphasis upon the personal. A warm, personal presentation of biblical truth related practically to life can be a means of leading children into meaningful worship of God.

---

11. Sara Covin Juengst, *Sharing Faith with Children: Rethinking the Children's Sermon* (Louisville: Westminster/John Knox Press, 1994), 90–92.

CHAPTER 11

BAPTISM
AND THE
LORD'S SUPPER

S
ince New Testament times, baptism and the Lord's Supper have
been considered central among the many acts and expressions of
public worship. In the history of the Christian church, various doctrinal and liturgical viewpoints have been held. Some churches have called
these acts "ordinances," while others have designated them "sacraments";
however, the New Testament does not use either of these terms in referring
to these rites of worship. The biblical terms are simply baptism and the
Lord's Supper.

Although historically most liturgical churches have freely used the term
"sacrament," many of the Free Churches object to the use of the term because of its historical connotation. It is generally conceded that the term
"sacrament" is valid when interpreted to mean a symbol representing some
aspect of God's redemptive revelation. In that sense, all of God's creation is
sacramental, but some Free Churches prefer the term "ordinance" as applied to baptism and the Lord's Supper. There is a danger, of course, that
much of the rich significance may be lost from these acts of worship if they
are spoken of as "mere ordinances," for they were commands of Jesus Christ

to be practiced by his church throughout the ages. They are more than ordinances; they are acts of worship.

SYMBOLIC ACTS AS WORSHIP

If baptism and the Lord's Supper are to be meaningful acts of worship, churches need a true understanding of their relation to symbolism. Although the search for transcendence can take on various dimensions, the climate of our time—skepticism, industrialization, scientific realism—tends to reduce all dimensions of life to the pragmatic level and to lose sight of the mystical and supernatural implications. The Free Churches, caught up in this spirit of materialism, have tended to speak of the ordinances as "mere symbols" instead of sacraments. There is a trend back toward a more serious use of symbolism in worship. As Samuel H. Miller says, "Reality can no longer be seriously described or adequately comprehended in non-symbolic terms."[1]

Early Christian worship combined both the inward attitude and the outward symbols representing the gospel as revealed in Jesus Christ. Paul emphasizes both spirit and symbolic acts in his writings. Christians are in a dynamic relationship to Christ, "brought into one body by baptism, in the one Spirit, . . . and that one Holy Spirit was poured out for all of us to drink" (1 Cor. 12:13, NEB). The entire body of Christians shares in the blood and body of Christ: "Because there is one loaf, we, many as we are, are one body; for it is one loaf of which we all partake" (1 Cor. 10:17, NEB). The truth of the gospel is embodied in symbols such as words and objects and also in rituals or actions. Both in Old Testament and New Testament worship, the term translated "to worship" emphasizes the physical act of bowing down or prostrating oneself before God. Baptism and the Lord's Supper are acts which convey the truth of the gospel. When they are performed as acts of worship, they witness to God's grace.

Although the ordinances are symbols of God's revelation, they are not vehicles of God's grace as set forth in the sacramental view. God communicates the truth concerning his grace through the written word, the preached word, and the acted word (such as in baptism and the Lord's Supper); but God's grace is effected only by direct personal communion through the Holy Spirit.

None of the historic views (Roman Catholic, Lutheran, Calvinistic, Zwinglian) adequately delineates the dynamic, revelational aspects of baptism and the Lord's Supper as acts of worship. The view that they are "mere

---

1. Samuel H. Miller, "Reducing the Reality of the Lord's Supper," *Foundation*, 1:4 (October, 1958), 24–29. See also chapter 13 in this book on "The Use of Symbols."

symbols" seems to deny the revelational aspect they were intended to convey. In worship a symbol must stand for a present, spiritual reality.

Genuine religion is a faith-relationship, not an exercise in magic. The magical attitude is that we may strongly influence or even coerce God to do our will by adhering to proper rituals or invocations. External acts in and of themselves have no effectual spiritual power. These acts must become a part of a relationship in which the human soul is engaged. To assume such power without relating oneself to God's redemptive grace is to attempt magic.

God reveals his truth through various worship acts. We come to know God in direct, personal relationship through a response of faith based upon the knowledge gained through these acts. Baptism and the Lord's Supper are two means of expressing God's revelation. In public worship, every church should practice the two permanent elements appointed by Christ: the preached word and the enacted word, baptism and the Lord's Supper. Although these elements differ in practice and expression, they are unified in essential purpose or function. Their purpose is to communicate the gospel of redemption.

The symbols of water, bread, and wine are deeply significant for Christian worship. One reason these symbols and actions are important in Christian worship is that we did not choose them; they were chosen for us in the acts of God in history. Baptism and the Lord's Supper are the earliest gospel, for they occurred before the writing of the New Testament. They point to the redemptive action of God in the life and death and resurrection of Jesus Christ.

God uses symbols to communicate. All of creation is in a sense symbolic of a deeper meaning—God's sovereignty beyond creation. A symbol points to reality and communicates ideas and awakens responses. Symbols speak to the mind, call forth emotion, and may lead to decisions. A symbol may become effective as a medium of God's grace, when it inspires faith and personal communion with God. The term "mere symbolism" is inadequate to express the meaning of the ordinances because greater significance is present in the experience, such as faith, obedience, commitment, and gratitude.

The Bible is the written word, symbolizing and communicating the living Word as incarnated in Jesus Christ. Preaching is the spoken word, symbolizing and communicating the living Word—God speaking through persons.[2] Baptism and the Lord's Supper are the acted word, symbolizing and communicating the living Word—God's speaking through signs. Neither the written word, the spoken word, nor the acted word is an effective

---

2. For more information, see Charles Rice, *The Embodied Words: Preaching Arts and Liturgy* (Minneapolis: Fortress Press, 1991).

medium of God's grace without the faith and commitment of the worshiper. Given the faith-response of the worshiper in personal commitment, each of these media becomes effective in the action of God's grace in the experience of the believer and in the unified experience of the congregation in worship. The ordinances as acts of worship, performed as a pledge of devotion and loyalty, help to enforce and complete the meaning of worship. In the ordinances, the actions and elements are secondary; the persons involved are primary. God speaks through the symbols and actions, and we respond to God through faith. In this dialogue there is personal communion, which is the essence of worship.

There are at least four ways in which the ordinances speak the gospel. In baptism and the Lord's Supper, God speaks in a sign; the officiant speaks in the written word; the believer or candidate speaks in an open act of commitment; the church speaks in the perpetuation of the ordinances as acts of worship.

BIBLICAL ORIGINS

Churches that take biblical authority seriously are much more concerned about the biblical account of baptism and the Lord's Supper than with tradition.

ORIGIN OF BAPTISM

Baptism was a significant act in the life of the early church. Water symbolized divine cleansing in the Old Testament (Ezek. 36:25). Baptism seems to have been a practice among the Essenes and also in the Qumran community.[3] The Jews practiced proselyte baptism. This is seen in the *Didache*, chapters 1 through 6. John the Baptist practiced a baptism of repentance. G. R. Beasley-Murray does not believe that a connection exists between the baptism of John the Baptist and Jewish proselyte baptism. John's baptism inaugurated the new life of the converted, assuring forgiveness and cleansing from sin; and it anticipated the messianic baptism with Spirit and fire, giving assurance of a place in the Messiah's kingdom.[4]

The baptism of Jesus is the foundation for Christian baptism. Jesus was baptized by John in the Jordan (Mark 1:9–12; Matt. 3:13–17; Luke 3:21–23). The purpose of Jesus' baptism was "to fulfill all righteousness" (Matt. 3:15). Jesus' baptism was a deliberate act of self-identification with humanity in at least four different ways: (1) He identified with us in our search for righteousness. We seek to do God's will; therefore, Jesus fulfilled the will of his

---

3. See Beasley-Murray, *Baptism*, (London: SCM Press, 1950), 12.
4. Ibid., 39.

Father. (2) He identified with us in our preparation for the coming of the kingdom of God. (3) He identified with us in our search for God. (4) Jesus identified with us in the sin and sorrow of humanity.[5]

The baptism of Jesus was in some sense the fulfillment of the purposes of God for his redemptive work. For Jesus, the event of baptism had deep meaning, as was indicated in the voice from heaven, "This is my beloved Son" (Matt. 3:17). It was for Jesus the moment of enlightenment and self-dedication.[6]

The whole context of baptism in the New Testament reflects Christ's ministry: his baptism, his endowment by the Spirit, his life of service, his death, and his resurrection. The Great Commission places baptism in proper relationship to discipleship and teaching (Matt. 28:18–20). This passage is important both for the authority it gives to baptism and for linking baptism with the mission of the church in making disciples.

ORIGIN OF THE LORD'S SUPPER

A common meal shared in a spirit of love, trust, and mutual acceptance has always been an expression of community. The Last Supper of Jesus with his disciples is considered by most scholars to have been a Passover meal. It took place in the evening and extended into the night. Jesus and his disciples reclined together for this last meal, an act practiced in the keeping of the Passover. Jesus took bread and broke it and gave it to his disciples. Then he took the cup of wine and gave it to them, commanding them to drink of it. The Supper concluded with the singing of a hymn, which may have been a portion of Psalms 114 or 115 to 118, the *Hallel* which closed the Passover meal.[7]

The New Testament contains only a few specific references to the Lord's Supper, but these are very significant. References include Matthew 26:17–30, Mark 14:23–26, Luke 22:14–23, and 1 Corinthians 11:17–34. Other references which may refer to the Lord's Supper or to incidental meals which the Christians had together are found in the following: Acts 2:42, 46; 20:7, 11; 1 Corinthians 5:17 (KJV); 10:3–4, 16–17, 21; and John 6; 15. Various terms in the New Testament refer to the Supper: "the Lord's supper" (1 Cor. 11:20), "the cup of the Lord" and "the table of the Lord" (1 Cor. 10:21), "the cup of blessing" and "the bread which we break" (1 Cor. 10:16), "the breaking of bread" (Acts 2:42, 46; 20:7), and "the communion of the blood . . . of the body of Christ" (1 Cor. 10:16, KJV).

---

5. See William Barclay, *The Mind of Jesus* (New York: Harper & Bros., 1961), 26.
6. Ibid., 27–29.
7. Higgins, *The Lord's Supper*, 13–21.

The historical facts concerning the institution of the Supper may be summarized as follows: (1) The place was an upper room, perhaps the home of John Mark. (2) The time was in the evening or night. (3) The Supper was related to the Passover, the Old Covenant, though the New Covenant is being inaugurated. (4) The persons present with Jesus were his disciples. (5) The elements used were bread and wine. (6) Jesus gave thanks to the Father in a spirit of worship. (7) Jesus broke bread and distributed it, then took the cup and passed it among his disciples. (8) Jesus commanded his disciples to partake of the bread and wine, giving his reasons for their participation, and indicated the act was to be repeated until his return. (9) Following the Supper they sang a hymn. (10) Jesus and his disciples went out to the Mount of Olives, where he prayed in the garden of Gethsemane in preparation for the crucifixion.[8]

In the history of the church, the Supper has been observed under various designations: Lord's Supper, Memorial Supper, Eucharist, Communion, and Mass. Some see it as a sacrament in the highest sense, while others look upon it as a symbol and nothing more. Some churches have observed it as a central part of every service of worship, while other churches observe it rarely or neglect it altogether. The term *Lord's Supper*, mentioned in 1 Corinthians 11:17–34, may have been a combination of what came to be called the "love feast" (*Agape*, Jude 12) and the Last Supper.[9] The term *Memorial Supper* is based on 1 Corinthians 11:24, "Do this in remembrance of me." The term *eucharist* is derived from a New Testament word which means a "thanksgiving." Mark says that Jesus took bread and blessed it and then gave thanks for the cup (Mark 14:22–23; see also 1 Cor. 11:24). The participles for "giving thanks" (*eucharistesas*) and "blessing" (*eulogesas*) are used interchangeably. The term *communion* used by many Christians is based upon Paul's use of the term in 1 Corinthians 10:16, where he speaks of "the communion of the blood of Christ" (KJV). The Greek word for *communion* is *koinonia*, referring primarily to the unity of the body of Christ. The Lord's Supper was described as a "communion" or *koinonia* in Acts 2:42. Dale Moody believes that Ephesians 5:18–20 is a liturgical passage referring to the Lord's Supper or Eucharist in Christian worship. This brief celebration is very similar to the details found in 1 Corinthians 11:17–34.[10]

---

8. Curtis Vaughn, "The Biblical View of the Lord's Supper" Sound recording, (Fort Worth, Southwestern Baptist Theological Seminary), Pastor's Conference, June 28, 1962. See also Alfred Edersheim, *The Life and Times of Jesus the Messiah* (Grand Rapids: Wm. B. Eerdmans Publishing Co., n.d.), 2:490–512.

9. See Oscar Cullmann and F. J. Leenhardt, *Essays on the Lord's Supper*, trans. J. G. Davies (Richmond: John Knox Press, 1958).

10. Moody, *Christ*, 112.

A THEOLOGY OF THE ORDINANCES

A theology of baptism and the Lord's Supper is essential for their proper observance as acts of worship. They are related to salvation-history, the kerygma, to Jesus Christ, to the Holy Spirit, and to the Church. They must be considered within a christological, ecclesiological, and eschatological context if they are to be given full content and meaning.[11]

Baptism and the Lord's Supper are related to evangelism. As a part of the gospel revelation, they persuasively present the offer of God's grace. The church's invitation to fellowship, the individual experience in repentance and faith as a responsible response, a commitment to a new way of life, and nurture and growth in a personal relationship with Christ are all included in evangelism. Participation in the Lord's Supper brings fresh experiences to the believer's conscious commitment in the salvation experience.

The ordinances are part of God's revelation of redemptive truth. Just as God is revealed in the written word (the Bible) and in the spoken word (the witness of a redeemed person), God is revealed also in the enacted word through baptism and the Lord's Supper. Since Jesus gave the command to make disciples, "baptizing them in the name of the Father and of the Son and of the Holy Spirit" (Matt. 28:19), we must reason that God speaks in the very act of baptism. H. Wheeler Robinson believed that baptism has spiritual value for worship. Since revelation has objective-subjective aspects, which are united in experience, the event of baptism becomes a worship experience in the commitment of the individual. Baptism is filled with the gospel of Christ; therefore, it is "charged with a new spiritual power." The outer act and the inner experience of forgiveness and faith are closely related—the New Testament never considers them apart.[12] Since Jesus commanded that his followers regularly take the bread and the cup as a reminder of his atoning death, we must conclude that God speaks in the very act of eating and drinking. Robinson saw baptism and the Lord's Supper as "acted parables" or dramatic acts in which God speaks and the believer identifies with Christ.[13]

Since salvation is based upon a personal faith-experience and is not a sacramental act, infant baptism has no place in Christian theology. God does speak to the church through baptism but not without the witness of the individual's faith to the saving gospel. The absence of infant baptism in the New Testament, together with the clear teaching of salvation by personal faith, prompted Karl Barth and Emil Brunner to denounce infant

---

11. See Neville Clark, *An Approach to a Study of the Sacraments* (London: SCM Press, 1958), 8.

12. H. Wheeler Robinson, *Baptist Principles* (London: Carey Kingsgate Press, 1938), 14–15.

13. H. Wheeler Robinson, *The Life and Faith of the Baptists* (London: Carey Kingsgate Press, 1946), 77f.

baptism.[14] The Church and the parents have a responsibility to dedicate and train the child, but they cannot act for the child in saving faith. Baptism is for believers only.

The Lord's Supper reaffirms the Christian's eschatological hope. At the Last Supper Jesus referred to "that day when I drink it new with you in my Father's kingdom" (Matt. 26:29). Paul reminded his fellow Christians that, as often as they observed the Lord's Supper, they proclaimed the Lord's death (the atoning gospel) "until he comes" (1 Cor. 11:26).

The Lord's Supper has meaning only as it refers to the relationship between Jesus and his followers. Participation in the bread and the wine implies participation in the death of Jesus. Paul sees a threefold significance in the celebration of the Supper: (1) remembrance of the Christ-event, (2) the presence of Christ in the act of worship, and (3) the eschatological hope of Christ's return.

The Supper represents the continuing presence of the crucified, risen Christ to remind his people of what he promised. When Jesus said, "This is my body and my blood," he implied that the observance with bread and wine would always be a reminder that he is present with his people at worship. The Supper is the Lord's appointment with his people.[15] Those who keep this appointment with Christ can confidently expect that he will assuredly come to meet them. This confidence produces joy and thanksgiving in this act of worship.

Some Practical Considerations

Since baptism and the Lord's Supper are acts of worship, several practical matters deserve serious attention. They should never be practiced carelessly but should be observed with care and sensitivity.

Concerning Baptism

1. The act of baptism should be made a part of a regular worship service. Whether it comes at the beginning or the close of the service, it should be performed in a spirit of reverence.

2. Each church is responsible for the administration of baptism. Jesus gave his commission to his church, a body of baptized believers; therefore, the local church is representative of the universal body of Christ and is responsible for the fulfillment of its mission in a particular place.

---

14. See Karl Barth, *The Teaching of the Church Regarding Baptism* (London: SCM Press, 1950); Emil Brunner, *The Divine-Human Encounter* (Philadelphia: The Westminster Press, 1944), 132.

15. See *A Theological Wordbook of the Bible*, ed. Alan Richardson (New York: Macmillan, 1955), 257.

3. The person to be baptized should be thoroughly instructed about the meaning of baptism and the manner in which it is to be performed. The candidate should approach baptism in a spirit of commitment and reverence.

4. Equipment for administering baptism should be properly prepared. The baptistry should be filled to a depth of approximately forty-two inches and the water warmed to body temperature. Appropriate apparel should be provided for the baptizer and the candidates. Most churches have a baptism committee that is responsible for physical preparations.

5. The baptizer should perform the ordinance with reverence and dignity. The person administering baptism should enter the baptistry, read (or have someone else read) an appropriate passage of Scripture pertaining to Christian commitment, and then indicate when the candidate should enter the water. The baptizer will instruct the candidate to fold his or her hands across the chest; then, holding firmly the candidate's hands, place the other hand at the base of the candidate's neck. The baptizer will then repeat the following or similar phraseology: "(Name), upon confession of your faith in Jesus Christ as Savior and Lord, and in obedience to his command, I baptize you in the name of the Father, and of the Son, and of the Holy Spirit. Amen." The candidate will then be lowered slowly into the water until the face is barely covered and then slowly lifted from the water to an upright position. The more slowly and smoothly this act is performed, the more likely it will be perceived as worshipful.

6. Among the ways of making baptism a more meaningful part of worship are the following: (1) Bring the candidate from the congregation and introduce him or her. (2) Consider allowing persons other than the pastor to baptize (parents baptize child, friend baptize friend, etc.). (3) Lay hands on newly baptized persons as an act symbolizing setting aside for ministry. (4) Allow the candidate to share a testimony or answer brief questions or dialogue with the candidate about his or her salvation experience. (5) Observe baptism outside when weather is appropriate. (6) Schedule several baptismal candidates together and focus an entire worship service around baptism. (7) Observe baptism on high worship days such as Easter and Christmas so that the memory of baptism is associated with an easy-to-remember day. (8) Photograph the baptismal candidate coming out of water and present the photo with a baptism certificate to the candidate. (9) Observe the Lord's Supper in the same service as baptism to allow candidate to observe both ordinances. (10) Provide invitations for the baptismal candidate to send to friends and relatives.[16]

---

16. See Appendix I for a sample invitation.

CONCERNING THE LORD'S SUPPER

The manner of observance of the Lord's Supper varies according to the customs and traditions of various congregations. The frequency of the Lord's Supper observance ranges from weekly, monthly, or quarterly, to in some instances annually or semiannually. Most of the Free Churches observe it either monthly or quarterly. Traditionally, most Free Churches have felt that the Lord's Supper should not be observed so often as to make it a perfunctory rite, nor so infrequently as to cause a spirit of neglect; however, churches are beginning to realize that frequent observance cannot be equated with commonness.

1. The Lord's Supper, like baptism, should always be observed as a central part of a worship service and not an addendum. In too many instances, it has been customary to have a full-length service and then add the Lord's Supper at the end as an afterthought. Such a careless observance is not worthy of this act of worship.

2. The order of worship should be planned to emphasize the significance of the Lord's Supper. It is appropriate to observe the Lord's Supper in a regular worship service where the hymns range from adoration and praise to devotion and commitment. A full-length sermon is unnecessary when the Lord's Supper is observed. A brief meditation consistent with the spirit of the service is preferable in order to keep the service within the regular time limit. However, the Scriptures and the sermon should not be limited to the biblical passages which are specifically related to the Lord's Supper. Themes of redemption and the Christian life are appropriate.

3. The administration of the Supper will vary in different churches. Many churches practice the following: (1) In a regular worship service, at the appropriate time usually following a brief meditation, the presider will stand behind the Lord's Supper table. (2) Those who assist will take their places on the front pews if they are not already seated there. The appointed leaders take their places at each end of the Lord's Supper table. (3) The presider may read an appropriate Scripture or make an appropriate remark pertaining to the Lord's Supper. (4) The presider may or may not break a portion of the bread. The presider will then have a prayer of thanksgiving and dedication asking God's blessings upon the people as they partake of the bread. (5) The bread trays are then passed to the assistants by the appointed leaders. The assistants will in turn go to their stations and proceed to distribute the bread among the congregation. When they have finished, at a given signal they will return to their places at the front of the sanctuary and pass

their plates back. Assistants will then be served by the appointed leaders, after which they will be seated on the front pews. The presider may then quote an appropriate Scripture verse such as Romans 12:1: "I appeal to you therefore, brethren, by the mercies of God, to present your bodies as a living sacrifice, holy and acceptable to God, which is your spiritual worship." After this, the presider and the congregation will partake of the bread. (6) The presider will then quote an appropriate Scripture passage or make an appropriate remark pertaining to the cup as representing the blood of Christ; then follows a prayer of thanksgiving and dedication, asking God's blessings upon the church as they partake of the cup. Distribution of the cups will then proceed in the manner of the distribution of the bread. When all have been served, the presider will quote an appropriate Scripture verse and then partake of the cup as a signal for the congregation to join. (7) It is the tradition in most churches to sing a hymn following the observance of the Lord's Supper. A benediction may then be pronounced, and the congregation will leave in a spirit of worship and devotion.

4. Among the alternative ways of observing the Lord's Supper are the following:

- Come forward to receive communion.

- Serve from stations around the worship room.

- Serve from tables in fellowship hall.

- Serve from a common cup and a common loaf.

- Dip bread into cup (intinction).

5. To make the Lord's Supper more meaningful, consider the following: (1) Make elements highly visible—real loaf of bread, pitcher of juice, fruit, use flowers, table cloth other than white. (2) Vary solemn and joyful celebrations.

6. Always notify the congregation in advance of the Lord's Supper observance so that parents can prepare their children for this meaningful act of worship. Unbaptized children need to be prepared for the Lord's Supper before the worship service.

7. Communion should be served to shut-ins on a regular schedule.

8. George Buttrick observed that church members should prepare before participating in the Lord's Supper. The following suggestions may guide the worshiper's thoughts and prayers during the Lord's Supper:

- Our Lord Jesus Christ—God's gift of love and power through Jesus to all humankind.

- The church—its steady witness in Christ's spirit and our witness through the church by prayer, gift, and service.

- Our failures—low aim, insensitive deeds, and wasted opportunities; our forgetting that all people belong to God's family; and our part in social wrongs such as racial intolerance, economic strife, and war.

- Our relationships—those we have hurt and those who have hurt us; our families, friends, employers; the sad and suffering; missionaries, ministers, peacemakers, and a host of those by whom our days are guided.

- Our need—of strength and joy for daily living in Christ's name. If these thoughts and prayers consume us as we partake of the Lord's Supper, then by faith we shall receive the power of Christ.[17]

ADMINISTRATION OF THE ORDINANCES

The ordinances are related particularly to the doctrine of the church—they were given as commands of Jesus to his church to be perpetuated by his people. The ordinances were given in the context of the body of believers and not primarily to individuals; however, the individual's participation in these acts of worship is first in relation to God and second, to the church.

The practical approach to the administration of the ordinances comes to focus in the local church. It is not limited to a local church, but each church is autonomous and is responsible for the administration of the ordinances according to its understanding of the biblical teachings. Each local church is responsible only to Christ as its head; however, in a secondary sense, each local church is related to all other churches of God's people. The local church represents the entire body of Christ and the kingdom of God. Whatever its practice, it must come under the judgment of the Scriptures.

The procedures of the ordinances in a local church are not spelled out in the New Testament; however, the spirit of the observance is clear. There must be loyalty to Jesus Christ and unity in the body of his people. The ordinances must always be interpreted in relation to the person of Christ. Believers are baptized in the name of Jesus Christ, which implies that they are committed to Christ and will be loyal and obedient to him. The observance of the Supper implies that those who partake are related to Christ and to one another.

---

17. Buttrick, *Prayer*, 290.

In the New Testament the primary emphasis is given to the experience and relationship of the believer to Christ, not to the administrator nor to the method of the administration of the ordinances. Historically, the administration of the ordinances has created divisions among the people of Christ. Methods of administration have varied even within denominations. For example, although Baptists have generally agreed on the basic meaning of the two ordinances—immersion of believers, and the Lord's Supper for believers only—they have not always agreed on the authority and methods of the administrator, the church, and on the relationship of the individual to the church. For four hundred years Baptists have varied in their interpretation of church membership as related to baptism and the Lord's Supper. Some have favored a closed or restricted membership, others an open or unrestricted membership.

Baptists still vary in their particular practices:[18] (1) some maintain open membership and open communion, (2) some keep both membership and the table only for baptized believers, (3) some feel the table should be open and that membership should be closed. Payne observed that in the New Testament the case for believer's baptism is clear. The exact relationship of the right to the membership of the church is not always clear.[19]

While Baptists have generally agreed on the immersion of believers only, they have not always agreed on what constitutes valid or proper immersion. Generally speaking, there are three viewpoints concerning the validity of immersion: (1) Some churches accept into their membership, without rebaptism, persons who have been baptized into the membership of non-Baptist churches, provided that at the time of baptism, the individual held the same doctrinal concept of baptism in relation to salvation that Baptists generally hold. (2) Some churches receive into their membership, without rebaptism, persons who have been baptized into the fellowship of a church of another Baptist general body. (3) Other churches require rebaptism of persons who come from any church outside their own denominational affiliation. They hold that the administrator is "alien" theologically and is not authorized by the proper authority. Thus they call this "alien immersion." W. W. Barnes observed that those who reject alien immersion have never come to agreement among themselves as to "how alien must an alien immersion be in order to be alien."[20]

The majority of Baptists are in accord with other Christians on the basic doctrines governing the observance of the Lord's Supper. Most denominations agree that the Supper should be restricted to those who have made a

---

18. For more information see Leon McBeth, *The Baptist Heritage: Four Centuries of Baptist Witness* (Nashville: Broadman Press, 1987).

19. Payne, *Fellowship of Believers*, 88–89.

20. W. W. Barnes, "Alien Immersion," *Encyclopedia of Southern Baptists*, 1:32.

Christian profession and have been properly baptized into the fellowship of God's people. Because Baptists have had a strict doctrine concerning baptism, some of them have been very restrictive in the observance of the Lord's Supper. There have generally been three points of view relative to the Lord's Supper, sometimes referred to as open communion, closed innercommunion, and closed intracommunion.[21] Some Baptist churches practice open communion, inviting all individual Christians who feel themselves to be qualified to participate at the Lord's table. Other Baptist churches practice closed innercommunion, inviting only those who hold membership in other Baptist churches to participate with them. Still other churches practice closed intracommunion, holding that only persons who are members of a particular local church may participate in the Lord's Supper when it is administered by that church.

Robert A. Baker observes that it is impossible to estimate what proportion of Southern Baptists hold to one of these views or to some similar position. It is the practice of many of the churches to make no statement as to the qualifications of individuals for participation when the Lord's Supper is observed. When the elements are passed to all who are present, each person must decide for himself or herself.

In perpetuating baptism and the Lord's Supper, worship is primary; procedures are secondary. Problems in administering the ordinances should not be allowed to hinder the spirit of worship. The local church as a responsible institution is autonomous, but it does not exist in isolation from other Christian bodies. To place the institution above the living fellowship is idolatry—the local church is representative of the larger body of Christ. There is a place for the denomination, but to place any given denomination above the body of all believers is presumption and idolatry.

Those who ignore the basic doctrines of the New Testament in relation to the administration of baptism and the Lord's Supper are guilty of disrupting the unity of Christ's people; and those who ignore the spirit of faith and worship by giving priority to detailed methods and procedures in perpetuating the ordinances are also guilty of disrupting the fellowship of Christ's body. Let each church be firm where the New Testament is clear and specific, and let all be charitable and flexible where the New Testament is not clear. Jesus prayed that

> They may all be one; even as thou, Father, art in me, and I in thee, that they also may be in us, so that the world may believe that thou hast sent me. The glory which thou hast given me I have given to them, that they may be one even as we are one, I in them and thou in me, that they may become perfectly one, so that the world may know that thou hast sent me and hast loved them even as thou hast loved me (John 17:21–23).

21. Robert A. Baker, "Requisites to the Lord's Supper," *Encyclopedia of Southern Baptists*, 2:794–95.

CHAPTER *12*

OTHER ACTS OF WORSHIP

THE CALL TO WORSHIP

T he call to worship is an appropriate way to begin a worship service. It calls a congregation to give attention to the primary objective for which the church is assembled, to "stand at attention" before God. The first words and movements of the leader will often determine the spirit of the entire worship service.

Purpose. The purpose of the call to worship is (1) to direct the minds of the congregation toward God, (2) to remove distractions from the attention of the congregation, (3) to call for participation of the congregation in every act of worship, (4) to call for a unity of all the people, and (5) to create the proper attitude or atmosphere for worship.

Nature. (1) The call to worship may be a passage of Scripture, such as Psalm 100:2, 4–5 (KJV): "Serve the LORD with gladness: come before his presence with singing. . . . Enter into his gates with thanksgiving, and into his courts with praise: be thankful unto him, and bless his name. For the LORD is good; his mercy is everlasting; and his truth endureth to all generations." (2) The call to worship may be a stanza of a hymn or some appropriate poem. (3) It may be an appropriately worded invitation for the people to unite in worship.

Presentation. (1) The leader may proclaim the call to worship alone. (2) The leader and congregation may read together:

Leader: I will bless the Lord at all times;

Congregation: His praise shall continually be in my mouth.

Leader: O magnify the Lord with me,

Congregation: And let us exalt his name together (Ps. 34:1, 3).

(3) The leader and choir may give the call to worship, the leader speaking a line and the choir singing a line alternately. (4) The choir may sing the entire call to worship. The mood of the call to worship may range from meditative and reflective to celebrative and extroverted.

THE OFFERING OF GIFTS

The offering of gifts has been a universal practice in the history of worship. Motivation for the giving of gifts has been prompted by superstitious fear and attempts to placate angry gods; however, in Christian worship the offering of gifts is an expression of gratitude and appreciation to God—a concept found in both the Old and New Testaments. The psalmist sang, "Bring an offering, and come into his courts!" (Ps. 96:8); the writer of Hebrews exhorted his fellow Christians, "Through him then let us continually offer up a sacrifice of praise to God . . . . Do not neglect to do good and to share what you have, for such sacrifices are pleasing to God" (Heb. 13:15–16).

Protestant worship has often neglected the act of giving. An outsider observing Protestant worship might report, "At a certain point in the service, money was collected." The church certainly needs money, but the raising of money to support the church should not dominate the motivation in giving. Some churches make a practice of collecting their gifts for the budget through the Sunday School classes, a practice that tends to detach the act of giving from the main worship service of the church. It is entirely possible that by this method, churches may have raised more money and made bookkeeping simpler, but it may have taken away the seriousness of making an offering as an act of worship.

Since worship is dialogue, with upward movement as well as downward movement, the offering of gifts should be considered seriously. The offering of gifts is a symbol of sacrifice—it is a positive act which symbolizes an inner attitude of homage. In an hour of physical need, King David asked for a drink from the well at Bethlehem. Men risked their lives to bring him a drink, but he would not drink it; it was too precious, and "He poured it out to the LORD" (2 Sam. 23:16). Worship needs the spirit of sacrifice. The offering of money in the offering plate is no less an act of worship than are the offerings of hymns and prayers.

A theology of giving. There is a sound theological basis for offering gifts as an act of worship to God. In the Old Testament, sacrifice was the essential act of external worship. In the very act of sacrifice a personal union with God was achieved, for God accepted the offering and also the worshiper who made the sacrifice. Paul refers to this act of sacrifice: "Are not those who eat the sacrifices partners in the altar?" (1 Cor. 10:18).

Proper motivations grow out of a Christian theology of giving as an act of worship. Christian giving is prompted by grace, not by legalistic fear.

The following theological principles are basic to giving as an act of worship:

1. In Christian worship, making an offering is a symbolic act representing the giving of one's self. Paul commended the Christians in the churches of Macedonia for their generosity. The real value of their giving is attested to by the fact that "first they gave themselves to the Lord," and their sacrificial giving attested to their sincerity (2 Cor. 8:5).

2. Unselfish sharing is proof of our love for others. All true benevolent giving is based upon love. John challenged his fellow Christians to share the world's goods with someone in need: "Little children, let us not love in word or speech but in deed and in truth" (1 John 3:18).

3. Generous giving expresses our missionary zeal. All world missionary enterprises depend on the gifts of God's people. Indeed, "How are they to hear without a preacher? And how can men preach unless they are sent?" (Rom. 10:14–15).

4. Worshipful giving is proof of our gratitude to God for his gifts, especially the gift of grace in Christ. The motivation for Christian giving is based primarily upon gratitude rather than upon law. Paul's appeal to the Corinthian Christians to share their material goods with the needy people of Jerusalem concludes with a paean of praise, "Thanks be to God for his inexpressible gift!" (2 Cor. 9:15).

5. Worshipful giving is a quality of life. Paul speaks of it as a grace, listing it alongside faith, utterance, knowledge, earnestness, and love. He exhorted, "See that you excel in this gracious work also" (2 Cor. 8:7).

Procedure in giving. Since giving is an act of worship, the manner of presenting gifts in worship is significant. A careful approach toward the presentation of gifts will help to prevent careless and indifferent attitudes.

1. A proper motivation for giving may be inspired by the use of an offertory sentence preceding the presentation of gifts. A brief statement or a Scripture verse concerning the meaning of our giving may be used to prepare people's minds and hearts for presenting their gifts. Second

Corinthians 8:9 is a good example: "You know the grace of our Lord Jesus Christ, that though he was rich, yet for your sake he became poor, so that by his poverty you might become rich."

2. All members of the congregation should be encouraged to participate in the act of making an offering. Every member of the family should have the privilege of placing gifts in the offering plates.

3. Appropriate offertory music, either instrumental or vocal, may enhance this act of worship.

4. The offerings of the people should be gathered in an orderly manner.

5. The presentations of the offerings at the altar is the climax of this act of worship. A well-worded prayer dedicating the gifts may imply God's acceptance and serve as a symbol of communion between God and the worshipers. A hymn response or a congregational "Amen" may be used at the conclusion of the prayer of dedication.

THE AFFIRMATION OF FAITH

An affirmation or confession of faith may be used effectively in public worship. The Apostles' Creed has been used traditionally in many Protestant churches, though some Free Churches reject the use of a fixed creed. Confessions or affirmations of faith may be used effectively in any service of worship.

The affirmation of faith is a confessional statement in which the congregation participates. A brief contemporary affirmation may be more meaningful than the Apostles' Creed. The affirmation should be read by the congregation. Affirmations of faith may help to keep worship alive and in dialogue with the living God.

An affirmation of faith may sometimes be presented in the form of a litany, a statement to be read responsively. At other times it may be read in unison. The following litany is an example.

Reaffirming Our Common Faith

Leader: In the living God our Father, maker and sustainer of the universe, who in Jesus Christ has perfectly revealed himself and his redeeming love to us,

Response: We reaffirm our faith.

Leader: In Jesus Christ our Lord, God's only Son, who for our salvation came to earth in human flesh, lived a sinless life, died for our sins, and rose again in accordance with the Scriptures,

Response: We reaffirm our faith.

Leader: In the blessed Holy Spirit, revealer of truth, convicter of sinners, and ever-present helper of all who believe,

Response: We reaffirm our faith.

Leader: In God's eternal purpose of grace, whereby, through the gospel of Jesus Christ, redemption, forgiveness, reconciliation, and the gift of eternal life are accomplished in the experience of every believer,

Response: We reaffirm our faith.

Leader: In the power and authority of the Scriptures as God-breathed writings which are able to make us wise unto salvation and equip God's servants for every good work,

Response: We reaffirm our faith.

Leader: In the church, the body of Christ, fellowship of the redeemed, set apart for worship and witness, teaching and ministry in the midst of an unbelieving, lost, and suffering world,

Response: We reaffirm our faith.

Leader: In the surpassing worth, immediate urgency, and certain victory of the kingdom of God,

Response: We reaffirm our faith.

It is appropriate for churches to write their own affirmations of faith. Another way Free Churches use affirmations of faith in public worship is to provide opportunity for individuals to make a public commitment when they desire. In response to the acts of worship, particularly to preaching, an invitation is extended to persons who wish to commit themselves publicly. While a hymn of dedication or invitation is sung, they present themselves to God in the presence of the congregation. The invitation is extended to nonmembers who desire to confess their faith in Jesus Christ in response to a conversion experience or to persons coming from another church by transfer of membership. Other motives for public commitment include response to the call of God to a life vocation and a rededication of life asking the church's forgiveness and prayers for past errors.

THE RECEPTION OF NEW MEMBERS

The presentation of the individual for membership deserves attention. The individual is enlisting in the service of Christ, and his or her initiation should be worthy of both the lordship of Christ and the sincere commitment of the individual. This should be a memorable occasion.

Churches vary in their methods of receiving new members. Some churches invite individuals to present themselves following the sermon as the hymn of dedication or invitation is sung. Upon the individual's request he is received by letter from another church, upon confession of faith as a candidate for baptism, or upon a statement that he has been a member of a church of "like faith and order." Members may also be received under watchcare: they remain a member of another church; but while they attend school or work away from home, they participate with the church who has received them under watchcare.

Many churches immediately receive new members by a vote of the congregation. Some churches request them to meet with a membership committee that will hear their personal witness and later recommend them for membership. Other churches have a "waiting period" during which the candidates attend a class of instruction.

However members are received, they should be received graciously. The pastor may ask the candidates to stand facing the congregation and then read their names, giving essential facts about them. They may be asked to confess their faith in Christ and their allegiance to the church, which may be done in the form of questions asked by the minister or by the reading of an affirmation prepared by the church. The congregation may then stand with the candidates and sing a hymn of commitment. The pastor may follow this with a prayer of dedication and the benediction, after which members of the congregation may file by and welcome the new members with a hand of fellowship. Whether churches receive new members with simply an affirmative "Amen" or by some of the suggestions above, new members should always be received with sensitivity and joy.

THE CONGREGATIONAL "AMEN"

It might be good to restore the use of the congregational "Amen" to public worship. It was evidently used in Old Testament worship. Moses' directions for worship included, "And all the people shall say 'Amen'" (Deut. 27:14–26; see also 1 Chron. 16:36 and Ps. 106:48). After hearing Ezra read the law, all the people raised their hands and shouted "Amen, Amen" (Neh. 8:6).

The Hebrew "Amen" has the force of strong affirmation or assent, usually to something spoken by another. The early Christians used "Amen" in their worship as an expression of the entire congregation in assent to praise. Paul refers to the people's "Amen" of thanksgiving (1 Cor. 14:16). It is also used in an exalted passage of worship in the book of Revelation (5:6–14). In the second century Justin Martyr wrote: "Then we all rise together and pray, and . . . bread and wine are brought, and the president in like manner offers prayer and thanksgiving, according to his ability, and the people assent, saying, 'Amen.'" The term was used later in the liturgy by the priest or the choir alone. During the Reformation, Luther interpreted the "Amen" as an expression of "firm and hearty belief, and its use was restored to the congregation in a number of cases."[1]

The "Amen" may be expressed by the congregation, sung by the choir at the end of a prayer or following the reading of a Scripture passage, or at the end of a hymn even if it is not encouraged as an emphasis in response to some part of the sermon. The punctuation of the worship service by frequent "Amens" should not be discouraged. "Amen" offers the congregation opportunities to become verbally involved in worship—especially prayers and sermons, acts which have been traditionally seen as monologue.

THE GREETING

Since God's people are called out of the world to gather for worship, a time of gathering followed by a greeting is a usual part of worship. The best time to greet the church and welcome guests is at the beginning of worship—perhaps even before the prelude. When words of greeting are offered later in the service, they may easily be perceived as an interruption to acts of worship such as praise and confession which are vertical—humanity to God, instead of horizontal—person to person.

When offering a greeting in worship, consider the following: (1) Make a statement of purpose such as, "We are the body of Christ gathered to worship." A statement of purpose distinguishes the body of Christ, the church, from other gathered groups; it reminds the congregation of its purpose; and it informs the guest about the nature of this unique gathering. (2) Encourage hearty participation in worship by regular attenders and guests with a statement such as, "I hope that you will give your best gifts to God today as you join in each act of worship." This helps the guest and regular attenders to join the worship as participants instead of spectators. (3) Perhaps offer a general statement concerning the congregation's openness to each other and to newcomers: "We are an accepting congregation. We accept each other, and we welcome guests among us. If you are a guest, I hope you have already been openly received by our members, and I am sure you will be greeted numerous times before you leave today." A statement such as this confirms for the guest the positive nature of this body and affirms the congregation in its hospitality ministry.

Avoid singling out guests and taking the risk of embarrassment. Many guests prefer to remain anonymous and any effort to introduce them—

---

1. *The New Schaff-Herzog Encyclopedia of Religious Knowledge*, 1:501.

having them stand, having them remain seated while they are greeted by members—can result in the guests' being offended. Guest attendance can be registered in many ways, including pew cards, registers at entrances, and attendance sheets passed down aisles. No one way of registering guests is appropriate for all congregations; however, guests will register their attendance if *they* choose; they should not be manipulated or coerced to register. The worship leader who announces the method of guest registry should assure guests that they will not receive an unannounced visit from a church member. Church members and ministers must *always* visit guests by appointment. Guests should be given opportunity to request on the guest card that they not receive a visit, phone call, or other correspondence. Individual privacy must be respected, and guests must be assured that coming to church does not violate their desire to remain anonymous.

ANNOUNCEMENTS

According to Anne Ortlund, "Announcements are the only part of a service which, by their very nature, edify nobody. They do not build up the Body or introduce unbelievers to the Savior. Hearts do not beat faster over announcements."[2] Announcements are not worship, even though some form of verbal reminder may be important from time to time. Worship is not an opportunity to promote the activity of the church; it is an opportunity to commune with God. Churches should be expected to depend on newsletters, bulletin boards, bulletins, bulletin inserts, word of mouth, telephone, and other means for church communication. Anne Ortlund offers the following suggestions for giving announcements: (1) Announcements should not repeat what is already in the bulletin. (2) Announcements should not pertain to a part of the congregation. (3) Never announce appeals for volunteers for anything.[3]

When announcements are necessary, Martin Thielen's suggestions are helpful: (1) Keep announcements brief. Do not announce regularly scheduled services and meetings. (2) Review the announcements before giving them in order to be as precise (and concise) as possible. (3) Think of announcements as opportunities for service and growth.[4]

Announcements can come at the beginning of the service in the gathering, or they may be at the end as opportunities for service. Under no circumstances should they interrupt acts of worship.

---

2. Anne Ortlund, *Up with Worship: How to Quit Playing Church* (Regal Books, 1982), 134.
3. Ibid.
4. Martin Thielen, *Getting Ready for Sunday: A Practical Guide for Worship Planning* (Broadman Press, 1989), 96.

CHAPTER 13

THE USE OF SYMBOLS

T
he *total* person is involved in a relationship to God and the universe;
therefore, we speak of embodied worship. God reveals himself
to us through outward forms—even God's highest revelation
through Jesus Christ comes in the Incarnation, a person embodied in the
physical. Our inner devotion requires outward expression in words and
deeds and in personal and social activity. Our communion with God and
with other persons takes place by some bodily means of communication.
Material symbols represent our intangible relationship with God that is
shared in worship.

The word *symbol* is derived from the Greek verb *symballo*, meaning "to
compare or infer." The noun *symbalon* means a sign by which one knows or
infers something. Edwyn Bevan in *Symbolism and Belief* has defined a symbol
as "something presented to the senses which stands for something else."[1]
Symbolism in worship is the use of outward objects and actions which stand
for some inner religious meaning.

Beauty is not its own excuse for being; rather, beauty in nature points to
the nature of God. A sense of feeling for the beautiful, the good, the true is
a part of our natural experience.

Symbols bridge the gap between the sensory and the spiritual. Symbols
can be aids to attention; therefore, symbols can help us keep our attention

---

1. Edwyn Bevan, *Symbolism and Belief* (London: George Allen & Unwin, 1938).

155

upon God. Objects are symbols, useful in worship because they represent certain facts, ideas, or feelings.

The Old Testament recognizes beauty and order in the universe and attributes these qualities to God, who created them. God created the earth and the forms within it and saw that "it was very good" (Gen. 1:31). The expression "good" conveys the idea of excellence. Our sense of the aesthetic is a part of the "image of God" in which we were made. The design and appointments of the tabernacle and the temple were beautiful, for they were "holy places" where God promised to meet God's people. The "holy garments" prescribed for Aaron, the first high priest of Israel, were "for glory and for beauty" (Exod. 28:2).

The early Christians recognized the value of symbolism, and they used it freely in the catacombs—the symbol of a fish was a password among the faithful. (The five letters in the Greek word for fish are the initials for "Jesus Christ, God's Son, Savior.") Although the use of symbolism was carried to an extreme and was abused in the Middle Ages, symbols properly used are acknowledged to have value in worship. Paul Tillich questions the use of symbols that must be interpreted. Symbols grow out of the life and thought of human culture and must be related to the particular period in which they are used.

Worship needs to include powerful and meaningful symbols. They are essential for proper communication between persons. Many of the great realities are not accessible to us without symbols. Symbolism is the very texture of human life.

God and the world are beyond our sensible experience and cannot be conceived except through symbols. The Word of God is expressed in the written words of the Bible which are symbols. J. Allen Kay says, "We are not pure spirit, but are embodied in flesh and blood, and our life is inseparably connected with matter, time, and place. This means that we can only express the spiritual reality of our thought and feeling by material things and by actions in space and time."[2]

THE VALUE OF SYMBOLISM IN WORSHIP

Symbols are concrete methods to call us away from ourselves to God. We acknowledge the presence of God by using symbols. In worship, symbols have a twofold direction, an ascending and a descending action. They are agents for God to show himself to us, and they are agents by which we express ourselves to God.

We must always remember that Christian symbols do not compel God's presence. God remains free, for God is God. Symbols can be used, however,

---

2. J. Allen Kay, *The Nature of Christian Worship* (London: Epworth Press, 1953), 66.

to acknowledge that God has acted in history and that God is continuously present in history. Symbols point beyond themselves to a greater reality. Tillich says, "They point to the ultimate reality implied in the religious act, to what concerns us ultimately."[3]

Symbols are valuable for communication. They may be used to re-create the thought or feeling which originally gave them birth. They often describe more accurately than words concepts such as God, Christ, salvation, atonement, and eternity. Symbols begin with us where we are and take us to the great mysteries of God. For example, the descriptions of heaven as presented in John's Book of Revelation point to some greater truth than the object pictures presented.

To awaken the senses, persons usually require objects which are tangible, touchable, or visible. To reject symbolism in religion leads to a false dualism of life, a separation of the "spiritual" from the "material" or "physical." In the biblical context the spiritual life is discovered through the physical life. Spirituality is the desired end, and the physical symbol is the necessary means.

Symbolism expressed in the arts can aid the church in maintaining a "newness within oldness," the retention of its ancient truths by means of contemporary expression. Even the "absurdity" of our existence expressed by the modern artist may point us to our only hope—God, who creates and communicates in the form of revelation.

SOME DANGERS OF SYMBOLISM IN WORSHIP

The tendency in the Free Churches to play down the value and use of symbolism stems mainly from the dangers and abuses of symbolism in the history of the church. When the Reformers broke with Rome, many of them smashed the sculptures in the churches and destroyed the stained glass and other visual symbols. Most, however, considered this excessive.

Today, many evangelical churches are reintroducing symbolism into their worship. Appropriate use of symbolism will aid in worship. Appropriate use of symbolism will enhance worship; however, there are possible dangers.

(1) Symbols are always in danger of being taken for the things symbolized. Instead of being aids to worship, they can become objects of worship. (2) Once symbols lose their meaning, they tend to become superstitions. To use them as mere decoration is unworthy of the Christian faith. (3) Symbols may convey no ethical suggestions. They may simply become a fascinating study. (4) Symbols may be entirely detached from personal fellowship with

---

3. Quoted in *Symbolism in Religion and Literature*, ed. Rollo May (New York: George Braziller, 1960), 77.

God. One may become absorbed in symbolic meanings without having an experience or personal relation to God. (5) The real value of symbols depends on the individual person. The mind of the worshiper must be filled with the right Christian content in order to make the proper use of symbols in Christian worship. There is the constant danger that false concepts may creep into the mind of the worshiper.

Although symbols are powerful, they are inadequate in themselves. They cannot take the place of reality nor express truth fully. A symbol should never be treated as if it contained God, for then it becomes an idol. For example, when the "sign of the cross" is thought to contain power and protection against evil, it becomes an idol and a hindrance to the worship of the crucified, risen Lord.

Even though the use of symbols in worship can be dangerous, our hunger for beauty is a God-given desire. In religious symbolism, properly used and controlled, the sense of beauty rises to its highest level and is most fully satisfied.

Symbols Suitable for Christian Worship

All Free Churches have made some use of symbolism in their worship. Today theologians, poets, novelists, and dramatists acknowledge the penetrating power of symbols. The arts are being rediscovered as a means of inspiration and teaching. Music, art and color, drama, and poetry may all be used as means of expressing worship and as aids in directing the mind in worship. Our worship is directed toward God, but worship provides also for God's action toward us.

All the arts depend on what they suggest, as well as on what they represent. Worshipers in Free Churches need to become aware of the meaning of the symbolism which they use. A more thorough understanding of symbolism's meaning can enrich the experience of worship. The following are suggested as appropriate symbols for Christian worship.

Language. The most obvious symbol in Protestant worship is that of language. H. Wheeler Robinson reminds us that words in themselves mean nothing until they are referred to life. "Life is continually moving beyond vocabulary which was evolved to describe it, continually putting new wine into old wineskins."[4] Words are never capable of permanent definition. They have to be interpreted in the light of their historical setting. Our use of language in worship appears to be symbolic in two ways: (1) the word is a symbol of some experience; (2) that experience is the symbol of something beyond itself.

---

4. H. Wheeler Robinson, *Redemption and Revelation in the Actuality of History* (New York: Harper & Bros., 1942), 43.

In religion, symbolic language is often used to express realities which otherwise cannot be expressed. Donald M. Baillie mentions many spatial metaphors which point to spiritual realities: "When we say: 'The Lord is in his holy temple,' or 'Lift up your hearts' ... or 'Come down, O Love divine,' or 'Feed me with food divine,' we are using spatial and material metaphors, 'up' and 'down' and 'come' and 'feed.'"[5] The writers of Scripture used anthropomorphic terms to express divine, eternal realities. The Bible symbolizes truth beyond the words it contains. The written words are symbolical of the living Word.

Robinson suggests that of all the arts, poetry comes nearest, in combined effect, to the adequate expression of unseen spiritual reality. As compared with painting, architecture, and music, poetry makes a much more primary demand on the reader or hearer; and the printed page is far more removed from life than the outline and color of the canvas, carved stone, and painted glass on the building, in directing the sensuous excitation of sympathy. In spite of the limitations of language, the articulation of poetic language, the unlimited range of imaginative portrayal, and the greater scope of its descriptive power make poetry supreme in the representation of spiritual reality.[6]

Church architecture. The church building itself symbolizes a congregation which assembles within its walls to worship. The building is not the church, but it does symbolize the church which makes use of it. As Stafford notes, one can worship God in a barn or a hall or any other structure completely devoid of Christian symbolism or churchly character, but under such conditions there is great need for discipline of the spirit. Secular and paganizing influences must be overcome, and the symbolism of the building may point away from the distracting influences of the world to a life of personal communion with God who is higher than humanity.[7]

Church architecture should express both the transcendence and immanence of God. Architecture presents the opportunity to show God's power through its symbolism. The sanctuary should also be constructed to emphasize the fellowship of the congregation. The arrangement of space and pews should bring the congregation close together.

The Cross. The cross is probably the most universal symbol of Christianity. It is a reminder of the redemptive work of God through the offering of God's Son, Jesus Christ. Most evangelicals prefer the symbolism of a cross rather than a crucifix because the empty cross is a reminder of an act which

---

5. Donald M. Baillie, *The Theology of the Sacraments: And Other Papers* (New York: Charles Scribner's Sons, 1957), 51.

6. Robinson, *Redemption and Revelation*, 47.

7. Thomas Albert Stafford, *Christian Symbolism in the Evangelical Churches* (New York: Abingdon-Cokesbury Press, 1952), 104.

was completed and which is symbolized in the resurrection triumph of Christ over death.

The Bible. The open Bible symbolizes the acts of God in history—it contains the written Word that points to the living Word. The open Bible should always be in view of the congregation. Some churches make a practice of displaying the open Bible on the Lord's Supper table. Others argue that the proper place for it is on the pulpit.

In some Free Churches a worshiper brings the Bible in and places it on the pulpit, opening it at the desired place and arranging the bookmark properly as a signal for morning worship to begin. In most churches, the Bible is opened for the public reading of God's Word. In both instances the dramatic action calls attention to the significance of God's Word in worship.

The pulpit. The pulpit symbolizes the centrality of the Word of God. From the pulpit the Word is proclaimed; therefore, it seems appropriate for the pulpit to be in the center rather than at one side. The Lord's Supper table, the pulpit with the open Bible, and the baptistry all symbolize the gospel; thus, it is appropriate for them to be in the center of the building facing the congregation. The center aisle may symbolize the free accessibility of the gospel and a welcome invitation for the acceptance of Christ.

The baptistry. The baptistry is a visible symbol of the believer's commitment to Jesus Christ as Lord. It symbolizes death to sin and resurrection to a new life. The baptistry has particular significance for churches that believe in the immersion of believers only. It symbolizes responsible decision to follow Christ. Located at the front of the sanctuary, behind the pulpit and in line with the Lord's Supper table, the baptistry is a constant reminder of the death, burial, and resurrection of Jesus Christ.

The Lord's Supper table. The Lord's Supper table should be located in front of the pulpit on the level of the congregation. This emphasizes the fellowship of believers and a sense of common unity of the entire congregation. The design of the table should be simple, without heavy decoration. It should be shaped to look like a table, not like an altar.

Dramatic action. From Old Testament times drama has been the servant of worship. Bodily actions are symbolic of our inner attitude in worship. Standing to show praise and adoration toward God, the bowing of the knee or head to show humility and an attitude of prayer, gestures of the hand to acknowledge the majesty of God, and other actions all have symbolic significance in expressing attitudes of worship. The processionals of the choir and minister, the new convert walking down the aisle, and the common handshake as a greeting of fellowship all symbolize the various aspects of worship. The dramatic play also has been used to communicate the truth of the Christian gospel through the centuries.

The visual arts. The church may well be given the credit for developing the visual arts. The dedicated Christian artist may capture religious attitudes on canvas that the average person is incapable of capturing. Thus, artists share their convictions and ideals with those who view their art.

Stained glass may have a powerful influence upon the emotions of the worshiper. Bailey suggests that stained glass arouses the feelings associated with worship—awe, reverence, and aspiration. These attitudes lead to insight, idealization, and the will to do and to be.[8]

Sculpture as a part of the building itself is acceptable in the Free Churches. However, many object to the use of sculpture if it is standing alone because it may suggest idols and idol worship.

Light and color are among the primary elements in the expression of beauty. Von Ogden Vogt reminds us that the same color in nature that moves us to praise can be used inside the church for the same purpose.[9] Various colors are used throughout the year to symbolize events of the Christian faith.[10]

All symbols should contain two elements if they are to be useful in worship: (1) beauty to inspire the senses, and (2) form to point to some Christian truth. God created us with a sense of aesthetic appreciation. Since beauty has come from the hand of God, it should be used to point to the God of truth and beauty.

Symbolism should be used sparingly and in good taste. Symbols which are mere embellishments are always superfluous and evil.[11] The quantity of symbols can never be an adequate substitute for a few well-chosen symbols that convey deep meaning.

BANNERS IN WORSHIP

Although widely used in liturgical churches for centuries, banners have only recently gained wide acceptance among Free Churches. As persons have become more visual in their perception of their world and churches have sought ways to respond to this shift, banners have provided an effective way for persons to worship with their eyes.

The use of banners in worship varies widely among different churches. While some churches use banners of a more general theme to enhance their regular worship, other churches use banners only for special seasonal emphases. As congregations become more aware of the possibility for enhancing worship through visual stimuli, churches will use banners more often.

8. Albert Edward Bailey, *Art and Character* (New York: Abingdon Press, 1938), 293.
9. Von Ogden Vogt, *Modern Worship* (New Haven: Yale University Press, 1927), 110.
10. See chapter 15, "The Christian Year and Other Special Days," for a discussion of colors used in various Christian seasons.
11. Douglas Horton, *The Meaning of Worship* (New York: Harper & Bros., 1959), 36.

Banners vary in construction from elaborate and expensive to simple and direct. Resources for making banners are becoming increasingly available from a wide range of publishers. Many churches have begun to use the term "Banner Ministry" to name the group of persons who design, construct, store, and maintain banners. This group is also responsible for banner bearers and coordination of processionals when multiple banners are used for special services.

When constructing banners for worship, consider the following: (1) Recognize the banner as a symbol. It will receive varying interpretations by individuals. Resist the urge to overexplain a visual worship aid. (2) A banner should contain only one primary message. Do not distract from the banner's effect by cluttering it with too many messages. (3) A banner should be primarily symbolic and should contain few or no words. Banners should speak primarily through pictures, not text. (4) Allow the colors, textures, and graphics to speak to the theme of the banner. A banner for a season (such as Easter, Christmas, or Pentecost) should be constructed of colors and fabrics and graphic styles that portray these seasons as festive, whereas a banner for Advent or Lent should be constructed of contrasting medium and style since these seasons are penitential and introspective. (5) Allow the banner to speak in visual language understood by the culture of the congregation. Not all symbols speak equally well to all cultures. (6) Utilize persons in the design and construction of banners who have interests and skills in these areas. Evangelical worship has traditionally provided few opportunities for persons not skilled in speaking and singing to offer their gifts in corporate worship. Banners provide these persons with an opportunity for leadership.

CHAPTER 14

ARCHITECTURE, ACOUSTICS, AND WORSHIP

F rank Lloyd Wright, the famous architect, once said, "We shape our environment, then our environment shapes us." While the intention of his statement was not directly related to church buildings, it is nevertheless true at least to some extent. The ability of surroundings to affect the mood of a group of people, and the ability of the group to model their environment over time are both significant.

It is easy to recognize the difference setting makes when we reflect on a group of people who first begin worshiping in a home, then in a storefront, next in a school building, and finally in their new facility designed for worship. Worship in each location is strongly influenced by the surroundings. The differences between worship in a rural evangelical church and a massive liturgical city cathedral occur not only in doctrine and liturgy, but also in surroundings.

ARCHITECTURAL PHILOSOPHY

Before beginning a new worship structure or remodeling an existing structure, basic questions must be asked. Beyond givens such as space for congregation, choir, baptism, Lord's Supper, and proclamation, basic questions must be asked, such as "For whom is a worship room built?" "What will be the primary activity to take place?" and "What theology will our worship structure reflect?"

Worship space is first of all built for the congregation. Congregational participation in worship is of utmost importance; therefore, every architectural decision must be considered in light of the congregation. Preaching and music preferences are second in importance to a design that encourages maximum congregational participation.

The primary activities in which congregations participate are singing and speaking, and the room should be designed architecturally and acoustically to make both of these possible. While a leader's speaking can be enhanced through electronics, congregations cannot sing and speak through sound systems.

For worship space to be effective, it must first meet the functional needs of the worshiping community. Aesthetic amenities must be secondary to function in worship space design. Also, careful consideration should be given to long-range maintenance when choosing design and furnishings. Only after worship room design fulfills all functional criteria should concerns such as furnishings and beauty be considered. Aesthetic concerns must be limited when they begin to override functional issues.

The function of worship space is worship—worship by all persons. Geometric forms may be architecturally pleasing but inhibit a "sense of community." Wall-to-wall carpet may give the room warmth and intimacy but prohibit the congregation's full-throated singing. An acoustical environment may allow for studio-quality recording but limit the congregation's full participation.

Historically, the church has vacillated between space that emphasized "the house of worship" (home church model) and "the house of God" (sanctuary model). Effective worship space must meet both of these needs; it must be intimate so worshipers do not feel alone and ostracized, and it must also point toward God. Worship space should not look or feel like the family room in a domestic dwelling, nor should it be cold and indifferent to the individual. Worship space must, however, facilitate and encourage worship as action, for its design will have much to do with the congregation's participation in the Word of God proclaimed, the prayers of the people, the congregation's voice through music, the choir's offerings of choral music, and the gift of instrumental music.

ARCHITECTURE AND ACOUSTICS

The design of the worship building determines the action which will or will not take place within. Many congregations are severely limited by persons who designed their worship space for another time in the church's history without thought of the church's future needs. Designers of worship space should be willing to lay aside their particular biases and focus on the needs of the future church, for the building will most surely outlive those who designed, built, or paid for it.

A worship room, especially one designed for a large group of persons, must accommodate the need for intimate experiences yet accommodate large numbers of persons as well. Invariably when a group of persons joins in an outdoor space to sing or to listen to a story, people gather close together, in a circle if the participants are to be the audience; therefore, spaces which encourage togetherness are desirable.

Although fan and circular shapes achieve togetherness by eliminating straight surfaces and parallel ceilings, they often fail to accomplish acoustical goals. Better acoustics and togetherness are often found in rectangular rooms where the platform is on the long wall with seating angled toward the platform. Central to architectural design is the acknowledgment that corporate worship—hence, corporate worship space—is public, not private.

According to David L. Klepper, four architectural designs are common in the United States:

Cathedral Style: *A large, rather traditional space housing an impressive pipe organ. Choir music is usually very important, and the space tends to be highly reverberant. Speech intelligibility is problematical, and a sophisticated electronic sound reinforcement system is usually necessary.*

Intimate Meeting House Style: *A relatively small space with a low ceiling. Unreinforced speech is usually highly intelligible. An organ may be present, but the type of music usually selected sounds good in a relatively nonreverberant space.*

Evangelical Style: *A large evangelical church has more in common with an auditorium or a television studio than with either of the styles of churches mentioned above. Reverberation is carefully controlled. All speech and music are reinforced, usually via very sophisticated amplification systems.*

Concert Hall Style: *This type of sanctuary represents an effort to compromise between the acoustical needs of a strong, traditional music program and the importance of speech intelligibility in modern worship. Although moderate in size, the concert hall style church usually requires a properly designed electronic speech reinforcement system.*[1]

Worship space must avoid domes, exposed beams, and porous or scalloped surfaces. High walls and ceilings are important for good acoustics, as are parallel surfaces. Generally speaking, for good congregational acoustics, the height of the room should be equal to or exceed its width. Many believe that high ceilings help worshipers turn their thoughts upward to God, giving worshipers a sense of awe and freedom.

---

1. David L. Klepper, "Considerations for the Design of Worship Space Acoustics: An Acoustical Consultant's Viewpoint," *Acoustics of Worship Spaces*, E. D. Lubman and E. Wetherill, Acoustical Society of America, 1985, quoted in "Acoustics of Worship Spaces," James F. Yerges, *Reformed Liturgy and Music*, 22, (1988): 87.

Designers of a worship building must consider interior and exterior noise. The acoustical environment inside the room will obviously center on the worship activities taking place; however, the noise outside the room and the undesirable noise within the room must not detract from worship. Consideration must be given to outside noises such as automobile traffic, aircraft flight patterns, proximity to fire and police stations, railway crossings, athletic and sporting complexes, and industrial complexes. Inside noises include heating and air conditioning units, fluorescent lighting, dimmers, and facilities in close proximity to worship space such as meeting rooms, classrooms, choir rehearsal rooms, church office, kitchen, and bathrooms.

Noises can be transmitted in three ways: (1) directly in the air (the voice or a musical instrument), (2) by impact (slamming a door or banging on the floor), and (3) by vibrating machinery. These noises can travel throughout the building through the air or by vibrations of the solid structure of the building (such as those caused by motors and fans). Airborne noises are transmitted through openings and forced vibration. Open windows and doors are the most common transmitter of these noises with heat ducts being the second most common cause. Gaps around water pipes and electrical fixtures also provide space for these noises to be transmitted. Forced vibration occurs when the noise in one room causes the walls to vibrate, resulting in a reproduction of the original sound.

Structure-borne noise and vibration must be suppressed at the source. Careful attention must be given to placement of plumbing, air conditioning and heating units, and other kinds of machinery so that their vibrations are insulated from the worship space. Noise that is transmitted through ductwork can be reduced by lining the ducts with sound-absorbing materials. To reduce external noise, a barrier must be constructed. For this reason and others an entry or gathering space is recommended for worship buildings. External noise can be prevented by constructing a sound barrier. For this barrier to be effective, it must be massive and airtight.[2]

Architecture and acoustics cannot be considered as separate, for acoustics is completely dependent on architecture. Worship space will inevitably become the sound reinforcer of the congregation and will ultimately (whether acknowledged or not) determine the quality of the congregation's participation. Each architectural decision must be made in light of its acoustical implication, for worship rooms that are too "live" can be easily and comparatively inexpensively deadened, whereas dead rooms are difficult and expensive to liven. Carl Schalk summarizes:

---

2. William J. Strong and George R. Plitnik, *Music, Speech and High Fidelity* (Brigham Young University Publications, 1977): 133–135.

The building itself is an instrument which must be designed so that the praise of God—whether spoken or sung, whether with voices or instruments—is a thing of beauty, lifting the spirits, bringing God's people together in a unified whole, encouraging and reinforcing their song, rather than draining its vocal energy as it attempts its praise and prayer.[3]

When beginning the construction of a new facility or remodeling an existing worship structure, the church should enlist the services of an experienced and successful acoustical engineer. The person should have specific experience with worship room design, for the architectural and acoustic needs of worship spaces are different from those encountered in designing auditoriums, convention centers, and workplaces.

The single most important acoustical property within the worship space is the room's reverberation characteristics. The size of the room, its shape, and even the furnishings will influence its reverberation. When a sound wave strikes a wall in a room, part of that wave's energy is reflected and part of the energy is absorbed by the surface. Highly absorbent surfaces cause the wave's energy to die quickly; low-absorbing surfaces cause the wave to continue to reflect, resulting in increased reverberation. The amount of time required for a sound to die is termed *reverberation time*.[4] Reverberation must not be confused with echo, for reverberation results when a single sound is heard once and decreases over a few seconds. Echo results when the initial sound is repeated two or more times with decreasing volume. Reverberation is desired, whereas echo is not. Ideal reverberation time is difficult to determine since each person hears differently. Even within a discipline such as music, the ideal changes with medium, style, and compositional technique. See the chart on the following page.

The unique function of a worship room makes the design of its acoustics difficult, for ideal acoustics for one of worship's activities is not necessarily ideal for another. According to Carl Schalk "a worship space sufficiently reverberant for spirited singing can easily be made suitable for public speaking. But a worship space designed only with the speaking voice in mind has effectively been ruined for the music-making of congregation, choir and organ. Since the people's song . . . is such an important and vital ingredient in worship, it is not only natural but imperative that the public speaking voice accommodate itself to an environment that is sufficiently live for effective congregational song."[5]

---

3. Carl Schalk, "A Lament for Resounding Praise," *Christian Century*, 100 (1983): 270.
4. Strong and Plitnik, *High Fidelity*, 142.
5. Schalk, 271.

Table 14.1
Acoustical Reverberation

Activity	Ideal Acoustical Environment (reverberation time*)
Choral Music	1.8–2.5 seconds
Congregational Singing	1.8–2.5 seconds
Organ Music	2.0–3.5 seconds
Orchestral Music	1.8–2.5 seconds
Contemporary/rhythmic Music	.5–1 seconds
Speech/drama	.7-1.8 seconds *Reverberation time is the amount of time that sound will linger in a given acoustical environment after the initial sound stops.

GATHERING SPACE

Every congregation should have adequate space for gathering, since worshipers are called out of their daily lives to gather for the express purpose of worship. In the past, this space often consisted of only a small entry or vestibule—there was little transition from the parking lot to the worship room. Churches are realizing more and more the need for this space which allows for transition and encourages fellowship of the congregation prior to and after worship. If adequate gathering space is not available, congregants will invariably use worship space and time for this missing ingredient.

CONGREGATIONAL SPACE

Congregational space should allow for maximum flexibility. Moveable seating allows accommodations for different group sizes, different focuses of worship, and for small group experiences within corporate worship. Flexible seating also allows for movement space to adjust for communion when worshipers come forward, for processionals, for weddings and funerals. It also allows for kneeling and other worship postures. Seating should be comfortable, but pew cushions should not interfere with acoustics. Seating that is designed with the body's natural contour may, in the long run, help more than pew cushions. If cushions are necessary, use fabrics with latex or vinyl backing instead of the usual upholstery fabric.[6]

---

6. Dennis Fleisher, "Acoustics for Congregational Singing," *The Hymn* 41, no. 2 (1990): 9.

While the room should not be elaborately decorated, it should have simple elegance. The room should be pleasing aesthetically and should point the worshiper toward God. Colors that inspire worship, accommodate the Christian year, and are positive and hopeful should be used. The room should make use of appropriate Christian symbols.

Congregational space should be well ventilated and well lighted. When the congregation is too hot or too cold, their attention will be taken from worship. Congregational space temperature should be separately controlled from choir and speaking spaces. Platform and choir space is higher (warmer), and since worship leaders often wear different garments (suits, robes), they are often too warm while the congregation is too cold. Natural light within the room is desirable; however, the ability to darken the room by the use of pulled shutters can be helpful if an electronic visual medium is to be utilized. Light strongly affects mood, and rooms that are too dark will encourage congregations to be introspective instead of vibrant and hopeful. The ability to gradually raise and lower lighting can be used for occasional special effects.

Congregational singing is a foundational act of worship and should be given high priority. According to Dennis Fleisher, the following assumptions for congregational singing are reasonable: (1) The environment should provide support and encouragement for the untrained voice. (2) The acoustic response of the space should impart to each individual in the congregation a sense of being a part of the assembly. (3) The environment should convey to each worshiper the awareness that, as small as one's contribution may seem, it is a meaningful part of the whole.[7]

The acoustical qualities of congregational space are unique, since the sound sources (the worshipers) and the receivers (other worshipers) are in virtually the same location.[8] In a sense, all congregational space is stage space, since the congregation's singing is heard by the congregation itself. The congregation has a number of distinct acoustical disadvantages: (1) They are surrounded by sound absorbers. (The fully clothed person provides about as much sound absorption as four to six square feet of conventional acoustical ceiling tile.)[9] (2) The untrained voice projects forward and down at a slight angle. (3) The congregation is typically on one level and cannot take advantage of the benefits of elevation. (4) There are few, if any, close proximity sources to produce sound reflections and to distribute sound. (5) The sound energy is usually directed toward another person, a sound absorber.

7. Ibid., 8.
8. Ibid., 9.
9. Ibid., 8.

Therefore, the introduction of pew cushions and carpet to this already difficult situation can be deadly. Furthermore, pew cushions and carpet absorb sound because of their proximity to the source; they eliminate the floor and pew surfaces as sound reflectors. While pew cushions (seat only) may have validity for some congregations, especially older congregations, carpet is purely cosmetic and can be eliminated. If carpet is mandatory, use the thinnest possible and use only for aisles and passageways. In addition, noise from other parts of the building, heating and cooling units, and other sources can also reduce the effectiveness of congregational singing, since they become sound competitors.[10] If window treatments are necessary, curtains and drapes should not be used, since they further deaden congregational space.

While balconies can allow for more seating within a worship space, they present interesting acoustical problems. Overhanging balconies should be avoided because the worshiper who sits under the balcony is, in a sense, sitting in another room which has an opening on one side. The worshiper will have difficulty feeling included and may have difficulty hearing since the acoustical environment under a balcony is usually inferior to the larger room. Balconies themselves, especially when deep, can also inhibit participation, since worshipers have the feeling of looking on instead of being a part of the action.

CHOIR SPACE

Choir space, like congregational space, should allow for maximum flexibility. Seating should be individual and moveable, and partitions should be easily removed. Adequate and flexible room should be designed for instrumental ensembles, handbells, additional choirs, and orchestra. Choir space should be built for growth and should be designed to accommodate the church's two largest choirs at once. Choir space should be within the congregational space, not a recess or nook to a larger room. When overhanging ledges and railings frame the choir space, the choir is heard as if in another room adjacent to the congregational space. The temperature in the choir space should be controlled separately from the congregation. The controls should be located within the choir space so that they can be controlled during worship if necessary.

The floor of the choir space and the surrounding surfaces should be hard in order for sound to be reflected. Drapes and other sound absorbents should not be near the choir space. Most choir spaces contain risers in order for the choir to see the director and to avoid the sound's being absorbed by the person in front; therefore, riser height should be graduated a minimum of twelve inches. Even greater distance between choir risers is advised.

10. Ibid., 9–10.

When risers are graduated adequately, sound is less absorbed by other persons, and singers can be placed according to musical demands instead of height. Riser width should accommodate a chair and allow for plenty of room for a person of any age to walk in front of the chair without fear of falling. Ideally, riser width will accommodate a chair and a music stand for an instrumentalist.

Although not a part of choir space within the worship room, adequate choral rehearsal space must be available. This space should allow for adequate storage of music, instruments, robes, etc.; should contain large, well-ventilated robing rooms (separate for men and women), restrooms, space for at least two choirs; should be located near the worship space; should be isolated acoustically from the worship space; and should contain adequate musical instruments.

BAPTISMAL AND LORD'S SUPPER SPACE

In most Free Churches, furnishing for the Lord's Supper is limited to a central table, usually on the congregation's level, symbolizing to the congregation that the Lord's Supper is an act of community. The Lord's Supper table should be easily accessible from all parts of the room so that communion can be easily served to the congregants, and they can easily come forward to receive communion as well.

Baptismal space is usually central and is elevated above the choir, though this placement prevents the choir from participating visually in this act of worship. Baptismal space should be easily accessed by baptismal candidates. Separate dressing areas for women and men should be located immediately outside the baptistry. Within these dressing areas, small stalls should be provided so that each candidate's privacy is respected.

MUSICAL INSTRUMENTS

Musical instruments must be planned at the architectural stage of the building process. A pipe organ takes much space, and building this space as new construction is much easier than rebuilding later. If a pipe organ is not purchased immediately, this space can often be used for other purposes in the interim. Grand pianos cannot fit into spaces designed for smaller pianos. No church would want to refuse a gift of a pipe organ or a grand piano because it had lacked foresight to plan for these instruments.

Congregational singing is reinforced and encouraged by musical instruments; therefore, adequate instruments must be given highest consideration. When purchasing a piano for a worship space, do not buy an upright piano smaller than a studio size, and do not purchase a small grand piano. Pianos designed for home use are not designed for the heavy use that most church pianos receive. In addition, studio pianos have much greater use in other parts of the church when new worship instruments are purchased, and they have high resale value. Small grand pianos do not provide proportionately more or higher quality sound than do studio uprights. A large grand piano is ideal for a worship space.

When purchasing a piano or organ, always check with a professional. The person should be knowledgeable about instrumental companies, should not work for or endorse a particular manufacturer, and should understand the distinct nature of church instruments. Companies that manufacture musical instruments are often bought by other companies and are consolidated with other manufacturers. Quality can be affected when these changes occur; a company that may have been completely reliable several years ago may be much different today.

When purchasing an organ, only organs designed for church use should be considered. Many organs are designed for home entertainment. These organs usually have many amenities not needed by the church organist, and they lack many essentials. Well-meaning committees are often misled to believe that a home organ will be less expensive and adequate for church use. An organ designed by a reputable church organ maker will always provide better value for the church's future worship.

The placement of musical instruments is fairly established: the piano is usually on the congregation's left (so that the piano opens toward the congregation) and the organ is on the congregation's right. The piano and the organ should not be surrounded by low walls, and the instruments should be on the same level as the platform. This allows for the piano to be heard better; for the instrumentalists to see each other, the congregation, and the choir; and for the instruments to be moved onto the platform for special programs. The piano should be on a hard surface so that its sound reverberates well, and the organ should be far enough into the room so that the organist can hear the actual sound from the pipes or speakers. Sound reinforcement should be discouraged or, if necessary, should be minimal. The sound of the piano loses much of its distinctiveness when heavily reinforced.

Pipe organs have many distinct advantages and considerations. Pipe organs are more expensive than electronic organs; however, in most cases, they are preferred because of their ability to reinforce congregational song. When plans are being made for a pipe organ, the room is required to support and carry the sound—the room itself becomes the sound reinforcer for the instrument. Organs have a wider frequency spectrum than the human voice; therefore, acoustics which are adequate for singing may not support the highest and/or lowest frequencies of the pipes.[11] Pipe organs work best

11. George Taylor, "Acoustics and Organs," *The Hymn* 41, no. 2 (1990): 17.

in very reverberant acoustical environments with high ceilings. The pipes and speaker boxes should be placed high so that they may be heard without the interruptions of furnishings and persons. The organ should project its sound directly toward the congregation, and the organ should face the long axis of the building.[12] Pipe organs can produce very loud volume without becoming offensive because they are part of the room's acoustics. Often electronic organs are offensive at louder volumes.

Synthesizers are gaining wide popularity in worship because, through interfacing, they allow wide usage of various instrumental colors not readily available to most congregations on a regular basis. Because technology evolves rapidly and synthesizers are outdated quickly, a piano and an organ should normally be the church's first priority when purchasing instruments. Many church organs now contain computer capabilities; greater flexibility will continue to be available.

PLATFORM SPACE

Acts of worship such as preaching, solo singing, choral singing, Scripture reading, and drama are focused in a single direction. These require a platform area with good visibility. The platform should be tall enough so that leaders can be clearly seen, but leaders should not tower above the congregation. Every attempt should be made to connect the congregation with worship leaders. Furnishings on the platform should be moveable, and seating should be flexible. Chairs should be of average size, simple in design, and no more comfortable than pews. Overstuffed, throne-like platform seating gives the impression that worship leaders are more important than other worshipers. Worship leaders, even by the chairs in which they sit, should make every attempt to be servant leaders. The pulpit should be large enough to be visible, but not so tall or large as to overpower smaller persons. A pulpit should never be designed to accommodate a particular person, for from behind this pulpit many persons of various physical statures will proclaim God's message through word and song. If the platform has low walls or barriers, these should also be moveable.

The floor surface of the platform area must be hard in order to reverberate well. Consider surfaces such as marble, hardwood, or parquet. These surfaces are both aesthetically pleasing and have good acoustical qualities.

SOUND REINFORCEMENT

Many churches reinforce sound through electronic means. While sound systems are the norm for most worship spaces, they are often overused by

---

12. Ibid., 19–20.

speakers and singers, and often they encourage poor vocal habits. Sound systems are rarely needed in small rooms. No sound reinforcement can make up for poor acoustics. Sound systems should reinforce existing good acoustics and should not draw attention to themselves. At its best, a sound system is unnoticed. Sound systems should always be kept simple. The sound systems of many worship spaces are far too complex for the simple needs of the space and for the inexperienced persons who are often asked to run them.

Most sound experts suggest that the sound should come from a central cluster of loudspeakers located slightly in front of the platform area. This placement allows the worshiper to hear the speaker or singer from the direction of the sound source. Sound system controls should be near the back of the room on the main floor and within the worship room, not in a booth. The sounds heard by the technician must be the same sounds heard by the congregation.

Sound systems should always be purchased with the advice of a professional who understands the needs of worship as well as sound reinforcement. Civic buildings are often designed to be dead acoustically so that the sound system will control the sound. This principle is valid for civic buildings but violates good worship practice because the congregation must hear itself and its leader. The sound from the platform must be enhanced, not fully controlled. No sound system is better than the microphone signals it reinforces.[13]

THE USE OF COLOR

The use of color for a worship room has great significance. Color affects our moods. Wise color choices not only help to avoid frequent remodeling but also can enhance worship. The following colors are generally associated with particular feelings:

Red, yellow, orange: restlessness

Blue, beige: neutrality

Green: hope, growth

Worship rooms should be designed to incorporate neutral or positive colors. The style of other furnishings should not be trendy. Many congregations worship in buildings that, due to their trendy architecture, color, wall texture, or furniture choice, give the guest the sense of visiting a congregation of persons who still live within a certain cultural period. On the

---

13. James F. Yerges, "Acoustics of Worship Spaces," *Reformed Liturgy and Music* 22 (1988): 90–91.

other hand, many older churches worship in rooms with timeless design and color choice.

Colors should harmonize with colors of the Christian year and other seasonal emphases. Stained glass, tapestries, and other art work must be designed with primary colors so that when paint color is changed, the artwork will neither control the change nor require discarding the art.

UPDATING EXISTING WORSHIP SPACE

Although difficult, congregations with poor worship-space acoustics can be led to update their existing worship space. When the acoustics of a worship space discourage good congregational participation, no amount of spiritual fervor will make up for this loss. Sometimes when a worship room has good to average acoustics, a well-meaning committee of uninformed persons updates the existing structure by adding a thicker carpet, replacing hard surfaces with carpet, adding pew cushions. Too often this puts a permanent damper on congregational worship. On the other hand, congregations can also update their worship structures by removing carpet, rails, acoustical tiles, and pew padding, and by adding hard surfaces. These worship-conscious congregations find the sermons are better, the singing more enthusiastic, the instruments clearer and more effective, and their worship more fervent.

CHAPTER 15

THE CHRISTIAN YEAR AND OTHER SPECIAL DAYS

T here is a time for everything, and a season for every activity under heaven:

a time to be born and a time to die,

a time to plant and a time to uproot,

a time to kill and a time to heal,

a time to tear down and a time to build,

a time to weep and a time to laugh,

a time to mourn and a time to dance,

a time to scatter stones and a time to gather them,

a time to embrace and a time to refrain,

a time to search and a time to give up,

a time to keep and a time to throw away,

a time to tear and a time to mend,

a time to be silent and a time to speak,

a time to love and a time to hate,

a time for war and a time for peace.

Ecclesiastes 3:1–8 NIV

USING THE CHRISTIAN YEAR IN WORSHIP

Throughout the course of the history of the church, the church has devised its own calendar. The church has established a logical cycle that reflects the major events in the life of Christ. This cycle has resulted in what is commonly called the "Christian year" or "church year." The Christian year is organized around the two primary events in the life of Christ—the birth and the Resurrection. Hence, the two highest days of the year, Christmas and the Resurrection, are given the most prominence; the two major preparatory seasons, Advent and Lent, are also particularly significant. Through observing the church year, the church gives appropriate emphasis to the major events in the life of Jesus in the hope of following Christ more fully.

The Christian year allows the church to have a balanced approach to its worship life. It avoids the tendency for worship leaders to become sidetracked into less significant events while leaving out the major tenets of the church's faith. The Christian year helps churches to seek a balance among the celebrative and the penitential, the extroverted and the introspective. It encourages us to deal with the dark moments in Jesus' life as well as the joyful and celebrative. The Christian year unites Christians of all worship backgrounds by focusing on the events we hold in common. Therefore, it offers Christians an opportunity for unity as we seek to proclaim the good news of Christ to others.

ADVENT

Advent is the time of preparation for Christmas. The season of Advent begins on the fourth Sunday before Christmas Day. Since Christmas Day is the day of Christ's birth and begins the season of Christmas, Christmas Day is not a part of Advent. *Advent*, from the Latin *adventus*, means "coming." Inherent in the Advent season is the incarnation of Christ and the escatalogical theme of his second coming. As Christians have sought alternatives to the excessive commercialism of Christmas, evangelicals have turned to

Advent for help. Advent gives Christians an opportunity to prepare for Christmas, and it puts the Christmas season in proper perspective.

Advent is a penitential season and, at its best, saves the celebration of Christmas for Christmas Day and the Sundays following. However, since Advent does not have a long tradition in many churches, postponing the use of Christmas elements altogether until after Christmas Day may not be possible or desired. Most congregations will blend Advent and Christmas. Advent Scripture should focus on Old Testament prophecy, on John the Baptist, and on preparing for the birth of Christ. The season of Advent is progressive and can become more celebrative as the season develops. As the candles of the Advent wreath light the darkness, the worship of the church can become less penitential. Purple, the primary Advent color, represents royalty and penitence.

Advent wreath. The Advent wreath is a circular wreath of evergreens with four candles (three purple and one pink) around the circle. A fifth candle (white) is in the center of the circle, although it may be in the circle with the purple and pink candles. The candles are lit, one on each of the Sundays of Advent and the white candle on Christmas Eve or Christmas Day. The pink candle, representing joy in the midst of longing, is lit on the third Sunday. Although purple and pink candles are more commonly used, blue (symbolizing hope) or green (symbolizing everlasting life) candles are also appropriate. The Advent wreath is usually placed on the table, and the appropriate candle, with those of previous weeks, is lit in the worship services. Candles from previous weeks are usually lit prior to the service. Churches light candles in many different ways; however, the following worship service excerpt seems to represent a typical lighting:

Scripture

Lighting of the candles

Prayer

The candles may be lit by individuals, family units, Sunday School classes, missions groups, or others. This section of the service may be expanded by the use of music, explanatory remarks, or additional readings. The candles may take on various kinds of significance; churches interpret the four Sundays in many different ways. The most common significance is first Sunday, hope; second Sunday, peace; third Sunday, joy; and fourth Sunday, love. Advent celebration is flexible and may be adapted to a church's particular situation.

Hanging of the Green. A Hanging of the Green service is a service during which the church, in a time of worship, adorns the sanctuary for the Advent season. Hanging of the Green is usually held on the first Sunday of Advent. During this service, carols are sung and readings about the symbolism of such things as evergreens, poinsettias, and candles are presented. The church begins the Advent season by preparing the place of worship for the upcoming Christmas season. A Hanging of the Green service can be a highly structured or an informal occasion.

Lessons and carols. A lessons and carols service is a service of Scripture and carols. It was popularized at King's College, Cambridge, England, in 1918 and has been observed there since.[1] The following model includes the most commonly read Scriptures:

First Lesson: Genesis 3:8–15

> God announces in the Garden of Eden that the seed of woman shall bruise the serpent's head.

Second Lesson: Genesis 22:11–18

> God promises to faithful Abraham that his seed shall the nations of the earth call blessed.

Third Lesson: Isaiah 9:2, 6–7

> Christ's birth and kingdom are foretold by Isaiah.

Fourth Lesson: Micah 5:2–3

> The prophet Micah foretells the glory of little Bethlehem.

Fifth Lesson: Luke 1:26–35, 38

> The angel Gabriel salutes Mary.

Sixth Lesson: Matthew 1:18–21

> Matthew tells of the birth of Jesus.

Seventh Lesson: Luke 2:8–20

> The shepherds go to the manger.

Eighth Lesson: Matthew 2:1–11

> The wise men are led by the star to Jesus.

---

1. Ray Robinson, "The Service of Lessons and Carols," *Choral Journal* 31 (December 1990): 13–20.

Ninth Lesson: John 1:1–14

John unfolds the great mystery of the Incarnation.

A carol is sung following each of the passages.

Chrismon tree. The word Chrismon means "Christ monogram." A Chrismon tree is an evergreen tree adorned with symbols of Christ. The symbols are white and gold, and the tree has white lights. Chrismons can be made of various types of material including fabric, sequins, and styrofoam. The ornaments can be very elaborate or simple. Patterns and information are available from bookstores, although many churches trade patterns and information.

Jesse tree. A Jesse Tree is a tree that has symbols which relate to the lineage of Christ. The tree is evergreen and is usually adorned with symbols, artwork, craft projects, and other items which relate to the heroes and heroines of the faith. Sometimes Jesse Trees are children's Christian education projects. While studying the heritage of Jesus, they create projects which are displayed on and under the tree.[2]

Home devotional booklets. Many churches provide home devotional booklets for church members during the Advent season. The booklets, designed to encourage personal devotion and Bible study, can be written by ministers or members, or can be purchased from a local bookstore.

CHRISTMAS

The Christmas season begins with Christmas Day and is followed by the twelve days of Christmas, ending on Epiphany, January 6. Christmas Day is the celebration of the birth of Christ, and the Sunday after Christmas continues the celebration. In reality, the Christmas season is the season for singing Christmas carols, placing creches on the table, and using symbols which are directly related to the birth of Christ.

Christmas Eve. Christmas Eve is the transition period between Advent and the Christmas season, culminating the period of preparation and beginning the celebration of Christmas. Since many people do not attend church on Christmas Day unless it falls on a Sunday, many churches begin the Christmas season with a Christmas Eve service. Christmas Eve services usually include candle lighting in some form and often celebrate communion. Services are sometimes held early in the evening to accommodate schedules, while many churches have traditions of late-night or midnight services.

---

2. For more information, see Darcy James, *Let's Make a Jesse Tree!* (Nashville: Abingdon Press, 1988); and Raymond and Georgene Anderson, *The Jesse Tree* (Minneapolis: Fortress Press, 1966).

Christmas. Christmas Day is observed on December 25, the date when the sun begins to move along the north horizon and the days begin to lengthen in the northern hemisphere.[3] Although no one knows the actual date of Jesus' birth, this seems a fitting time to observe it. By the fourth century this date was well set. During the Christmas season, the Christian calendar may be at odds with the secular calendar. For the secular calendar, Christmas is over at midnight on December 25; for the Christian calendar, the real celebration has just begun. Churches should, therefore, continue the celebration of Christmas until Epiphany.

EPIPHANY

Epiphany is from a Greek word meaning "manifestation" or "showing forth." Epiphany is "the manifestation of the Word made flesh" or "the showing forth of God in Christ." This season brings together several different themes, all of which show forth "God in Christ" as "God with us" and as "Christ, the light of the world." The Western church traditionally focused on the visit of the Magi during Epiphany, while the Eastern church focused on the baptism of Christ in the Jordan. These themes, as well as the wedding feast at Cana, are appropriate focuses for Epiphany. White and gold are appropriate colors for this season, for both represent Christ's shining forth into the world.

LENT

The word *Lent* means "the lengthening of days" and is the term used for the period of preparation before Easter. The Lenten season begins with Ash Wednesday and continues for forty days, excluding Sundays. (Sundays are excluded because they are celebration days; and since Lent is a penitential season, Sundays are not actually part of Lent.) The period of forty days draws its significance from the Jewish Passover and from Jesus' forty days of fasting and prayer. Historically, the Lenten season is a time for fasting and for instructing baptismal candidates. Lent remains a time of corporate and personal spiritual renewal. Worship during Lent should focus on self-examination in light of Christ's life, deepening of spiritual disciplines, opportunities for public and private dedications, and an overall emphasis on commitment. This season is an excellent time for doctrine studies, Bible studies, revivals, and other forms of spiritual emphasis. Many churches encourage small-group prayer and accountability during this season. Churches

---

3. Donald Wilson Stake, *The ABCs of Worship* (Westminster/John Knox Press, 1992), 44.

should provide materials for these groups and should consider publishing or purchasing materials to aid all congregants in deepening their spiritual lives. Like the Advent season, Lent is an excellent time to produce devotional booklets.

The colors for Lent are purple (penitence) and other dark earth colors, and somber hues. Rough, coarse textures such as muslin and burlap are appropriate for table and pulpit drapes.

ASH WEDNESDAY

Ash Wednesday is forty days before Easter, excluding Sundays. Ash Wednesday focuses on the humanity of all Christians and is summarized by the phrase, "ashes to ashes—dust to dust." While Ash Wednesday services are not as common in Protestant churches, they are rapidly becoming more common with Protestants of varied worship practices. The ashes for Ash Wednesday come from the burned palm branches of the previous year's Palm Sunday. As the ashes are placed in the shape of a cross on the forehead of the people, it is customary to recite, "Remember that you are dust and to dust you shall return" (see Gen. 3:19). This act begins the worshiper on the journey of self-examination during the season of Lent.[4]

The day before Ash Wednesday is sometimes called "Shrove Tuesday," "Fat Tuesday," or "Mardi Gras." The word shrove comes from an Anglo-Saxon word referring to confession. "Fat" is used to describe this day since, in preparation for the Lenten fast, all the food in the house was to be used on this day. Some churches have a pancake supper on this day to signify using all fat and butter before the Lenten season. The tradition of having pancake breakfasts after sunrise service on Easter symbolizes that the season of Lent is over and the fast can be broken.[5]

PALM SUNDAY

Palm Sunday, sometimes called Passion Sunday, is the Sunday before Easter Sunday. The major theme of Palm Sunday is Jesus' triumphal entry into Jerusalem preceding his Crucifixion. Palm Sunday may be celebrated with the whole church's gathering outside or in the fellowship hall; and after the Scripture announcing Christ's entry has been read, the congregation processes into the worship room waving palm branches and shouting, "Hosanna! Blessed is he that comes in the name of the Lord," and other appropriate

---

4. Ibid., 19.
5. Ibid.

phrases. Many churches also have processionals led by children or choral groups. Palm Sunday contrasts the joy of the triumphal entry with the Cross that looms on the horizon. Palm Sunday's role is to put Holy Week into perspective. If Holy Week services are not held, it is imperative that Palm Sunday worship reflect a gradual progression from the celebration of waving palm branches to the gloom of the Crucifixion. Without this progression on Palm Sunday, the whole of the Cross will have been overlooked. Worship leaders are cautioned to resist the tendency to share the joy of the Resurrection on Palm Sunday. Palm Sunday should end with the Crucifixion, and the congregation should be allowed to experience the grief of death before the joy of Easter. The color for Palm Sunday is deep, blood red.

HOLY WEEK

There is no particular emphasis usually assigned to the first three days of Holy Week. Noon services and evening services that focus on aspects of the passion week are appropriate.

Maundy Thursday. Maundy Thursday gets its name from the Latin *mandatum novum*, literally "new mandate" or "a new commandment" (see John 13:34). Maundy Thursday is also frequently called "Holy Thursday." Two acts—the Last Supper and footwashing, associated with Jesus' last meal with the disciples—are observed on Maundy Thursday. While churches are accustomed to observing communion, many churches have never observed footwashing. Among the ways in which footwashing can be observed are the following: (1) as a dramatic act, two or more persons symbolize footwashing for the congregation; (2) twelve persons, representing different aspects of the congregation, wash each other's feet after the minister has washed the feet of the first person; (3) open participation from the congregation is encouraged and adequate basins and towels are available.

Good Friday. Good Friday, or Black Friday as it is often called, is observed on the Friday before Resurrection Day. The term Good Friday is probably the remainder of what was once called God's Friday. Others believe that the contradictory word Good is used to describe this day because the eventual outcome was good. Good Friday is the most somber day of the Christian year, and the worship room should be stripped of any adornment. Several worship options are available for this day; among them is *tenebrae* (Latin for "shadows"). In a tenebrae service, twelve candles representing the disciples and a central candle representing Christ are lit. As the passion narrative is read, the candles are blown out one at a time until only the Christ candle remains. The Christ candle is extinguished as the reading is completed.

Harsh noises or harsh music may follow the reading to symbolize the desperateness of this moment. The worshipers should depart silently in virtual darkness. Tenebrae may also be observed on Maundy Thursday. If Maundy Thursday is not observed, communion and/or footwashing may also be observed.

Holy Saturday. On the day before Easter, sometimes called Holy Saturday, the church often gathers for an Easter vigil. Churches sometimes have the building open for members to come during the day and night to offer prayers. Churches may choose to have members sign up for continuous prayer as the church waits for the day of Resurrection.

EASTER

Easter is a day of pure celebration! Lent has passed and celebration is the order of the day as the church celebrates the triumph of Christ over death and sin. Easter is the first Sunday after the full moon on or after March 21 and can fall any time from March 22 to April 24.[6] Since Orthodox churches follow a different calendar, Easter in the Eastern church is celebrated on a different day. The Easter season lasts for fifty days until Pentecost Sunday.

Easter services are characterized by hymns of the Resurrection, trumpets and organs played at full capacity, and choral processionals. While the Lord's Supper is appropriate for Easter, it should take on a more celebratory mood. The room should be elaborately decorated with the Easter colors: white and gold. Easter lilies, fine-textured fabrics, and colorful banners are all part of this season. Easter is the highest day of the Christian year and should be a model for all worship of the Christian church as we gather weekly to celebrate Christ's birth, life and death, and the promise of his return!

ASCENSION DAY

Ascension Day is the fortieth day after Easter, the sixth Thursday. (See Acts 1:3–11.) Although Ascension Day is always on a Thursday, it can be celebrated the Sunday before Pentecost when the readings about Ascension are usually read.

PENTECOST

The Easter season ends at Pentecost which is fifty days after Easter Sunday. Pentecost (sometimes called Whit Sunday) is taken from the Greek and means "fifty days." Pentecost celebrates the sending of the Holy Spirit and

---

6. Ibid., 69.

the establishment of the church as described in Acts 2. At Pentecost the church was commissioned to proclaim the Word of God in Jesus Christ to all people, and the good news was spoken in every tongue.

Bright festive colors such as red and gold are the colors for Pentecost; symbols include tongues of fire and the dove. Worship on Pentecost may contain a reading of the Gospel contrasted in several languages. Since the Holy Spirit represents the creative aspect of the Trinity, emphasis should be given to the creativity of the congregation. Arts and crafts displays, multimedia presentations, creative uses of instruments and movement are all appropriate to celebrate this festive day of the church year. Pentecost is the birthday of the church, and the mood of the day should be appropriately joyful.

THE SEASON AFTER PENTECOST

The season after Pentecost is called "Ordinary Time." This season begins the Sunday after Pentecost, "Trinity Sunday," and continues until the Sunday before Advent. The Sundays of this season are referred to as the "First Sunday after Pentecost," "Second . . . ," and so forth until Advent. The time after Pentecost gives the church greater freedom in choosing the direction of its worship.

Trinity Sunday. Now that Pentecost has come, the revelation of the Trinity is complete; thus, Trinity Sunday is celebrated the Sunday after Pentecost. This day should recognize the doctrine of the Trinity, but worship should concentrate on worshiping the Trinity, not explaining the doctrine.

All Saints' Day. November 1 is All Saints' Day and is the day when the church recognizes its forebearers. The Day's origin was to honor Christian martyrs; however, it has come to be a day for remembrance of God's faithful people who have died. Hebrews 12:1 is the key biblical reference for this day. All Saints' Day is an appropriate time to recognize persons in the congregation who have died in the previous year as well as all Christians who form a "cloud of witnesses." The color for the day is white. All Saints' Day is an ideal time for a homecoming; a day for people to share about Christians who influenced their lives; and a time to share about denominational, congregational, or ecumenical saints.

Some churches celebrate the Reformation instead of All Saints' Day. Reformation Day is associated with All Saints' Day because Martin Luther nailed his 95 Theses on the door of the Wittenburg church on All Saints' Eve October 31, 1517, the day before All Saints' Day.

Christian Year Summary

Advent	Time of preparation
	Four Sundays before Christmas Day
	Emphasis on birth and Second Coming
	Liturgical color: Purple
	Symbols: Advent Wreath, Chrismon Tree, Jesse Tree
Epiphany	Twelve days after Christmas
	Manifestation of the Word made flesh
	Events: Visit of the Magi, Baptism of Jesus, Wedding at Cana
Lent	Season of preparation, like Advent
	Forty days before Easter, excluding Sundays
	Begins with Ash Wednesday
	Liturgical color: Violet
	Time of personal reflection and repentance
	Emphasis on teaching of Jesus and personal relationship with God
	Symbols: Ashes, forty days
Palm Sunday	Commemorates Jesus' triumphal entry
	Celebrated with palm branches
	Joyful day contrasting the Cross
	Liturgical color: Deep red
	Symbols: Palm branch, young colt
Maundy Thursday	Celebration of the upper room
	Footwashing is often observed
	Also called Holy Thursday
	"Maundy" from Latin word *mandatum*, meaning commandment
	John 13:34
	Symbols: Chalice, bread, towel, basin
Good Friday	Day of Crucifixion
	Good because of what God did for all persons by resurrecting Christ
	Sometimes called Black Friday
	Symbols: Cross, darkness, crown of thorns
	Other Holy Week symbols: Rooster, gavel, dice

Christian Year Summary (Continued)

Easter	Day of Resurrection	
	Liturgical colors: White and gold	
	Symbols: Sun, empty tomb, butterfly, lilies, pomegranate, peacock	
Pentecost	Fifty days after Easter	
	Celebrates the coming of the Holy Spirit	
	The official birthday of the church	
	Acts 2	
	Liturgical Colors: Red and gold	
	Symbols: Flames, doves	

USING THE SECULAR CALENDAR IN WORSHIP

Although specific days in the secular calendar have religious connotations, many, such as Valentines Day, have taken on a secular rather than a religious significance. In contrast, some secular calendar days, such as Independence Day, have been so widely observed by many churches that they have taken on religious meaning far beyond their original intention. Whether or not a particular day is a part of the Christian calendar, if it is observed in the corporate worship of the church, it must be observed so that the primary focus is on God. Church celebrations which focus on specific individuals, groups, national celebrations, etc., with minimal attention to God, have no place within the church's regular worship. Worship leaders must guard worship as an experience which in its purpose and practice honors God.

MOTHER'S DAY

Mother's Day became a national celebration in the United States in 1913 when Anna Jarvis of Philadelphia, whose mother had recently died, determined to have a national day to honor mothers. Mother's Day is on the second Sunday of May, the same day as Mothering Sunday in Britain. As are some other national recognitions, Mother's Day is nearly viewed by many churches as biblical instead of traditional. Mother's Day can be utilized as a meaningful worship celebration when it is (1) focused on God, and (2) does not exclude all persons who are not mothers.

When planning a worship experience for Mother's Day, consider the following: (1) not all women are mothers—some choose not to have children, others want to be married and are not and some women are infertile. For those who would like to have children, Mother's Day is among the most difficult days of the year. (2) Some persons do not have positive relationships with their mothers, and Mother's Day is a stark reminder of this unpleasant reality. (3) Many people who would like to be with their mothers on Mother's Day cannot because of death, distance, or other circumstances. Mother's Day should avoid practices that draw attention to these negative realities. Mother's Day should be a day to recognize the positive influence of women in our lives and to express gratitude that, because of the willingness of a woman, our mother, we are God's children.

Many churches use Mother's Day as an opportunity to recognize the importance of family within the Christian community. Some churches recognize new births on Mother's Day, while others rotate this practice between Mother's and Father's Day. Whatever the emphasis, this potentially important worship day must focus on God as the object of our worship and must recognize God as our heavenly parent.

FATHER'S DAY

Father's Day has been observed since approximately 1920, and it is always held on the third Sunday of June. Although worship on Father's Day is usually less sentimental than on Mother's Day, the above caveats apply to both days. Father's Day can be a good opportunity to recognize the role of godly men and the importance of family in church and society, as well as the Mother's Day suggestions above.

INDEPENDENCE DAY

Independence Day celebrations by the church must be approached with great care and caution, for often God and country are not distinguished as separate entities: patriotism is mistaken for spiritual fervor, and gross violations of church and state occur. While the church is a part of society, the church must carefully guard its unique identity as separate. Civil government must be kept at arm's length from the church. The church must not, in an attempt to take advantage of government's amenities, become too friendly with government lest the church find itself in a position of compromise of its theological aims. Services which can hardly be distinguished from civil patriotic rallies have no place within the church's worship and should be avoided. Worship services built around national celebrations must praise God as the sovereign God of all times and places and not mistakenly honor God only for his role in the formation and preservation of the United States.

God is sovereign, whatever does or does not happen within the civil government of the United States.

Worship around national holidays must poignantly remind the worshiper of his or her role as a Christian citizen, for national change can best occur as Christian citizens take seriously their roles to share the reality of God's grace with the world in which they live and work. Encouraging involvement in political process without affirming the Christian's larger role in society can be misleading.

Many churches participate in services near national holidays which involve pledges of allegiance to the United States; singing of patriotic music (national anthem, military songs, songs associated with particular wars and victories); processions of flags by honor guards; elaborate red, white, and blue decorations; fireworks; and recitations of national documents. These services can easily fail to recognize the humility with which the Christian approaches a personal relationship with the nation. These services may fail to focus on God as the sustainer of all persons and God's being higher than civil authority, and they may confuse patriotism's emotionalism with worship of God. Worship centered around national days which fails to boldly recognize God as the supreme authority and the source of true freedom and which fails to challenge the worshiper concerning individual social responsibility, fails to accomplish the true aims of the church's worship.

MEMORIAL DAY

Memorial Day was originally called Decoration Day, since it was a day to decorate the graves of dead soldiers. Memorial Day now occurs most often on the last Monday of May, although some states still observe it on its original date, May 30. This holiday dates to 1868 and is recognized as a day to honor persons who have given their lives for the good of their country. It is a patriotic day for remembering and for expressing gratitude for the price of national freedom. As a day observed in the church's worship, Memorial Day should not simply be a reverent, more passive patriotic celebration than Independence Day as celebrated in some churches. Memorial Day as a part of the church's worship may be viewed as a day for the church to celebrate the heritage left by members who have died. This day also may be a day for recommitment by worshipers of their opportunity to leave a legacy for the church of the future. Many churches use this service to recognize persons within its body who have died in the previous year. (Some churches do this on All Saints' Day.) While a worship experience of this type has merit, it must express continued faith in God as the source of all life and hope.

LABOR DAY

Labor Day, always held on the first Monday of September, was recognized as a legal holiday by Congress in 1894. Its purpose is to honor the "working person." Labor Day's becoming a national holiday was strongly influenced by the American Federation of Labor. Although Labor Day is exclusively a secular calendar observance, churches can utilize implicit themes of this day in worship. Since Labor Day recognizes the national working force, it can also be an opportunity to recognize the importance of persons who work in and outside the church to accomplish God's will. While overt recognitions, such as having persons stand or presenting certificates, can utilize much worship time and can focus too strongly on persons instead of God, the service can effectively utilize Scripture, music, sermon, and testimonies that focus on the joy of serving God. Labor Day is a perfect time to focus on the calling of Christians to share God with persons with whom they come in contact in the workplace and in leisure settings.

Services which inspire deeper Christian commitment may become trite if used every year. A good secondary emphasis for Labor Day is a focus on Jesus' words, "Come unto me, all ye that labour and are heavy laden and I will give you rest" (Matt. 11:28, KJV). Many persons within the church are tired and need to be assured that there is rest and refuge in God. A service focused on this theme could be a fresh approach to the sometimes burdensome challenge to greater service when some persons are overburdened and over-committed.

THANKSGIVING DAY

The national observance of Thanksgiving Day on the last Thursday of November dates to 1863, when President Lincoln issued the first national Thanksgiving proclamation. Since Thanksgiving occurs in late autumn, it is a fitting time to focus on God's generous provision for God's people. Thanksgiving services are often closely tied to harvest celebrations, although Thanksgiving in many areas of the country occurs well within winter. Thanksgiving services should be celebrative and joyful. They should be full of opportunities for the congregation to express their praise to God for divine acts. Since Thanksgiving comes near the end of the year and barely precedes Advent, Thanksgiving worship can be a time of reflection on the previous year. With Advent and Christmas yet to come, Thanksgiving may be the last time in the calendar year to reflect on God's goodness, since after Christmas, worship will likely center on the new year or on Epiphany.

GRADUATION

During May, most churches recognize persons who are graduating from various educational institutions. While this recognition is important and is seen by some as a "rite of passage," the focus, as on other special days, should be on God as the sustainer during days of preparation and on God as the hope for the future. Services in which graduates are recognized should include opportunities for the congregation to commit itself to active involvement in the future of the graduates. Responsive reading in which the congregation pledges to pray for the graduates and corporate prayer in which the leaders pledge the support of the congregation are possibilities. This service should look primarily toward the future and should not be a time simply to dwell on past accomplishments.

SERVICES OF ORDINATION

Ordination services for deacons and ministers will occur within the life of the church. Churches have varying views on ordination; therefore, ordination services will reflect the particular church's views. Ordination is the "setting aside" by the church of a person for a certain or specific ministry. While most churches recognize particular callings within the body of Christ and choose to ordain persons specifically for these, churches also recognize that each person is called to ministry. Ordination services contain many usual worship elements such as hymns, Scripture readings, and a sermon; however, these general elements are usually focused toward the ordination theme. In addition, ordination services often contain at least some form of the following elements:

• Questioning of the Candidate, Report of the Ordaining Council, and Personal Testimony

In some instances the candidate is asked representative questions within the service to assure the church that the individual is sound in doctrine and life. In other cases, a representative member from the ordaining council reports to the congregation the council's approval of the individual for ordination. Other churches assume that any discrepancies would have previously been discovered and that, by the time of the ordination service, the candidate is theologically sound. Usually the candidate will give a testimony during the service which serves somewhat the same function as questioning the candidate. During the testimony, the candidate's calling to Christian ministry should be told.

- The Laying on of Hands

This act is the most distinguishing act of the ordination service. Churches vary in their practice of laying on of hands. In most cases, the candidate kneels facing the congregation, and the congregation or ordained persons, one by one, come forward, lay their hands on the head of the candidate, and quietly pray a brief blessing or whisper words of encouragement to the candidate. Some churches view ordination as an act of the entire church; thus, all persons who desire participate in the laying on of hands. Other churches reserve laying on of hands as an act for only ordained persons. When the congregation is not allowed participation in the laying on of hands, the act may appear secretive and exclusive.

- Ordination Prayer

If the congregation is not free to participate in the laying on of hands, it is important that someone pray a prayer, representing the congregation, affirming the candidate's recognition of God's call. If the congregation does participate in the laying on of hands, this prayer will be a summary prayer.

- Sermon or Charge to the Candidate and the Church

Some ordination services contain a single sermon which addresses the candidate and the church concerning their unique responsibilities. Other ordination services contain two separate sermons, a charge to the candidate and a charge to the church. These sermons may be given by the same person or two different persons.

- Presentation of Ordination Certificate and Bible

Near the end of the service many congregations present an ordination certificate to the candidate. Often the congregation also presents a Bible. These acts are usually accompanied by appropriate words regarding the significance of this service in the life of the candidate and the centrality of the Bible in the candidate's ministry.

CHAPTER 16

DRAMA IN WORSHIP

*A*s worshipers have become more and more visual in their perception of the world around them, churches have used drama more frequently to portray the biblical story. The church embodies the acts of God, and drama is an ideal mode of communication for retelling God's acts in history and contemporary life.

Church drama is, according to Everett Robertson, inclusive of "all dramatic mediums in the church." It is the "portrayal of the basic human situation as interpreted through the Bible. It is the expression of [our] relationship to God as stated through the inspired writing of the Bible." By its purpose, church drama is centered on Christ. [1]

Church drama differs from secular drama in purpose and intent. Secular drama is designed to move the human spirit toward various cognitive or emotional responses that may or may not have any inherent moral or spiritual goals. Christian drama uses many of the same techniques but is intentionally directed toward the purposes of the church, honoring God through worship, building up the body of Christ through nurture and education, and reaching out to persons who have not yet met Christ. Church drama should not intend to remake or redirect secular drama but should seek to gain its own identity by emulating the best artistic models within a philosophy that supports the ministry of Christ through the church.

---

1. Everett Robertson, *Introduction to Church Drama* (Nashville: Convention Press, 1978), 4.

Much of the Bible was oral tradition before it was written, and drama was primary to the Bible's being passed from generation to generation. Therefore, the biblical narrative is replete with drama. The Passover is a highly dramatic event that used the didactic purpose of drama to teach succeeding generations of God's choosing Israel (Exod. 12:25–27). Prophets such as Jeremiah and Elijah dramatized vital truths of God to the people (Jeremiah 13:1–9; 27:2–11, 1 Kings 18:20–39). The parables of Christ contain drama because they are narrative. Baptism and the Lord's Supper are dramatic events of the highest significance.

Throughout history the church has used drama to portray religious experiences, though at times the church has banned dramatic performances. The Middle Ages are known for their mystery plays, in the ninth century, drama began to grow out of Catholic worship. Drama as an alternative to opera during Lent led to the development of oratorio—a musical form much like opera but without staging and costumes. As an art form within the church, drama has made its most marked progress in recent decades.

Drama contains action, plot, character, language, and spectacle. *Action* is the moving of the human spirit from one place to another, tracing the development, conflict, or change in human essence—a movement from pride to humility or from goodness to evil.[2] Dramatic action involves the interaction of the observer with situations and emotions of the characters resulting in a change of position or a change of character on the part of the observer. The change results from the observer's having participated vicariously in the action as portrayed by the characters.

Plot is the sequence of events through which the action occurs.[3] The plot traces the actions of the characters on their journey of change. *Character* always involves persons. Characters, in order to be believed and to make ultimate impact, must be seen as real people, persons with potential for good and evil. The believability of a character is in direct proportion to the character's portrayal as a real person—warts and all.

Language is a complex area of drama in that language "more than words, syllables, grammar, or syntax, actually has a very mystical or spiritual quality."[4] Hicks and Key suggest:

> When an actor speaks, more occurs than mere recital of lines and words. Symbols are being verbalized by the actor and, as a result, the audience begins to experience the emotion of the play. . . . The emotions and frequently the other senses are triggered by this spiritual interrelationship of language, senses, and emotions.[5]

---

2. Robert M. Hicks and Tom Key, "Drama and Education: The Medium for Modern Man," *Christian Education Journal* XI (1991): 103.

3. Ibid.

4. Ibid., 104.

5. Ibid.

The last element of drama is *spectacle*. This element includes the music, sets, and choreography, seen in many dramatic works.

Drama is a particularly good tool for the church because it involves all the senses. Drama can affect the conscience, the emotions, and the will simultaneously. Drama addresses both the left (logical, rational) and the right (emotional, sensory) sides of the brain.[6]

Drama can be effectively used in worship in many ways:

1. play—a dramatic presentation involving characters, plot, props, and so forth;

2. monologue—the portrayal of a character by one actor;

3. story telling—telling a story with one or more actors;

4. pantomime—the drama portrayed in silence or while a story is read;

5. tableau—a living picture, with actors portraying a "still" scene (effective with music or reading);

6. choral speaking—reading in a systematic form as a choir;

7. pageantry—a play involving music, sets, full-scale visuals;

8. readers' theater—drama by readers usually in black, sitting on stools, usually with no props;

9. puppetry—the use of puppets to portray drama;

10. sermon—some newer sermon forms are drama.

While drama is an effective worship tool, it can, as can other elements, have unique problems. The following guidelines are helpful in the preparation of drama:

1. Drama should point to God as the source of worship.

2. Avoid drama in which humor or special effects camouflage its meaning.

3. Puppetry and clowning must be used with caution in order for their spirit to point toward worship's aim.

4. In drama, as in art, less is more; therefore, understate dramatic effects, characters, scenery, special effects. Simple, direct drama is often more effective than elaborate presentations which draw attention to themselves.

---

6. Ibid., 105.

5. Drama always deserves the best in planning and preparation.

6. Sometimes the production of the drama and the entertainment value may detract from the gospel message.

All worship is drama, and drama as an art form is unique in its ability to serve effectively as a worship tool. The combination of words and actions can say much more than either can say alone.

CHAPTER 17

RITES OF PASSAGE

L ife is a dynamic journey in which events, predictable and unpredictable, mark the way. While these events differ from person to person and happen at various times, major events of birth, marriage, and death present unique transition points that call for particular ministries within the worshiping community.

The term "rite of passage" has its roots in cultural anthropology but is used widely to describe life's major thresholds. Arnold van Gennep is the leading figure in the concept of rites of passage.[1] He offers the following definition: "rites which accompany every change of place, state, social position and age." He describes three phases of transition: (a) symbolic detachment from an earlier social structure, (b) an intermediate period of ambiguity, and (c) symbolic visiture with the rights and obligation of a new status.[2] William Bridges states that all transitions begin with (a) an ending, followed by (b) a period of confusion and distress which must be experienced, leading to (c) a new beginning.[3] Rites of passage mark and define life's primary transition points as they enable us to define our current

1. Arnold van Gennep, *The Rites of Passage*, trans. M. Vizedom and G. Caffree (Chicago: University of Chicago Press, 1960).
2. Gennep quoted in *Liturgical Rites of Passage for the Later Years*, quoted in Thomas B. Robb's *Journal of Religion and Gerontology* (1991), 7.
3. William Bridges, *Transition: Making Sense of Life's Changes* (Readings: Addison-Wesley, 1980), quoted in Robb, 2.

(former) state, recognize our current (upcoming) change in social structure, understand the occurring transitional process, and integrate our new role into our community. Inherent in rites of passage is a concern for the future in which the individual will productively work and serve. The church in its worship life is uniquely positioned to help facilitate the journey in the life of its members. Specific rites (rituals) surrounding major life events allow the church to respond in a secure and predictable manner in times which may be characterized by instability and disorientation.

Many major life events, other than parent-child dedications, weddings, and funerals, are considered rites of passage, although they may not be observed as often. Rites of passage such as graduation, entering military service, going to college, change of jobs or careers, and summer missions deserve periodic recognition by the church. Observing these rites underscores Free Church theology that all of life is sacred and subject to theological interpretation and community prayer support.

PARENT-CHILD DEDICATIONS

Many Free Churches have rejected infant baptism, believing that valid Christian conversion is not a decision to be made by parents but a conscious decision prompted by God's Spirit and freely acknowledged by the individual at the appropriate time. Yet there is biblical precedent for dedicating children to God. Hannah gave Samuel to God for his service. There is much biblical support for the responsibility of Christian parents to live godly lives in the presence of their children and for parents to teach their children the ways of God.

From the pastoral care perspective, both for parents and other congregants, Free Churches have until recent years overlooked the need for a formal recognition of the unique roles of parents, the family of faith, and God in rearing children. Parents need to covenant with God in the presence of the congregation their vow to parent their children in a godly manner, and churches need to covenant with God their responsibility to nurture Christian families. Rearing children is a responsibility that must be shared by the congregation in prayer and other actions.

The preferable term for this observance is Parent-Child Dedication, since the bulk of the responsibility is on the parent and the child's role is passive. Terms such as "Baby Dedication" or "Child Dedication" should be avoided, since they do not adequately represent the theological perspective of most Free Churches. Parent-Child Dedication can be held on various Sundays. Many churches alternate this observance between Mother's Day and Father's Day, while other churches observe it on a neutral Sunday such as Thanksgiving. Other congregations observe Parent-Child Dedication on the first Sunday a new baby comes to church or at the parents' discretion.

When the service is observed once per year, the thrust of the service will center more on this observance, whereas observances on an individual basis are usually brief and may serve as an addendum to a regular service.[4]

Parent-Child Dedication offers opportunities to acknowledge the unique role of extended family in the religious upbringing of children. Care must be shown in acknowledging the difficulty of this worship experience for some worshipers. For couples unable to have children, this service can be a stark reminder of their childlessness. For single adults who would like to be married and have children, this day can be painful. For adults who grieve the loss of an infant or distress of a handicapped child, there is possible alienation. Experienced parents who feel like failures may feel guilt for their lost chance or envy toward the new parents for their fresh start. These mixed feelings *must* be acknowledged either through the pastoral prayer or the sermon.[5]

WEDDINGS

Perhaps in no other rite of passage do the church and society have as much at stake as in Christian weddings, for the church and society will be strengthened by strong Christian marriages. Nevertheless, many churches and their leaders stand idle, giving no or little direction to the formation of wedding services that honor God. Weddings are often seen as purely personal and are left totally to the discretion of the couple and their families—persons who usually have little training in service design, theological concepts, or appropriate etiquette. Any service sanctioned by the church should be controlled by the church and its leaders. Weddings when held at the church should be a unique blend of personal preferences of the couple, established church practice, and local custom, with the overarching principle that a wedding must first be God-honoring. All texts, actions, and intent must honor God!

Although there is less doctrinal certainty to wedding practices than most people would like to admit, churches must nevertheless make every attempt to assure that weddings held in their sanctuary reflect their beliefs. The government ultimately determines what makes a marriage legal; therefore, people have the option to choose the church's services for weddings, and the church has the right to give or withhold its services.[6] Wayne Brouwer offers the following four expectations from the church: (1) The church expects that a couple married within its walls believes in God and desires that God

---

4. See appendix D for a sample Parent-Child Dedication service.

5. M. Mahan Siler, "Rites of Passage: A Meeting of Worship and Pastoral Care," *Review and Expositor* 85 (Winter 1988): 54.

6. Wayne Brouwer, "Whose Wedding Is It?" *Reformed Worship* 16:12.

be the authority guiding their individual and corporate lives. (2) Given the Christian understanding of the permanence of marriage, the church expects the couple to recognize the importance of lifelong commitment to their marriage vows. (3) The church expects to have some normative influence on the shape of a wedding ceremony and all associated events. (4) The church can reasonably expect to have continuing involvement in the spiritual life of the marriage partners and the family that may develop.[7]

Brouwer offers the following guidelines to help the congregation assure that these expectations become reality: (1) Pastors should agree to officiate at a wedding only if the intended marriage relationship has been endorsed by the governing council of the congregation. This removes pastors from the pressure to act as marriage agents simply because they have that right. Knowing that the church must confirm their right to marry gives the prospective bride and groom a greater sense of community involvement. (2) The church should establish a period of premarital instruction or counseling. (3) The shape of the wedding itself should take its cue from the church's understanding of the meaning of marriage.[8]

BIBLICAL PERSPECTIVES

Although the Scriptures are virtually silent about wedding ceremonies, they do speak frequently about marriage. Marriage was established in the garden of Eden for the purpose of an individual's companionship (Gen. 2:24). Deuteronomy 24:5 (NASB), "When a man takes a new wife, he shall not go out with the army, nor be charged with any duty; he shall be free at home one year and shall give happiness to his wife whom he has taken." This passage speaks of the importance of newly married couples' spending time learning about each other. Genesis 29 tells the story of Jacob's long struggle to marry Rebekkah, and the book of Ruth is dedicated to the beautiful familial account of the love between Ruth and Naomi and between Ruth and Boaz.

The first of Jesus' sign miracles recorded in the gospel of John occurred at a wedding at Cana. Matthew 22 records Jesus' parable of the wedding banquet, which likens the kingdom of God to a great wedding feast replete with joyous celebration and many guests.

References to the roles of spouses and analogies to God's love for us and spouses' love for each other are numerous in the Pauline epistles. The ultimate wedding reference is Revelation 19, where John records the victory of Christ's bride, the church. Revelation 21:2 contains the wedding procession

7. Brouwer, 13.
8. Ibid.

of "the holy city, new Jerusalem, coming down out of heaven from God, prepared as a bride adorned for her husband."

HISTORICAL PERSPECTIVES

Throughout history weddings have vacillated between "civil service" and "church service." Boggende cites three historical models of weddings:

> The earliest model was the lay model: people simply decided to live together. Ancient laws indicate that the state was frequently involved in formalizing the relationship, but there was no evidence of religious ceremony. The second model, the ecclesiastical, resulted from the church's views of marriage both positive and negative. The Middle Ages can be regarded as a period during which these two models clashed. Although by the end of the Middle Ages the ecclesiastical model had become the norm, formalized by the Council of Trent, the lay model continued. The third model was inspired by the Reformation and was essentially a mixture of the previous two. The Reformers differed in emphasis: Luther tended to think more in terms of the lay model, while Calvin was more sympathetic to the ecclesiastical.[9]

Lay model. In the lay model, two aspects are stressed: legality and finance. The man was to file a formal marriage contract with the woman's parents, and money or goods were exchanged. Marriage was not necessarily a voluntary act on the part of the woman. She was seen as property for the purpose of producing children; she was a second-class citizen. The Hebrew Scriptures contain little about marriage rites; however, the betrothal (engagement) was almost as binding as the marriage itself. Boggende makes the following observations regarding weddings in this period: (1) Marriage usually included a contract to protect the wife from abuse and to insure financial stability. (2) Many marriages began with public announcements and ceremonies (Gen. 29:22; Judg. 14:10; John 2:2; Luke 12:35–38; Ps. 45:14; Jer. 7:34; Matt. 25:1–13). (3) Weddings could include blessings from parents, relatives, or friends (Gen. 24:60; Ruth 4:11). (4) Parental permission was not always required—Samson married against his parents' wishes (Judg. 14:3). (5) The ceremonies gave legal sanction to the marriage.[10]

Ecclesiastical model. The church model had its roots in ancient culture. The Greeks and Romans regarded marriage as important for the state and the family and, although primarily a social action, marriage was seen as a divine institution and took place in a religious context. During the first century two opposing views began to emerge—the status of women and sanctity of marriage vied with the esteem for celibacy. The idea that sex was evil gained

---

9. Bert Den Boggende, "A Historical Survey of the Rite of Marriage: Pre-Christian and Christian," *Grail* 3 (September 1987): 59.

10. Ibid., 62–63.

greater prominence, and marriage was seen as an escape from sin, an alternative for those not strong enough to choose virginity and sexual abstinence.

In the second century, marriage began to be seen as sacrament, although there was no agreement among church leaders until emperors Charlemagne in 802 and Leo VI in 900 legislated that marriages contracted without the church's blessings were null and void. By the end of the twelfth century, the church was fully in control of the wedding ceremony in most of Europe.[11] Its control of marital contracts continued nearly unchallenged throughout the Middle Ages.

Mixed Model. Martin Luther led in the breaking of the church's control over the wedding ceremony. In his 1520 treatise *The Babylon Captivity of the Church*, he wrote, "There is no Scriptural warrant whatsoever for regarding marriage as a sacrament. . . . Nowhere do we read that it was instituted by God in order to symbolize something." Luther denied that grace would be received by getting married. The Lutheran church did not dispense with weddings, but they did come closer to a lay model.

Calvin carried a mediating position between the Catholic tradition and Luther's. Calvin viewed the woman as an inseparable associate, while Luther viewed her primarily as a bearer of children. It is apparent from Calvin's *Institutes of the Christian Religion* that he viewed marriage as a holy estate. In England marriage (until 1835) was seen as an ecclesiastical event.[12]

Wedding ceremonies in the twentieth century remain mixed models with both civil and religious elements. Ministers today serve as agent of the civil government as well as of the church.[13]

THE REHEARSAL

Under no circumstance should a wedding be attempted without a rehearsal. Even a small wedding involving a few people should be rehearsed, perhaps immediately before the service. Larger church weddings should be rehearsed the day before. Although, according to some etiquette books, brides are to be in charge of the wedding rehearsal, this system rarely works well because most brides have observed few weddings, have limited awareness of church policies, and often have limited experience in supervising large groups of persons—especially close friends and relatives. For these reasons, the pastor or the wedding coordinator should run the rehearsal. The service should be carefully planned by the couple and the pastor, and every attempt, within good taste and theology, should be made to accommodate

---

11. Ibid., 68–70.
12. Ibid., 72–75.
13. Robert C. Rayburn, *O Come Let Us Worship: Corporate Worship in the Evangelical Church* (Grand Rapids: Baker Book House, 1980), 272.

the couple's needs. However, rarely will the wedding couple, or closer family members, be emotionally prepared for the rigors of guiding a rehearsal. The fact that wedding rehearsals are often run by inexperienced persons causes many ministers and musicians to dislike participation in weddings.

When all members of the wedding party have arrived, the minister should lead the group in prayer and speak to them briefly about the role of worship in the wedding ceremony. The wedding should first be rehearsed in reverse. The wedding party should be placed in their positions for the service. After each place is carefully marked, the recessional should be practiced without music. After the silent recessional, the processional should be practiced and the recessional reviewed, all with music. If needed, repeat the procedure. When everyone is comfortable with their places and procedures, dismiss all persons except the bride, groom, maid (or matron) of honor, and the best man. Rehearse the ceremony with these four persons. If others are out of the room, this procedure will go much faster. The custom of the bride having a "stand-in" for the rehearsal is antiquated and *not* recommended. The bride will feel more confident when she has rehearsed, rather than observed.

MUSIC

It is perhaps in the selection of music that couples are most sensitive and the greatest abuses of worship occur; for often texts and tunes are chosen which neither honor God in their original intent nor in their current application.

The traditional wedding marches—the processional "Bridal Chorus" by Richard Wagner from the opera *Lohengrin* and the recessional, Mendelssohn's incidental music for Shakespeare's *A Midsummer Night's Dream*—have been the subject of much debate and most agree that better choices should be made.[14]

Congregational singing should be included in all Christian weddings as an act of praise to God. It is appropriate for the bride to process while a hymn is sung; hymn tunes are appropriate for preludes, recessionals, and within the context of the service. Great hymns of praise are always appropriate as the service focuses on God, the source of love. Numerous new wedding texts by contemporary hymn writers are available in current denominational hymnals.

The wedding party must be provided with copies of hymn texts, responsive readings, and other corporate worship acts. Inconspicuous copies should be made and strategically placed so that members of the wedding party can fully participate in the various acts of worship. Often groomsmen

14. The processional occurs in the opera after the wedding, an event which ultimately brings death, and the recessional has inappropriate associations due to Shakespeare's light-hearted farce.

can have copies in their coat pockets. The copies can be shared with brides-maids at the appropriate times.

While favorite love songs from the pop repertoire may have their place in the total celebration, the wedding service should use solo material with a distinctively Godward text. Solos should focus on the wedding event in its future context instead of looking backward to remembrances of brief yesterdays. The service should focus on the many years that await the couple rather than the comparatively brief courtship.

THE ORDER OF SERVICE

The planning of the order of service should be a joint venture with the couple, minister, and musicians.[15] According to Rayburn, "a dignified simplicity should control all decisions."[16] The service should avoid elaborate decorations that take away from the focus on God.

Couples are encouraged to use existing vows, since most wedding manuals contain material that has withstood theological and liturgical scrutiny. Rarely does a couple have the literary skills and knowledge of tradition required to write wedding vows deserving of this important occasion. Often couples become sentimental while neglecting essential elements.

Printed orders of worship are used widely for wedding services and are a visual and tangible addition. A wedding bulletin should display appropriate artwork on its cover; the order of service, responsive readings, and perhaps hymn and prayer texts on the inside; and a list of the wedding party, minister, musicians, and others on the back.[17]

The preludes. Since guests at a wedding are generally seated by ushers, numerous preludes usually accompany this lengthy process. Preludes may be played by any soloist or group of instrumentalists. Recorded music is inappropriate. To spend money on elaborate decorations, clothing, and so forth, and then to use recorded music sends an incongruent message.

Vocal solos or ensembles. After the preludes and before the processional is a good time to use solos and vocal ensembles that do not fit in the context of the service.

Processional. Sometimes two musical selections are used, one for the bridal party and one for the bride. There are numerous ways in which the order of the processional may be organized.

Men first. In this tradition all the men enter from a side or front entrance and take their places at the front. When the men are in place, the attendants come

---

15. For helpful suggestions, see Jim Henry, *The Pastor's Wedding Manual* (Nashville: Broadman Press, 1985).

16. Rayburn, *Let Us Worship*, 277.

17. See appendix E for a sample wedding service.

down the aisle one at a time and take their places either opposite the groom and groomsmen or in couples. The bride is the last to enter the sanctuary.

The bride may come down the aisle alone, with her father, accompanied by both parents, or accompanied by another person of her choosing. The tradition of a bride's entering with her father recalls a time when a woman was owned by her father until her marriage, at which time ownership was transferred to her husband. For a woman who considers herself an independent person, to enter with her father and be "given away" sends a mixed message.

The bride and groom may also choose to process together or enter from two different doors, meet and process together. The bride and groom may each enter with their parents, or the bride may enter alone.

Men and women together. Growing in popularity is the practice of all attendants coming down the aisle in pairs with the minister and groom leading the procession.

However the processional is organized, it is a good idea to involve all parents, since, with a wedding, significant change is taking place in the bride's and groom's families. Both sets of parents should publicly express their approval of the marriage by promising their full support to the new union.

The call to worship. When the wedding party is in place, the minister will acknowledge the primacy of worship in the ceremony. This may be done with a scriptural call to worship, carefully chosen words, or a congregational responsive or unison reading.

Hymns of praise. A hymn in praise of God is appropriate following the call to worship. The couple should move to the platform or a higher position at this point.

Scriptural basis for marriage. Appropriate Scripture should be read by the minister or another person. The minister should avoid the archaic statement, "If either of you know any reason why you may not rightly be joined together, you may now acknowledge it." The wedding service is too late to acknowledge conflicts. A brief wedding sermon (homily) may be inserted after the Scripture.

The marriage vows. Traditional vows are spoken from memory or repeated after the minister.

The exchange of rings. The ring ceremony is spoken from memory or repeated after the minister.

Prayer. Prayer is spoken by the minister, the couple, the congregation, or another person. A sung prayer may also be used. Often the couple kneels at this time.

The lighting of the candle. Many couples choose to light an unlit central candle flanked by lit candles. This symbolism should be explained by the minister. The two flanking candles should *not* be extinguished after the unity candle is lit, for, although "the two shall become one," they each will retain their unique identity as God's creation.

The pronouncement. The minister pronounces the couple husband and wife and introduces them to the congregation according to their wishes, as, for example, Mr. and Mrs. John Doe, or John and Jane Doe, or John Doe and Jane Doe.

The blessing (benediction). Whether sung or spoken, the benediction affirms God's blessing on the union.

The recessional. The symbolism of the couple's exiting together as a unit is significant. Couples may choose to acknowledge their individual families as they exit. This symbolizes the couple's separating from their parents only to re-enter their old family systems as a unit.[18]

PHOTOGRAPHS

Photographs, either flash or non-flash, are strongly discouraged during the ceremony. Video cameras should be well out-of-sight and should in no way distract from the reverence of the service.

Quickly fading is the practice of not taking photographs of the bride and groom together until after the wedding. The superstition that the couple should not see each other on the wedding day until the bride walks down the aisle is not based on Christian principles and should be ignored. Many couples would have better photographs if all photographs were taken before the service when they are more relaxed, free from the crowd of well-wishers, and not preoccupied with their need to be at the reception. Many wedding attenders wait for long periods of time for a receiving line while photographs (which could have been taken earlier) are being taken. This practice is inconsiderate to guests.

WEDDING POLICIES

Every church should have a thorough set of wedding policies including every aspect of the wedding service. Thorough policies protect the service as a worship service, protect the church's property, and assist the minister in guiding couples and their families.[19]

WEDDING RESOURCES

Numerous books are available which have examples of various services and contain suggestions for alternative elements.

---

18. Siler, "Rites of Passage," 59.
19. See appendix F for sample policies.

FUNERALS

Funerals, like weddings, are unique worship opportunities. Although rarely would a funeral contain all the elements of a regular worship service, a funeral for a Christian should wholly center on God as the source of comfort and Christ's resurrection as the source for power to face the future.

PURPOSE OF THE FUNERAL

Leonard J. Vander Zee states that the Christian funeral has both a vertical and a horizontal dimension. The funeral should give opportunity to *remember* and *believe*.[20] Funerals are times of *remembrance* as family and friends express grief and emotion. "Funerals are public rituals in which profound grief is expressive, precious memories are released, and lifetimes are thankfully remembered."[21]

Funerals are also times to *believe*. The Christian response to death arises out of faith. We believe that God is the giver and creator of life, yet we do not fully understand the reality of death. The funeral service should affirm the faith that we know to be reality even in a time when our grief may not allow us to experience faith's full power. Funerals are about hope—hope in a God who has sustained our past and in whom we depend for our future: "At the funeral we listen to the death-defying words of Scripture, we sing of God's grace and Christ's victory and we place our loved ones in God's loving arms."[22] Although the truth of the gospel should be proclaimed, a funeral is not an evangelistic rally. Vander Zee states: "People feel cheated when their needs and emotions are overlooked in the interest of saving their souls."[23]

PLANNING THE FUNERAL

The funeral service should be planned by the minister, musicians, and family. When the service planning is a combined effort, each group will make its contribution. Planning funeral services should not be left to a family who is not trained or experienced in this task. Neither should the planning be left to the funeral director. While ministers desire always to accommodate special requests by the family, they should be quick to offer suggestions and alternatives. The minister must guard the service as a worship experience.

---

20. Leonard J. Vander Zee, "When Someone Dies," *Reformed Worship* 24 (June 1992): 4.
21. Ibid.
22. Ibid.
23. Ibid.

Although some people choose to plan their own service, families should feel freedom to change plans that seem unusual or outlandish. A funeral is to edify and comfort the living. The survivors' needs, not those of the deceased, must be the primary focus. However, requests by the deceased for a closed casket, particular song, favorite Scripture, no flowers, and other requests that are well within good reason, good worship practice, and good taste, should be honored.

Worship councils and other groups interested in worship would be wise to assist the minister in preparing appropriate guidelines for funeral services. Through this process, members would come to understand appropriate funeral elements and increase awareness of the church's resources.[24] Ministers should make uninterrupted time to discuss with the family their remembrances about the deceased so that the minister has a good knowledge of the unique nature of this individual.

When planning the funeral, the location of the service will have to be determined. Ideally, Christian funerals are best held in the church, which is designed for worship. The acoustics, instruments, and symbols in the church make the funeral more conducive to worship. In many cases, the church sanctuary is also the place where other significant life events have taken place, and the location itself is a comfort to those who grieve. Although many people object to having a funeral in the church because of anticipated low attendance, there is nothing inherently wrong in a few people gathering in a large room for a funeral. There are valid reasons for holding a funeral in a funeral chapel and these must be respected. In the case of a non-Christian, there is little rationale for a church service.

Increasingly, people are preparing printed orders of worship for funeral services. This practice has several values: (1) People are accustomed to printed orders of worship in regular worship services; therefore, a printed order for a funeral helps the family and congregation to see the funeral as worship. (2) People (especially families) often are not fully aware of the content of a funeral service and in days (and years) to come the printed order allows them to remember better. (3) When loved ones die, families hold to tangible evidence of the deceased person's existence. A bulletin serves as a concrete reminder of having recognized God's supremacy. (4) Bulletins serve as historical records for persons who, years later, want to learn more about a person. They also serve to guide other families in the planning of funeral and memorial services.[25]

---

24. Ibid.
25. See appendix G for a sample funeral service.

FUNERAL, MEMORIAL, AND COMMITTAL SERVICES

The main difference between a funeral and a memorial service is that the body is not present at a memorial service. Funerals are usually held in close proximity to the death date, whereas memorial services are sometimes held days or weeks afterward. The common pattern is for a funeral to be followed by a graveside or a committal service; however, many families are choosing to have a committal service (or a funeral service at the graveside) first, followed by a memorial service. The advantage of the second sequence is that the last (most remembered) event is the memorial (worship) service instead of the graveside. Graveside services are advisable unless extreme travel distances make this service prohibitive. Many see the graveside service as a necessary ingredient in the grief process. It is important for grieving persons to see the act of death as final. As a result, families and friends are taking a much more active role in this part of the service. Many families now choose to have the coffin lowered while they are present; to lower the coffin themselves; to throw a symbolic handful or shovelful of dirt on the casket; or to fully cover the casket themselves. These actions should be viewed as therapeutic. Vander Zee states:

> At Christian funerals, we go to the graveside as an act of defiant faith. There standing over the grave we say with Paul: "Where, O death, is your victory?" (1 Cor. 15:55) It is almost as though we shake our fists in death's face, believing in the bottom of our hearts that this is not the last word. The last word will be life everlasting.[26]

OPEN AND CLOSED CASKETS

The family should decide whether the casket should be opened or closed. Many feel that the act of viewing the deceased person helps the healing process, while others feel that this custom is nearly pagan. However, if the deceased has specifically requested a closed-casket funeral, the wish should be respected.

When the casket is opened for the visitation and before the service, it is best closed before the service actually begins. The open casket can make concentration on the funeral more difficult. It may be best not to re-open the casket after the service, for this custom may simply prolong the inevitable. Some believe that to re-open the casket has psychological value, especially when viewed only by the family with the minister standing at the head of the casket. Funeral practice varies widely among ethnic groups and within geographical regions. Local practice must be respected and wise ministers should not be attempt to impose their views on a grieving family.

---

26. Vander Zee, "When Someone Dies," 4.

USE OF A PALL

Many churches have recovered or begun the tradition of using a pall (covering for the casket). The pall is placed over the casket before its entrance into the sanctuary. A pall is usually made of white fabric and adorned with simple symbols of Christ. The use of a pall equalizes death in that attention is not drawn to the beauty or lack of beauty of the casket.[27]

ELEMENTS OF A FUNERAL

Processional. Most funerals have a procession that includes the entrance of the family into the church. H. P. V. Renner offers the following insights into this act:

> Processions are symbolic features in a rite. They proclaim the transitory, passage-like pilgrim nature of the Christian life, its movement from beginning, through time, to its end. . . . Processions also symbolize the progression of a rite: at this point a procession from the world, the role of tears outside the house of God, into the comforting presence of God. And, because processions are group movements, coordinated and regular marches, they create and actualize solidarity in a group. . . .[28]

Prayer and Scripture. These elements allow us to speak with God and to be spoken to by God. They are at the heart of all Christian worship.

Sermon, homily, or meditation. Some feel that Scripture alone should be used at a funeral, which is preferable if the minister has difficulty in knowing what to say.[29] Vander Zee states:

> The preacher's job at the funeral is not to exegete or expound the Word, but to express the feelings and thoughts of people who are too numb or afraid to name them—to express the swirling hopes and fears of grieving hearts. The preacher needs to be both the voice of God and the voice of the people, and this is an exceedingly demanding and delicate task.[30]

Music. No Christian worship is complete without song, for in Christian song we express both our joy and our sorrow. Le Roy Christoffels offers the following suggestions on developing the musical elements to be used for a funeral service:

---

27. For a thorough discussion of the use of a pall, see Eloise Van Heest, "A Symbol of Faith: Using a Pall in Christian Funerals," *Reformed Worship* 24, 14–15.

28. H. P. V. Renner, "A Christian Rite of Burial," *Lutheran Theological Journal* 26 (May 1992): 72–77.

29. For helpful suggestions see Paul Powell, *Gospel for the Graveside* (Nashville: Broadman and Holman Press, 1981); and Eugene H. Peterson, Calvin Miller, and others, *Weddings, Funerals, and Special Events* (Waco: Word Books, 1987).

30. Vander Zee, "When Someone Dies," 6.

1. *Express both grief and hope.*

   Music must express the reality of present grief and also affirm the hope in the eternal God.

2. *Make sure corporate music predominates.*

   A funeral is a community event and the community must be given a voice. The community must sing, even if with a lump in our throats.

3. *Focus on God.*

   Music for a funeral should focus on God, not us.

4. *Balance family choice with the considerations of the larger community.*

   The minister must respect a family's preference but must balance their desires with those of the larger community.

5. *Involve the choir.*

   If the church has a choir, then this group, whose primary purpose is to lead in corporate worship, should be in its place. A choral offering is a gift to a grieving family.

6. *Plan for the acoustical setting.*

   The acoustical environment of a funeral home will differ from that of a church sanctuary. Music should take these differences into consideration.

7. *Lead with strength and confidence.*

   Whether leading from the bench of a musical instrument or standing in front of the congregation, the leader must model Christ's victory over death.

PART THREE:

PLANNING
AND CONDUCTING
WORSHIP

CHAPTER 18

PLANNING THE ORDER OF WORSHIP

GeButtrick, for twenty-seven years pastor of the Madison Avenue Presbyterian Church in New York City, told a class in pastoral theology at Harvard University that he always spent about three hours each week planning the morning worship service. This time was calculated apart from the time spent in preparing the sermon. In other words, it included the selection of hymns, the preparation of prayers, and all the other elements of the worship service.

One of the explanations for ineffective worship in our churches is the lack of serious planning. The entire church has a large responsibility concerning public worship. The church determines the liturgy, the hymnal, the plan and appointments of the church building, and the general program for the Christian year. However, the church usually looks to its leaders for leadership in planning worship. Throughout the history of the Christian church, the bishop or minister has been considered responsible for planning and leading worship. The Free Churches are giving more attention to the training of ministers for leadership in worship. Most seminary curricula offer courses in worship, though the courses are not always required.

Some Guiding Principles

Planning a worship service should include all that will enrich worship. The following suggestions may serve as guidelines in planning worship:

1. Specific persons must accept the responsibility for planning worship. This responsibility should be taken seriously. Ordinarily, the pastor is primarily responsible for planning the order of worship in smaller churches, and the minister of music assumes much of the responsibility in larger churches. The worship planner should plan the design for each service of worship, keeping in mind the theme which will be emphasized. Attention should be given to every detail of the order. A church committee on worship can add strength to the creative planning of the order of worship.

2. Plenty of time should be devoted to planning an effective order of worship. Time should be set aside every week for the planning of the worship service. Worship should be planned far enough in advance for the musicians to have time to select appropriate music and to rehearse in preparation for the worship service.

3. The order of worship should be suited to a given congregation. There are times when members of the congregation have had experiences which call for a certain kind of worship experience. However, those who plan worship should beware of neglecting the needs of the larger congregation to minister to specific individuals. Worship is first of all a corporate experience.

4. The planner should have a definite purpose as the order of worship is planned. Micklem suggests that the planner should seek to bring the congregation to a new point of view or decision.[1] To achieve this goal, the planner will select the hymns, prayers, Scriptures, and sermon, carefully weaving them to lead the congregation into a well-rounded worship experience.

5. Although no one season is more important than another, many churches find it helpful to plan their worship according to the calendar of the Christian year. Every day is the "day which the Lord hath made." All time is holy, and every day is a day for worshiping God. However, the observance of certain days and seasons may remind the church that God who has acted in history is continuously acting in the lives of God's people.

---

1. Nathaniel Micklem, ed., *Christian Worship: Studies in Its History and Meaning* (London: Oxford University Press, 1936), 201.

To some extent, most of the Free Churches follow the Christian calendar in planning their worship. Worship and preaching are often planned to emphasize the Advent season, which focuses upon the Messianic expectation; Christmas, which stresses the Nativity and the Incarnation; the Lenten season, which emphasizes the suffering and death of Jesus and the consequent repentance and confession which it prompts; Easter, which is the season of the resurrection and ascension of our living Lord; and Pentecost, which comes fifty days after Easter and stresses the doctrine of the Holy Spirit and the Holy Spirit's empowerment of the church.

6. A certain amount of variety in the order of worship will keep the attention of people and stimulate their interest in worship. In general, it may be wise to conserve the overall design of the service with which a congregation is familiar. Ordinarily, variety should come by altering parts of the service within the general structure without radically changing the main structure. To surprise a congregation with a radically new and unexpected order of worship may prevent them from focusing their attention upon God.

7. Worship resources can help leaders in planning worship. Handbooks of prayers, hymnals, and manuals on order of worship prepared by many denominations may stimulate thinking and provide enrichment materials for those who plan worship. Attention to current and historical materials helps the worship planner continue a fresh approach to worship.

8. A printed order of worship can aid a congregation in worship. This visual aid is particularly helpful in directing the attention to the particular objectives of the various elements in worship. This should be made as attractive as possible.

9. Traditionally, the morning service has been more closely structured and is given more dignity, and the evening service is more flexible and provides for more freedom. The morning service is more objective in emphasis and the evening service more subjective. This variety in the kinds of worship services provides a balance for the emotional experiences of the congregation, as well as for the different perspectives which various people have.

10. Planning for worship includes the preparation of the building and facilities. The house of worship should be clean and attractive. Everything should be in order. The temperature and ventilation of the building should be properly controlled to make the place of worship comfortable.

11. Creativity in planning is essential for vital worship. Neither slavish dependence upon resource materials which others have provided, nor the naíve presumptuousness that no previous thought or planning is necessary for a public worship service is valid. Meaningful planning for worship will make good use of literary resources created by others, and it will call forth the best creative thinking and praying in the present. The Holy Spirit desires to work creatively in the minds of those involved in planning worship, and the Spirit will inspire and guide as vitally in the planning as in the actual experience of worship.

FORM AND FREEDOM IN WORSHIP

The Bible does not prescribe an exact order of worship, but it does acknowledge some essential form for worship. The Old Testament gives more emphasis to form while the New Testament stresses the spirit and freedom of worship without rejecting form.

Gene Bartlett points out two hindrances to a mature approach to worship in the Free Churches: a deep-rooted suspicion of "formalism" and the fear that the emphasis upon worship will result in a corresponding de-emphasis on preaching.[2] Do not assume that spontaneity and order are incompatible and that we must choose one or the other. Both are required, for spontaneity without order can become excess and even chaos, and order without spontaneity can become compulsive ritual.

The ideal, as in the early church, is an ordered service with which congregations are familiar so that they may easily participate, yet one which allows liberty for the Spirit to suggest.

The average Free Church, even while declaring its suspicion of ritual, has usually developed a ritual of its own. Every church, however "anti-liturgical," has its own ritual phrases with which it passes from one part of the service to another. B. B. McKinney, former professor of church music at Southwestern Baptist Theological Seminary, once declared that Baptists may not be ritualists, but they usually are "rutualists." If they do not plan some order or ritual, they usually drift into a rut which they follow as slavishly as the more liturgical churches follow their liturgies.

THE VALUES OF FORM

The dread of formality and ritualism must not cause people to repudiate all form in worship. It is never a choice between forms and no form, but between good forms and bad. Whatever speaks to the total person and aids in

---

2. Gene Barlett, "Worship: The Ordered Proclamation of the Gospel," *Review and Expositor* 62, no. 3 (Summer 1965):276.

personal communication with God is good form. The following values may be found in an order or a plan of worship:

1. A plan of worship is psychologically sound. People form and use habits in all the activities of life. This is also true in worship. There is value in following an order of worship, for familiarity and tradition aid the worshiper. Most people do not like too much variety in their order of worship; rather, they like variety to come in the content of the familiar order.

2. Form gives intelligent direction and purpose to worship; the minds of the people are directed toward God. Whatever turns the mind toward God is an aid to worship.

3. Good form leads the congregation into unified participation. All minds unite in praise and prayer and giving to God.

4. Form in worship gives concrete expression to inward attitudes.

5. An order of worship provides discipline for the worshiper. Too often people approach the worship service with a careless, indifferent attitude.

FACTORS DETERMINING THE ORDER OF WORSHIP

Orders of worship usually follow the traditional patterns of a given church or denomination. While tradition should be honored, it should not limit a congregation in its journey toward a more creative approach to worship.

Aesthetic and cultural tastes also help to determine the forms of worship. Some congregations desire the more elaborate and artistic forms, whereas others prefer simpler and fewer aesthetic forms.

The emotional level of a congregation often dictates the amount of subjective material and spontaneous response used in worship. Some groups will insist upon a high emotional intensity and more outward emotional expressions to satisfy their desires in worship, while others will desire a more objective and formal approach to worship. The diversity of worship services among American churches can be explained in the light of historical, sociological, and theological considerations. Services of worship will differ not only from culture to culture but also from one subculture to another.

Based upon these factors, three patterns of liturgy have developed: (1) the liturgical, as seen in the Roman Catholic, the Orthodox, the Episcopal, and the Lutheran churches; (2) the nonliturgical, in which there is no planned order (theoretically at least), as seen in the Quakers and other groups; and (3) the free or planned order of worship as seen in a majority of Protestant churches where they have no fixed order of worship, but they do plan the order of worship, allowing for a certain amount of freedom and spontaneity.

PRINCIPLES GOVERNING THE ORDER OF WORSHIP

Since some form in worship is a necessity, there are certain practical principles which should govern the order of worship.

1. An order of Christian worship should never contain anything contrary to biblical truth.

2. An order of worship should be consistent with good historical tradition.

3. A good order will be intelligible to the particular congregation and will make the gospel relevant to present life situations.

4. Every experience of public worship should have a definite purpose or objective.

5. A good order of worship must have unity.

6. Public worship, like a story or a drama, must have movement or progression.

7. Good form in worship necessitates alternation—contrasting moods and movements, silence and expression, standing and sitting, spoken words and music, and participation by the minister and the congregation.

The order of worship has movements like a symphony or acts as in a play. The movements of praise and prayer, listening and responding to the Word of God, offering and receiving—all move together toward a grand climax in bringing glory to God.

THE PLANNING PROCESS

Planning worship is somewhat like writing a paper or preparing a project—once you have an outline, the work is nearly complete. To begin planning worship from a clean slate is an overwhelming task. To have no set direction—with all the hymns in the hymnal at your disposal and all biblical texts as possible readings—is not the best way to plan a service.

Worship planning should always begin with a structure (outline), even if you do not wish the final product to appear to have a set structure. Even the most apparently spontaneous worship experiences have behind-the-scenes structure!

Traditionally, Free Church worship has been sermon-centered; therefore, worship planning has centered strongly around the theme of the sermon. The danger in planning thematic worship every week is that a well-rounded worship experience may not be possible, and certain important aspects of Christian worship may never be experienced.

In the beginning, worship planners must reconcile themselves to the fact that, although a worship service is a work of art, one cannot start from scratch each week and produce a completely new and innovative worship service. There are at least two inherent dangers in the above approach: First, congregations are not willing (nor should they be) to have every service completely different from every other service. When all elements of a service are different and in a different order, congregations struggle to find their place. They are therefore insecure and their energy is spent trying to keep up. (This is not to imply that worshipers should be allowed to be lazy and uninvolved.) Worshipers also desire for worship to be their worship— worship which they refer to as "our church." The analogy of "home" and "journey" is appropriate for worship. People are willing to journey in worship, but they want to begin at home and they want the leader to bring them home at the close. When congregations trust their leaders, over time they are willing to journey further and further for longer periods of time. Some congregations are primarily made up of travelers while others are made up of "home folks." The wise leader will know the make up of the congregation and will gently lead them to journey.

Second, leaders experience quick "burn out" when worship is a totally new experience every week. Often, worship leaders feel that each experience should not only be new but also bigger and better. When we are at our best, we are often inspired to great worship adventures; however, the wise worship planner learns the value of pacing and consistency. Though we should always give our best in worship planning, a constant diet of worship sugar sticks is unhealthy. The model on the next page by Brian Wren is helpful in considering worship planning.

While same place/same method (*Repetition*) becomes monotonous to the worshiper, the different place/different method (*Refreshment* and *Reposition*) leaves the worshiper struggling to keep up with the service. *Refreshment* and *Reposition* are both effective models for worship planning; therefore, they should be used regularly, saving *Refreshment and Reposition* for special days.

SUGGESTED PATTERNS OF WORSHIP

Various patterns may be helpful in planning an order of worship.

Seidenspinner speaks of three movements in worship: (1) adoration of God; (2) communion with God; and (3) dedication to God. He feels the unity of the service should be like a symphony.[3]

---

3. Clarence Seidenspinner, *Form and Freedom in Christian Worship* (Chicago: Willet-Clark & Co., 1941), 186ff.

A Model for Revitalizing Worship Design*

Repetition

Same place

Same method

Refreshment   *Reposition*

Same place   Different place

Different method   Same method

Refreshment and Reposition

Different place

Different method

*This model was presented by Brian Wren in a worship conference, February 20, 1991, St. Joseph, Missouri. Used by permission.

Based upon his principles, a fourfold summary is suggested as an outline for worship: (1) adoration and praise; (2) confession, petition, and intercession; (3) affirmation and the proclamation of the Word; and (4) submission and dedication to take the gospel into the world according to God's will. These four attitudes or movements suggest four major divisions of the order of worship according to purpose. The various elements or means of expressing worship—call to worship, hymns, prayers, the reading of the Scriptures, offerings, and so on—may be appropriately arranged under these divisions.

A RATIONALE FOR WORSHIP OUTLINES

A worshiper in a congregation once said to a minister of music, "I really like it when you plan our worship with headings because then I know what I am supposed to do in each section. Otherwise, I often find myself trying to decide what I am supposed to get from this element." Headings within the service offer the following benefits: (1) They guide worshipers. (2) They guide worship planners. (3) They provide education opportunities for the congregation.

Not all see headings as beneficial and some may perceive a structured bulletin as formal or stuffy. While headings alone do not make a service formal, if they are perceived as too structured it may be helpful for the worship planner to plan with headings and then remove them from the printed page. This method serves as an outline and provides direction for the planner. Consideration should also be given to offering the service structure by reading Scripture passages to delineate each section or singing a different stanza of a hymn to show different worship divisions.

A BIBLICAL MODEL

Many scholars agree that Isaiah's worship experience as recorded in Isaiah 6:1–9 is the most comprehensive biblical model. The Isaiah 6 model of worship is:

Revelation: "I saw the Lord" (v. 1).

Praise/Adoration: "Holy, Holy, Holy is the LORD of hosts" (v. 3).

Confession: "Woe is me! For I am lost" (v. 5).

Forgiveness/Atonement: ". . . your guilt is taken away, and your sin is forgiven" (v. 7).

Proclamation: "I heard the voice of the Lord" (v. 8).

Dedication/Commitment: "Here am I! Send me" (v. 8).

Commission: "Go, and say to this people" (v. 9).

The Isaiah 6 model is helpful as a general non-seasonal Sunday model and as a point-of-departure for planning other services. For many worship planners, even when another form is used, Isaiah 6 becomes a checklist to assure that worship is balanced. The following represents a service prepared on a modified Isaiah 6 model:

MAYWOOD BAPTIST CHURCH
MORNING WORSHIP SERVICE
April 25, 1993 10:50 A.M.

THE CHURCH . . . GATHERING FOR WORSHIP

The Chiming of the Hour	
Opportunities for Service	Bob Spradling
Welcome to Our Guests	Bob Spradling
Prayer Needs for the Congregation	Bob Spradling

. . . EXPRESSING PRAISE

Call to Worship
Leader:	God created us;
People:	Praise God.
Leader:	The Son re-creates us;
People:	Glory to the Son.
Leader:	The Spirit creates new life in us;
People:	Honor to the Spirit.
All:	Praise, glory, and honor
	To the Triune God,
	The cause of our worship,
	The source of our joy.
	We will ever praise the Triune God!

*Hymn No. 36	"Praise the Lord! Ye Heavens, Adore Him"	HYFRYDOL
*Hymn No. 37	"The Majesty and Glory of Your Name"	SOLI DEO GLORIA
*Invocation		Bob Spradling
*Hymn No. 462	"The Lord's Prayer"	MALOTTE

. . . CONFESSING OUR SIN

Responsive Reading No. 266:		Kathleen Wright
Hymn No. 272	"I Lay My Sins on Jesus"	AURELIA
Silent Meditation		

. . . EXPERIENCING GOD'S FORGIVENESS

Hymn No. 329	"Grace Greater than Our Sin"	MOODY
Prayer for the Offering		
Organ Offertory	"Holy Spirit Breathe on Me"	arr. Phillips

(Please join in singing "Jesus Loves Me" as children in pre-kindergarten and kindergarten exit for Children's Worship Workshop.)

. . . HEARING FROM GOD

Choral Proclamation	"Come, Sing to the Lord"	Wagner
(At the conclusion of the anthem, please join in singing Hymn No. 216)		
Message	"Hearing the Voice of God"	Bob Spradling
Hymn No. 604	"Come, All Christians, Be Committed"	BEACH SPRING

. . . DEPARTING TO SERVE

*Hymn No. 579   ** "Shine, Jesus, Shine"   SHINE

  Shine, Jesus shine,
  Fill this land with the Father's glory;
  Blaze, Spirit, blaze, set our hearts on fire.
  Flow, river, flow,
  Flood the nations with grace and mercy;
  Send forth Your Word, Lord and let there be light.

Organ Postlude   "Crown Him with Many Crowns"—   arr. Byrson

*Please stand.
**CCLI #169926. Used by Permission.

The Isaiah 6 model can also be varied, for example:

 Revelation and Praise

 Confession and Forgiveness

 Proclamation

 Dedication and Commission

Other popular biblical models include 2 Chronicles 7:14, Matthew 6:9–13 (The Lord's Prayer), and Psalm 23. Many Scripture passages can lend themselves to worship design when approached by an innovative worship planner.

MODELS FROM HYMNS

Hymns and other musical genres are well-suited for worship service outlines. While some planners feel the need to keep hymn phrases in sequence, not all see such sequencing as important. When using a hymn as a worship outline, look for general worship elements (such as those found in Isaiah 6) within the hymn stanzas. The chosen phrases should always represent a logical worship progression. The following is a service designed from "Worthy of Worship" (*The Baptist Hymnal*, 1991, no. 2):

MORNING WORSHIP SERVICE
NOVEMBER 3, 1992

WORTHY OF WORSHIP

The Chiming of the Hour
Opportunities for Service   Mike Weddle
Welcome to Our Guests   Bob Spradling
Prayer Needs of the Congregation   Bob Spradling

WORTHY OF ALL THE GLAD SONGS WE CAN BRING

Call to Worship   "This Is the Day"   Lewallen
*Hymn No. 3   "Worthy of Worship"   JUDSON
*The Invocation   Bruce Leafblad
*Prayer Response   **"Worthy of Worship"   JUDSON
    You are worthy, Father, Creator.
    You are worthy, Savior, Sustainer.
    You are worthy, worthy and wonderful;
    Worthy of worship and praise.

WORTHY OF BOWING AND BENDING OF KNEES

Scripture Reading   Ginger and Greg Carroll
    Luke 19:10; Acts 4:12;
    1 Timothy 1:15; 2 Timothy 1:12;
    Psalm 51:1–4, 7, 10–13.

Hymn No. 329   "Grace Greater than Our Sin"   MOODY
    Stanza 1: Women (unison); omit refrain
    Stanza 2: Men (unison)
    Refrain: All
    Stanza 3: All
Solo   "Love Lifted Me"   arr. Smith
    Carol Lopez

WORTHY OF ALL OF THE OFFERINGS WE BRING

*Hymn No. 486   "Lord, Here Am I"   BECK
Prayer for the Offering
Organ Offertory   "Jesu, Joy of Man's Desiring"   Bach

*Response   "Doxology"   OLD 100TH
    (Hymn No. 253)

WORTHY OF HONOR AND GLORY

Choral meditation   "Come, Thou Fount"   arr. Courtney
(Please join in singing "Jesus Loves Me" as children in kindergarten and pre-kindergarten exit
for Children's Worship Workshop.)
Message   "The Life of Worship"   Bruce Leafblad
*Hymn No. 296   "Jesus Is Lord of All"

WORTHY OF LOVE AND DEVOTION

| *Benediction | ***"Shine, Jesus, Shine"
(Hymn No. 579) | SHINE |

Shine, Jesus, shine, fill this land with the Father's glory;
Blaze, Spirit, blaze, set our hearts on fire.
Flow, river, flow, flood the nations with grace and mercy;
Send forth Your Word, Lord, and let there be light.

Organ Postlude

* Please stand
** CCLI #169926. Used by Permission

OTHER GENERAL OUTLINES

Worship planners should have outlines of worship that are both standbys for their congregation and yet offer flexibility for a given Sunday. The following outlines provide stability and flexibility:

1.	2.	3.
THE PRAISE OF GOD	WORSHIP IN PRAISE	ADORATION
***	***	***
THE HEARING OF THE WORD	WORSHIP IN PRAYER	COMMUNION
***	***	***
THE PROCLAMATION OF THE GOSPEL	WORSHIP IN AFFIRMATION	INSTRUCTION
***	***	
THE RESPONSE OF FAITH	WORSHIP IN DEDICATION	

The following model offers a flexible section that allows for a particular Sunday's focus:

The Church . . .

... Gathering for Worship
... Expressing Praise and Adoration
... (Insert a heading unique to this service)
... Hearing God's Word
... Departing to Serve

Headings which point to a particular theme or emphasis that can be used in the flexible section above include:

Focusing on Our Mission
Celebrating God's Faithfulness
Trusting in God's Strength
Bound for Greater Things
Focusing on God's Purpose for Us
Focusing on Our Experience with God
Focusing on the Holy Spirit
Moving toward the Cross
Discovering Our Mission
Searching Our Hearts
Deepening Commitment
Seeking to Follow God
Focusing on God's Authority
Experiencing Forgiveness
Sharing Our Lives with Others
Celebrating God's Promises

Many hymns work well as worship outlines. The hymn outlines on the following two pages are suggested.

Hymns as
Worship Outlines

Shine, Jesus, Shine *** Jesus, Light of the World, Shine Upon Us *** Search Me, Try Me, Consume All My Darkness *** Set Us Free by the Truth You Now Bring Us *** Mirrored Here, May Our Lives Tell Your Story *** (From "Shine, Jesus, Shine," No. 579, *The Baptist Hymnal*, 1991.)	Come, Ye Thankful People, Come *** Raise the Song of Harvest Home! *** All Is Safely Gathered In *** God, Our Maker, Doth Provide *** Raise the Glorious Harvest Home *** (From "Come, Ye Thankful People, Come," No. 637, *The Baptist Hymnal*, 1991.)
I'm Pressing on the Upward Way *** New Heights I'm Gaining Every Day *** Still Praying as I Onward Bound *** "Lord, Plant My Feet on Higher Ground" *** (From "Higher Ground," No. 484, *The Baptist Hymnal*, 1991.)	O Come, O Come, Emmanuel *** Rejoice! Rejoice! Emmanuel Shall Come *** Disperse the Gloomy Clouds of Night *** Fill the Whole World with Heaven's Peace *** (From "O Come, O Come, Emmanuel," No. 76, *The Baptist Hymnal*, 1991.)
Lord, Here Am I *** Master, Thou Callest, I Gladly Obey *** Only Direct Me, and I'll Find Thy Way *** Teach Me the Mission Appointed for Me *** Ready and Willing, Lord, Here Am I *** (From "Lord, Here Am I," No. 486, *The Baptist Hymnal*, 1991.)	Break Out, O Church of God *** Cry Out, O Church of God *** Cast Off, O Church of God *** Preach Christ, O Church of God *** Go Forth, O Church of God *** (From "Break Out, O Church of God," No. 401, *The Baptist Hymnal*, 1991.)

Hymns as
Worship Outlines (Continued)

World Hunger Day *** Let Your Heart Be Broken *** Give the Loaf of Bread *** Share Your Rich Resources *** Give and Give Again *** (From "Let Your Heart Be Broken," No. 611, *The Baptist Hymnal*, 1991.)	Where He Leads I Will Follow *** We Follow Him to Jerusalem *** Will You Go to the Cross? *** I'll Go with Him, with Him, All the Way *** (From "Where He Leads Me," No. 288, *The Baptist Hymnal*, 1991.)
Bless That Wonderful Name of Jesus *** Praise That Wonderful Name of Jesus *** Sing That Wonderful Name of Jesus *** Preach That Wonderful Name of Jesus *** Share That Wonderful Name of Jesus *** (From "Bless That Wonderful Name," No. 236, *The Baptist Hymnal*, 1991.)	Christ the Lord Is Risen Today, Alleluia! *** Raise Your Joys and Triumphs High, Alleluia! *** Love's Redeeming Work Is Done, Alleluia! *** Made Like Him, Like Him We Rise, Alleluia! *** (From "Christ the Lord Is Risen Today," No. 159, *The Baptist Hymnal*, 1991.)

God, Our Help in Ages Past
***
From Everlasting Thou Art God
***
Sufficient Is Thine Arm Alone
***
Our Hope for Years to Come
***
God, Our Eternal Home
***
(From "O God, Our Help in Ages Past," No. 74, *The Baptist Hymnal*, 1991.)

WORSHIP WITHOUT OUTLINES

Many churches do not use headings or outlines in worship, although they do use a fairly standard form. The following is an example of a service without headings:

Welcome		Paul Lucas
Organ Prelude	"Come Christians Join to Sing"	Carr
Call to Worship	"There's Something About That Name"	Gaither
Hymn No. 227	"Praise Him! Praise Him!"	Crosby
Morning Prayer		Paul Lucas
Responsive Reading No. 708		Bill Clem
Hymn No. 476	"Be Strong in the Lord"	Johnson
Children's Worship Feature		Paul Lucas
Hymn No. 484	"Higher Ground"	Gabriel
Prayer for Tithes and Offerings		Ken Livingston
Piano Offertory:	"More Love to Thee, O Christ"	Doane
Solo:	"It is Well with My Soul"	Starla Jones
Message		Paul Lucas
Hymn No. 301	"I Am Resolved"	Hartsough
Announcements		David Branning
Benediction Hymn No. 484	"Higher Ground" Stanza 1	Gabriel
Organ Postlude	"Be Strong in the Lord"	Fettke

THE PRINTED ORDER OF WORSHIP

Naming persons who lead in worship. It is better to call ministers by their given name instead of Pastor, Minister of Music, and so forth. This allows for consistency among worship leaders, breaks down barriers of "clergy vs. laity," and gives persons names instead of positions. Avoid giving titles such as Doctor, Reverend, Mr., Mrs., and Ms. Sometimes titles can create hierarchies among leaders.

Hymn designation. Each hymn should be identified in one of the following ways.

Hymn No. 1	"Holy, Holy, Holy"	NICAEA
Hymn No. 1	"Holy, Holy, Holy"	Heber

All hymns are given tune names (NICAEA above). The tune name designates the music as a particular tune always identified with this name even when used with another text. Tune names (in all capital letters) are appropriate for worship bulletins. Hymns may also be identified by the name of the author of the text (Heber above). The writer of a hymn is understood to be the writer of the text. The writer of the tune is the writer of a hymn tune, not a hymn. Hymns should *not* be referred to by page number, for often more than one hymn is on a page. Do *not* use "#" (number sign). Use "No." (number abbreviation).

Designation of other music. Music should not be labeled as "special music," for hopefully any music used in worship is special! Call the music by its function or presenting group, e.g., Choral Music, Quartet, Call to Worship, Choral Praise, Solo, or Vocal Meditation. Music, other than hymns, should be designated as follows:

+ Choral Music	"God Is Our Refuge and Strength"	**Pote
+ Choral Proclamation	"Come, Thou Fount"	arr. Courtney
+ Organ Prelude	"Prelude in a Classic Style"	**Young
+ Organ Offertory	"Jesus Loves Me"	*arr. Travis
Solo	"The Lord Is My Shepherd"	**Matthews
	++John Doe	
Vocal Meditation	"Face to Face"	*arr. Fettke
	++Jane Doe	

+ These titles are appropriate when the choir is understood to be the usual service choir and the name of the organist is listed.

** When there is no arranger, list the composer—not the author.

* When music is arranged, list the arranger.

++ This is the most appropriate way to indicate soloist or group other than service choir.

Additional Information—If there is too much material for one line, drop down a line for the title; for example:

Choral Proclamation arr. Martin
   "When I Survey the Wondrous Cross"

Do name everything because (1) people are relieved of curiosity; (2) people get to know each other; (3) names are important for a person's identity. (4) better preparation from all parties—organist, choir, pastor, and others—is encouraged; and (5) the bulletin will be a more informative historical document.

The order of worship should be appealing visually. Good use of fonts, print sizes, and white space can greatly enhance the look of a worship bulletin. Bulletins may be flat with no fold, bi-fold, tri-fold, or even more folds. The possibilities are endless; however, priority should always be given to the congregation's ease of reading.

THE WORSHIP COUNCIL

A worship council can greatly assist the worship planner. The worship council should be viewed as a work group, not an advisory council. Worship planners need people who can help them lead and plan more effective worship experiences. The worship council should be appointed by the worship leaders and not be chosen by the committee on committees, since it is mandatory that this be a group with whom worship leaders can feel comfortable and express ideas and feelings openly. Once a worship council is in place, the group may well be self-perpetuating. Consider the following qualifications for worship council members: (1) They should have a broad understanding of worship, its purpose, and priority. (2) They should have the ability to see the big picture. They should not represent a small group with particular issues. (3) They should be mature Christians and have the respect of the congregation. (4) They should be self-starters since they will be responsible for numerous contacts and details. (5) They should know many people within the church and be unafraid to enlist persons and boost their confidence.

The worship council should be composed of about five persons who represent various age groups within the congregation. The group should include both women and men. Once the council has begun, all members should remain for two years. At the end of year two, two members should rotate off; year three, two members; year four, one member, and so forth. The pastor and minister of music should co-chair the council.

One church has used the worship council in the following ways:

Quarterly Meeting (two hours). This meeting is for long-range planning. Prior to the meeting, the pastor has chosen sermon titles, themes, and Scripture focus. The minister of music has chosen choral music and soloists, and assigned various other ensembles to particular services. When the members arrive at the meeting, the room has newsprint around the walls with a section for each Sunday, for example:

October 1

Sermon:	"The Way of the Heart"	
Theme:	Personal Devotion	
Scripture:	Matthew 5:3–17	
Choral Music:	"Devotion"	Ness-Beck
Solo:	"Shepherd of My Heart"	Baldwin/Tunney
Other Music:	"Purer in Heart, O God"	
Invocation:		
Scripture Reader(s):		
Contact Person:		

The leader will discuss the services to be planned. The group will highlight special emphases, creative ideas, Sundays for drama, special effects, and other matters. These ideas will be added to the wall information. The group is then responsible for choosing persons to lead in prayer, Scripture readings, and other elements of worship. (Council members are provided with an ongoing list of persons who have previously led in worship and with a current church directory.) The group will select persons they plan to enlist. The list should include people of various ages, genders, and church responsibilities. Groupings for Scripture readings should be varied; combinations could include two children, youth and child, child and adult, married couple, parent and child, child and grandparent. After worship leaders have been chosen, the group will assign a contact person from the council for each week. The contact person is responsible for (1) contacting the worship leader at least two weeks in advance, (2) providing the Scripture passage or other material, (3) serving as a source of encouragement for the person, (4) enlisting replacements when needed, (5) contacting the church office when changes occur, and (6) coordinating rehearsal if needed with sound technician.[4]

After the meeting the pastor or minister of music transfers each week's information from the newsprint to single pages which are sent to each council member, music leaders, and others involved in the worship planning process. This sheet also serves as a weekly planning sheet for the pastor and minister of music.

Monthly Meeting (one hour). The purpose of the monthly meeting is to look with greater detail at individual services, to discuss changes, and to work on special projects such as special emphasis, Advent or Lenten booklets, and revivals.

Additional Suggestions. (1) Schedule quarterly meetings at least three weeks prior to the date when your existing plans expire. (2) Always schedule the next meeting before adjourning.

Benefits of a Worship Council. (1) Worship leaders often are overwhelmed with responsibilities in other areas and do not enlist worship leaders far enough in advance. Therefore, they call on faithful standbys or do it themselves. A worship council involves more people in worship leadership. (2) A worship council allows for a broad group of people to serve as worship leaders. Worship truly belongs to the people when they are allowed to lead. (3) Since a worship council represents all facets of the congregation, the church discovers the importance all persons have in the body of Christ. (4) Broader participation highlights good worship leaders whom pastor and music minister may have never discovered. Council members know the history of their church. Their contacts in some segments of the congregation will be broader than the staff. (5) A worship council serves as an educational process as

---

4. See appendix B for guidelines for prayer and Scripture readers.

different people are guided each week by a council member concerning the importance of worship, prayer preparation, and other matters. (6) The council builds competent worship leaders. (7) It models worship as a participatory event. (8) It allows the worship planner immense freedom as he or she comes to worship planning each week with much prior thought already having been done.

EVALUATING WORSHIP

Although worship leaders should evaluate their perceived effectiveness of each worship experience, the congregation should be given occasional opportunities to evaluate the worship experience, also. In order for congregational evaluation to be most effective, it should be preceded by teaching about the nature and purpose of worship. When this is not done, congregants may respond only from their tastes and personal preferences, giving little attention to the priority of God in worship.

Worship evaluation instruments are numerous and varied. Worship evaluation instruments using questions based on statements like "Leads me in worship" or "Points me toward God" are preferred over instruments with language such as "prefer" and "like." The evaluation instrument should seek to evaluate all aspects of the service, including the sermon.[5]

Worship leaders must be prepared for honest and critical evaluations; however, leaders must avoid overreacting to a survey, which can result in thoughtless change. Every worshiper worships differently and, since worship is an inclusive act, attempts should be made to allow each worshiper maximum opportunity to worship; however, not all worshipers may be pleased at all times. This is the nature of working with large groups of persons who have unique identities.

---

5. See appendix C for a sample worship evaluation instrument.

CHAPTER 19

LEADING WORSHIP

W orship must be well planned; however, if worship is to be effective, it must also be well led. Second only in importance to the form of the worship service is the method of conducting the service. Since worship is offered to God, it demands our very best in preparation, leadership, and participation. Above all else, the spirit of worship must be genuine.

THE LEADER OF WORSHIP

The worship experience depends upon three factors: the worshiper, the Holy Spirit's power, and the human leadership provided in the order and conduct of worship. Leadership is also necessary if worshipers are to feel secure and free to participate. Although there is no distinction between the so-called clergy and laity, the congregation selects leaders who are qualified to give direction in all its acts of worship and ministry. Ordinarily, the pastor and the minister of music are the primary leaders in worship, although in most churches other staff members and laypersons share in the leadership.

Worship leaders serve in the roles of both prophet and priest. The prophet contends for change and vitality; the priest seeks stability and instruction. The prophet speaks forth the ideal and eternal truth of God; the priest comes to God in behalf of humanity's temporal and partial grasp of truth and reality. These elements are always in tension in the work of the worship leader, and both affect his or her approach to leading in worship. Worship leaders do not act for themselves alone but for and with the congregation. The leader not only speaks God's Word to the congregation and speaks to God in behalf of the congregation the leader is also one of the congregants.

The leader's spirit. Charles Haddon Spurgeon once said that the person who guides others into the presence of the King must have journeyed far into the King's country and often looked upon his face. It is an awesome experience to come into the presence of God. Leaders must commit themselves anew for each particular occasion. The worship leader's private worship experiences with God are supremely important to his or her ability to provide spiritual leadership for the congregation. The leader should subordinate self and exalt God as the objective of worship. Worship should never be personality centered, for worship cannot focus on persons and on God at the same time. Worship leaders must resist the temptation to draw undue attention to themselves through careless speech or action. The spirit of the leader should be characterized by seriousness, reverence, joy, disciplined enthusiasm, hope, expectancy, and humility. These attitudes are dependent upon the grace of God through the Holy Spirit.

The leader's appearance. The leader should be properly dressed when entering the pulpit to conduct worship. Churches' and leaders' expectations vary widely, and no general custom prevails; however, a worship leader's dress should not distract from the message, verbal or nonverbal, that he or she is to proclaim. Moderation should guide the worship leader's choice of attire. Ministers usually wear the same style of clothing as that worn by the laity. Clothing should be in good taste in terms of style, color, fabric, and accessories. It must be noted that, right or wrong, congregations often have double standards for their leadership, especially ministers. While they may view casual worship attire as completely appropriate for themselves, they may expect the minister to dress more professionally. Ministers must be aware of the congregation's expectations for their worship appearance.

In some churches the minister's robe is acceptable or even preferred. A black academic robe is acceptable. The main objection by some to the clerical robe is that it tends to make a distinction between the minister and the congregation. One argument in favor of the robe is that it tends to make the minister less conspicuous by concealing personal taste.

The leader's conduct. The worship leader should enter the platform calmly and confidently. When seated, he or she should sit tall and confident without crossed legs. The worship leader must participate wholeheartedly in all aspects of the service. The pastor must *not* read sermon notes during the offertory or choral music. The minister of music must *not* read the hymnal or write notes during the sermon. Worship leaders seated together on the platform must not talk. When worship leaders talk, the congregation is distracted, wondering, "What are they saying?" "What has gone wrong?" "Are they talking about me?" When worship leaders talk they are showing the congregation that they have priorities other than worship. A leader should not leave the platform to check on unfinished details unless an emergency exists. Any behavior by a worship leader that distracts the congregation from worship must be avoided! Every aspect of the leader's deportment should exhibit total involvement. Decorum should indicate sincerity, not pretense. Simply to appear decent and well-mannered is not sufficient. The worship leader models worship involvement verbally and nonverbally—all aspects of the leader's countenance are readable.

PRINCIPLES OF LEADERSHIP

Since Christian worship involves the whole congregation, it is important that certain principles be observed in order to encourage participation. Leaders of worship must remember that the corporate life of worship is central in all that is done and said. The following principles are suggested as guidelines for leading in worship:

1. There should be complete preparation in the details of the service. The leader must know exactly what to do, step by step. All items should be in order: the Bible, the hymnal, the order of worship, the sermon notes, and all other notes pertaining to the details of conducting the service.

2. Proper mental preparation will lead to poise and a calm self-confidence. To lead others in worship, the leader cannot succumb to personal fears and doubts. A consciousness that he or she is God's leader will go far toward making that leadership effective.

3. The leader should seek personal rapport with the congregation. In this pursuit, the leader should be constantly aware that his or her own emotions are communicated. Actually, the congregation absorbs the "feeling tones" of the leader.[1] It is possible for the leader to communicate one message verbally and an entirely different message emotionally. However, worship leaders must realize that rapport is not created wholly within the context of worship. Congregations will not respond well to a warm, personable "up front" leader who is not warm and personable in interpersonal relationships.

4. A positive attitude is essential in leading others in worship. A positive, confident attitude will inspire confidence on the part of the

1. James T. Hall, "Measuring the Communication Feeling During Worship," *Pastoral Psychology* (October, 1963), 50 ff.

congregation. To avoid awkward expressions, words should be well chosen. In calling the people to prayer or to participation in music, the leader should be positive in his or her expressions. For example, "Let us pray" is better than "Shall we pray?" or "May we pray?"

5. The leader should speak in a natural tone of voice, never using the perfunctory tones of the "professional clergyman." The voice communicates either honesty or pretense; congregations accustomed to hearing voices on radio and television can instantly unmask a phony personality. A conversational tone is usually preferred.

6. The worship leader must begin on time and not allow any part of the service to drag or to consume more than its appropriate amount of time. People's habits condition them psychologically so that they are distracted and irritated when the timing is poor. Worship services should normally be completed within the appointed time. Congregations may be willing and eager to continue a service past a designated time if (1) they feel God's peculiar leadership or (2) the service has had a sense of forward movement and has maintained interest. A late service due to poor leadership will rarely be tolerated repeatedly.

7. Personal eccentricities and distracting idiosyncrasies of a leader are annoying and become a hindrance to worship. Almost everyone is subject to an occasional unusual facial expression or peculiar bodily movement such as adjusting the glasses; the leader should constantly seek to overcome such distractions. However, unavoidable handicaps are generally accepted graciously when worship leaders are not self-conscious and apologetic.

8. The spirit of a leader is contagious; therefore, a leader of worship should reflect a spirit of optimism, hope, and enthusiasm. Spiritual zeal may make a leader enthusiastic; however, enthusiasm will not necessarily result in heightened spiritual zeal. Worship is always an occasion of joy and hope. God has promised to meet his people when they approach God in worship. Every service should be approached with a spirit of expectancy. The difference between an "alive" church and a "dead" one can sometimes be attributed to the spirit of the person who leads in worship.

9. One of the privileges of the leader in worship is that of participating in worship with the congregation. The worship leader must worship *before* and *while* leading others. The leader should sing the hymns with the congregation and show interest and concern for every part of the service. People will follow a leader who shows genuine interest by participating in all acts of worship.

10. The worship leader should model genuine interest in people. An unselfish attitude in the worship service speaks of a wider concern for persons and may encourage people to come at other times for counsel and support. Worship leaders should be available to people as they exit the service; however, the leader must focus worship-related comments away from himself or herself and show interest in the worshiper's experience. Worship leaders should be available in warm, personal relationships.

11. Laypersons should be enlisted to lead in prayers and reading the Scriptures. Theologically, there is no distinction between "clergy" and "laity"; however, members should function according to their gifts and training. If the motive for enlisting laypersons is to involve the congregation in more meaningful worship, it may well be done; but if enlisting laypersons is done to exalt certain personalities or simply to pass the honors around, the practice will distract from worship.

Laypersons should be instructed regarding the purpose of each worship element and the manner in which each element should be led. Worship leaders should be enlisted far enough in advance to give them time to prepare thoroughly.

Ushering is an important function in worship. Ushers should model exemplary hospitality and set an example for all other congregants. The usher's main purpose is to make it easier for people to worship God. This ministry demands reverence, dignity, patience, courtesy, tact, and discipline. The responsibilities include greeting the people, seating them, distributing the order of worship, receiving the offerings, and handling minor emergencies. If ushering is to be effective, it will demand organization and training. Ushering involves total worship participation. Once guests are seated, ushers should sit at the back of the worship room and join the worshiping community while also remaining alert to latecomers. Ushers should also treat as worship all aspects of gathering the offering.

12. The choir has a major task in leading worship—their worship leadership can aid or distract the congregation. The choir should work closely with the worship planners in all parts of the service. A wandering mind, a roving eye, or a wriggling body in the choir loft can interfere with the close communication that should exist between God and the congregation. Choir members should give careful attention to entering and exiting the choir area as well as to their leading during the service. Choir members should avoid wearing excessive jewelry and other accessories that draw attention to them. The choir should enter in a

spirit of prayer and there should be absolutely *no* talking during the service. Being an effective choir member demands a spirit of reverence, cooperation, and self-discipline.

CONGREGATIONAL PARTICIPATION

"You are a chosen race, a royal priesthood, a holy nation, God's own people, that you may declare the wonderful deeds of him who called you out of darkness into his marvelous light" (1 Peter 2:9).

Medieval clergy monopolized worship. Because the liturgy was performed in Latin and the people could not understand Latin, the congregation ceased to be participants and became spectators in worship. The sanctuary was a "sort of stage for a mystery drama which they watched, to which they contributed little except the necessary fees to keep it going."[2] They seldom participated in the Lord's Supper more than once a year. Doubtless, many of them paid their fees and attended services to escape purgatory.

This description may well be applied to contemporary worship in many instances. Often the congregation listens too much and participates too little. The sermon is *listened* to, the prayers are *listened* to, the anthem is *listened* to. The congregation does not participate enough! Of what value is freedom without participation? It is dishonest to boast of a freedom which is not honored and exercised.

The doctrine of the priesthood of every believer does not mean that every person is merely his or her own priest, but that every person is priest to every other person. This doctrine necessitates a community in which all members of the congregation, as a "royal priesthood," have a responsibility in public worship. Just as Jesus our High Priest offered himself as a sacrifice for us, we must also offer ourselves to God and to each other. The congregation offers "spiritual sacrifices acceptable to God through Jesus Christ" (1 Peter 2:5).

The obligation of the individual to worship has a threefold theological basis: (1) to give God the glory and honor due to his name; (2) to witness to the spiritual needs of society; and (3) to receive the "unsearchable riches of Christ."[3] As a part of the church, the worshiper is God's representative to the contemporary world.

The congregation and its leaders are privileged to participate in worship. The worshiper participates in the music, the prayers, the offerings, the responsive reading of the Scriptures, and in God's Word as it is proclaimed. Participation may be both audible and visible, or it may be silent and unseen except by God. Congregations need guidance to enable more meaningful participation.

---

2. M. H. Shepherd, Jr., *The Worship of the Church* (Greenwich, Conn.: Seabury Press, 1952), 84.

3. John G. McKenzie, *Psychology, Psychotherapy, and Evangelism* (London: George Allen & Unwin, Ltd., 1940), 228.

Just as leaders prepare for public worship, so must the congregation be prepared before entering the worship room. Christians are to regard communion with God as their priority. When Christians have an active prayer life and regular devotional times, and seek to worship God in daily life, corporate worship becomes the gathering of the community of worshipers—people for whom worship is a familiar practice. Worshipers should not only expect to *receive* something from public worship, but should also *bring* something to public worship, for worship is humanity's response to God's initiative.

Worshipers can have more profound worship experiences when certain principles are followed: (1) Regular participation is essential. God has designed worship as an act of the gathered body of Christ—the church. Regular attendance not only affects the individual worshiper but also other worshipers as well. Through wholehearted participation, we inspire others to worship better. (2) The worshiper must approach worship with a spirit of reverence: respect for God and his Word, for the house of worship, for the day of worship, and for the leader of worship. (3) The worshiper must willfully cooperate with the worship leaders and unite with other worshipers in every act of worship such as singing praise to God and praying to God. Worship should be viewed both as a privilege and a duty. (4) Worship is enhanced when individuals are sensitive to the needs of other worshipers. Any behavior that is distracting to others should be avoided. (5) Fellowship within the congregation is a natural part of the church's gathering. Regular attenders are encouraged to show sensitivity to new persons who may not yet feel welcome and accepted.

If we are to grow in worship, we must cultivate a spirit of expectation. Growing as a Christian depends upon growing in the art and discipline of worship. The mind must engage all its powers in the exercise of imagination and creativity in order for worship to achieve its greatest potential. The "fruits of worship"—guidance, comfort, and inspiration—will come as a result of the higher action of giving glory and honor to God through the giving of ourselves to him.

As Kierkegaard pointed out, the leader and the congregation should not think of themselves as actors but as servants and responders.[4] The worship leader is not responsible for doing worship for the congregation. The leader guides other worshipers with a humble and sincere attitude. All worshipers are actors in the drama of worship, with God as the star of the action. The worship leader is the prompter and an actor in the worship drama.

---

4. Søren J. Kierkegaard, *Purity of Heart*, trans. Douglas Steere (New York: Harper & Bros., 1938), 163 ff.

CONCLUSION

Worship is experiencing renewal in our day. This is evidenced by the number of worship conferences, the great number of recent books and periodicals discussing worship, and the experiences we each share in seeking to sort through many new and innovative resources in our attempt to make worship more meaningful for the congregations to which we minister. Several key persons are contributing meaningfully to this revival and renewal of worship. Each has made a unique contribution and each seems to speak to a somewhat different audience. It is my hope that as these streams broaden, they will each spill over into the others so that, in time, all will benefit from the mix.

MOVEMENTS AFFECTING THE CHURCH'S WORSHIP

Robert Webber is, perhaps, the foremost writer and lecturer in the field of worship today. His books and their ideas are strongly influencing much current practice. Webber is a student of many styles of worship, and he is an advocate of convergence in worship. He seeks to choose from the unique traditions of all Christians, from the liturgical to the charismatics, and to blend them into a service that is the better from each of our contributions. He encourages churches to return to their liturgical roots, and he believes that worship must be experiential and must appeal to the senses.[1]

---

1. See Robert Webber, *Worship Is a Verb* (Nashville: Abbott-Martyn, 1992); *Signs of Wonder: The Phenomenom of Convergence in Modern Liturgical and Charismatic Churches* (Nashville: Abbott-Martyn, 1992); and *The Complete Library of Christian Worship*, 7 vols. (Nashville: Abbott-Martyn, 1993–94).

Don Hustad, in recent lectures and writing, is calling for a careful examination of the theology of worship and how it relates to practice. He is fearful that many Baptist and other non-charismatic Free Churches are beginning to borrow a charismatic model of worship without considering the theological implications. At the risk of oversimplifying, I will illustrate: Many churches that practice a "praise and worship" model of worship—i.e., a long period of singing at the beginning of the service progressing from exuberant, extroverted praise to intimate, hushed praise—are cheating their congregations because charismatic documents and practice authenticate that ultimate worship for charismatics will progress into a "holy hush" which will most often include glossolalia (speaking in tongues). When Baptists use the same model, we move through the progression of extroverted praise to introspective praise but stop before the Holy Spirit is released as the Spirit is in the charismatic model. What results, according to Hustad, is a giving up of some of the cognitive and didactic elements that have characterized non-charismatic Free Church worship. At the same time, we are not practicing worship which would allow for the intense "heart" experience of the charismatics. This results in a huge vacuum that is left unfilled. Hustad issues a warning call that non-charismatic evangelicals get their theology in line with their practice.[2]

Bill Hybels and Rick Warren, pastors associated with Willow Creek Church and Saddleback Community Church respectively, have exerted the most influence on Baptist worship in recent years through their "seeker friendly," "worship as the front door of the church" philosophy.[3] These leaders have helped us all by encouraging us to be considerate of those persons who have not grown up in our unique traditions. I sense that the worship and church growth movement, as we have experienced it, is beginning to lose some of its initial appeal. There seem to be fewer church growth conferences, and some of the more respected leaders in this area now recognize the need for balance in all church growth. Some recent worship fads seem to be giving way to depth and richness.

Richard Foster, while not generally seen as a leader in the field of worship, is influencing worship profoundly through his popular books.[4] His formation of Renováre groups and their emphasis on small group accountability in five great traditions of Christian life and faith are making a marked impression and, I believe, a life-changing difference in the lives of

---

2. See Donald P. Hustad, *Jubilate II: Church Music in Worship and Renewal* (Carol Stream, Ill.: Hope Publishing Company, 1993).

3. Bill Hybels and Rick Warren have exerted their influence through articles and through workshops in their churches for ministers. Both have written books particularly designed to assist the Christian's daily effectiveness.

4. See Richard J. Foster, *Celebration of Discipline: The Path of Spiritual Growth* (San Francisco: Harper and Row, 1978); and *Prayer: Finding the Heart's True Home* (San Francisco: Harper and Row, 1992).

many Christians in various denominations. Foster's strong emphasis on balance and on various aspects of worship is influencing the practice of worship in the churches where we serve.

Other writers and leaders in this stream are Baptists: Dallas Willard, Henry Blackaby, Avery Willis, and T. W. Hunt. I feel that it is this group that will exert the most influence on Free Church worship in the near future, and I hope that they will in the distant future as well. Their call is for churches to begin to rely on God's leadership in all of its actions. Since worship is the place where this happens, I feel that worship will be the basis for genuine spiritual renewal instead of its being used as a tool to pack pews and increase our vital statistics. In the years to come, these are some of the movements that I will watch in an effort to decide where we are going in worship.

OBSERVATIONS ON CURRENT WORSHIP PRACTICES

Following are some observations on current worship practices:

1. The instrumental movement continues to grow and blossom. This movement seems to be lessening the perceived need for an overabundance of taped accompaniments. Synthesized sounds are allowing us to have instant orchestral sound yet maintain a level of artistry and sacrifice that prerecorded accompaniment tracks do not allow. Accompaniment track usage does seem to be increasing on the small-church level where it is often needed because of limited keyboard and other instrumental resources.

2. The mix of liturgical and charismatic worship practices is slowly breaking down the fear of those in the middle. It is a given that those in the middle will be influenced when strong movements are taking place at the ends of the spectrum. Renewal seems to have begun at the ends of the spectrum instead of the center. Recent instances prove this point. (1) In cities worldwide, Christians of many denominations are coming together for "Marches for Jesus." These marches are held downtown and are led by persons carrying non-political, liturgical banners and chanting mutually agreeable texts such as the "Apostle's Creed." (2) Christian leaders, who have finally realized that evangelizing cities is a privilege to be shared by all Christians, are meeting in weekly prayer meetings for spiritual renewal. Other positive results of blending of liturgical and charismatics are (3) the breaking down of the fear of creeds and affirmations of faith, (4) use of different forms of prayer, from written prayers to corporate or simultaneous prayer, (5) increase in the possibility of movement and alternative worship postures, (6) openness to alternative ways of observing communion, (7) emphasis on the church year, especially Advent and Lent, and (8) the beginning of

a universal church repertoire of music through the increased use of ethnic music and other shared resources.

3. There is a perceived greater balance in the repertoire played by Christian radio stations. Christian radio seems to be playing a more balanced selection of hymn arrangements, contemporary Christian, classics, and praise and worship music. The influence of Christian radio on the person in the pew must not be overlooked.

4. In the popular music realm there is a greater use of *a cappella* music. This new trend gives churches an opportunity to restore the importance of beautiful choral music to worship.

5. Fewer church growth conferences seem to be taking place, while spiritual awakening conferences under the title *Fresh Encounters* are taking the country by storm. True worship can surely result from this movement.

6. Through efforts by those advocating spiritual disciplines, an environment in which worship will thrive seems to be developing. The "worship as church growth movement" has given worship a new visibility in Free Churches. Now, this new awareness of worship offers leaders the opportunity to lead their churches to see God as the source of worship. This renewed interest in personal piety is a very healthy sign for the future of the church's worship.

Practical Suggestions for Implementing Change

In the early eighties much time was spent contemplating how long this era of contemporary Christian music, praise choruses, and electronic media would last; today we accept each of these phenomena as here to stay in at least some form. We must now ask ourselves the pragmatic question: How will we use this broad repertoire of elements to enhance our worship? The world is open for us. We no longer have to shop for our worship service elements in a "mom and pop grocery." We can literally choose musical and artistic expression from the global market. This can be intimidating because choices are sometimes threatening. We often make excuses such as "the people in my church wouldn't respond to that" or "I'd get kicked out of my church for that," when we are actually excusing our lack of knowledge and openness. While I advise anyone to approach change carefully, change is positive and our ability to lead in change can be a true measure of our leadership ability. Balance and innovation are difficult. I became astutely aware of this fact a couple of years ago when I met for breakfast with a fellow minister of music and we discussed our churches and their feelings about their congregational music. We soon discovered that some persons in his church, which is more contemporary in its worship practices, longed for more hymns, while some persons in my church felt that we should be doing more new music. Balance is difficult!

I am increasingly learning the lesson of not saying, "I won't." If I am truly open to God's leadership, God may lead me to do what I once resisted. God can change my desires if I am open to his leadership. However, when in doubt, we must remember: don't rush to abandon your historical roots just to try something new. Experiment carefully, giving a new trend time to prove its enduring worth or ephemerality. If the worship practice is worthy, the new element will be around long enough for you to utilize it. If an innovation is truly great, you won't miss it even if you wait. If you fail to implement some new fad because it passes too quickly, you may simply consider yourself blessed!

Worship must, by its nature, be an inclusive act. It must provide genuine worship opportunities for all of God's gathered people. We as God's servants must do all within our powers to plan for genuine worship opportunities for children, youth, young adults, median adults, and older adults. While we recognize our limitations and our never being able to please all persons, we must keep their faces—the people in our church's pews—in front of us each time we plan our church's worship.

Change is all around us, and sometimes I am so overwhelmed with my struggle to keep up that I am tempted to give up. However, my calling is to continue ministry, to spend a lifetime giving my best! I am continually learning that to be a minister is to feel constantly tugged, and sometimes torn, in many directions. However, when I am totally honest, I recognize God's using movements and individuals who seem to tug and tear me to make me a more useable servant of God. My prayer for you and for myself is that we can see our ministries in the larger focus of God's plan as we "present [ourselves] a living and holy sacrifice, acceptable to God, which is [our] spiritual service of worship" (Romans 12:1, NASB).

C. Randall Bradley

APPENDIX A

THE ORDINARY OF THE MASS

Kyrie Eleison, Christe eleison, Kyrie eleison

Lord, have mercy upon us. Christ, have mercy upon us. Lord, have mercy upon us.

GLORIA

Gloria in excelsis Deo. Et in terra pax hominibus bonae voluntatis. Laudamus te. Benedicimus te. Adoramus te. Glorificamus te. Gratias agimus tibi propter magnam gloriam tuam. Domine Deus, Rex coelestis, Deus Pater omnipotens. Domine Fili unigenite, Jesu Christe. Domine Deus, Agnus Dei, Filius Patris. Qui tollis peccata mundi, miserere nobis. Qui tollis peccata mundi, suscipe deprecationem nostram. Qui sedes ad dexteram Patris, miserere nobis.

Glory be to God in the highest. And on earth peace to men of good will. We praise thee. We bless thee. We adore thee. We glorify thee. We give thee thanks for thy great glory. O Lord God, heavenly King, God the Father almighty. O Lord Jesus Christ, the only-begotten Son. Lord God, Lamb of God, Son of the Father. Who taketh away the sins of the world, have mercy upon us. Who taketh away the sins of the world, receive our prayer. Who sitteth at the right hand of the Father, have mercy

Quoniam tu solus sanctus. Tu solus Dominus. Tu solus Altissimus, Jesu Christe. Cum Sancto Spiritu, in gloria Dei Patris. Amen.

upon us. For thou alone, O Jesus Christ, art most high. Together with the Holy Ghost, in the glory of God the Father. Amen.

CREDO

Credo in unum Deum, Patrem omnipotentem, factorem coeli et terrae, visibilium omnium, et invisibilium. Et in unum Dominum Jesum Christum, Filium Dei unigenitum. Et ex Patre natum ante omnia saecula. Deum de Deo, lumen de lumine, Deum verum de Deo vero. Genitum, non factum, consubstantialem Patri: per quem omnia facta sunt. Qui propter nos homines, et propter nostram salutem descendit de coelis. Et incarnatus est de Spiritu Sancto ex Maria Virgine; et homo factus est. Crucifixus etiam pro nobis; sub Pontio Pilato passus, et sepultus est. Et resurrexit tertia die, secundum Scripturas. Et ascendit in coelum: sedet ad dexteram Patris. Et iterum venturus est cum gloria, judicare vivos et mortuos: cujus regni non erit finis. Et in Spiritum Sanctum, Dominum et vivificantem: qui ex Patre Filioque procedit. Qui cum Patre et Filio simul adoratur, et conglorificatur; qui locutus est per prophetas. Et unam sanctam catholicam et apostolicam Ecclesiam. Confiteor unum baptisma in remissionem peccatorum. Et expecto resurrectionem mortuorum. Et vitam venturi saeculi. Amen.

I believe in one God, the Father almighty, maker of heaven and earth, and of all things visible and invisible. And in one Lord Jesus Christ, the only-begotten Son of God. Born of the Father before all ages. God of God, light of light, true God of true God. Begotten, not made; of one substance with the Father: by whom all things were made. Who for us men, and for our salvation, came down from heaven. And was made flesh by the Holy Ghost of the Virgin Mary: and was made man. He was also crucified for us, suffered under Pontius Pilate, and was buried. And on the third day he rose again, according to the Scriptures. And ascended into heaven: He sitteth at the right hand of the Father. And he shall come again with glory to judge the living and the dead; and of his Kingdom there shall be no end. And in the Holy Ghost, the Lord and Giver of life, who proceedeth from the Father and the Son. Who together with the Father and the Son is adored and glorified: who spoke by the prophets. And in one holy, catholic and apostolic church. I confess one baptism for the remission of sins. And I expect the resurrection of the dead. And the life of the world to come. Amen.

SANCTUS

Sanctus, Sanctus, Sanctus Dominus Deus Sabaoth. Pelni sunt coeli et terra gloria tua. Osanna in excelsis.

Holy, Holy, Holy Lord God of hosts. Heaven and earth are filled with thy glory. Hosanna in the highest.

BENEDICTUS

Benedictus qui venit in nomine Domini. Osanna in excelsis.

Blessed is he that cometh in the name of the Lord. Hosanna in the highest.

AGNUS DEI

Agnus Dei, qui tollis peccata mundi, miserere nobis. Agnus Dei, qui tollis peccata mundi, miserere nobis. Agnus Dei, qui tollis peccata mundi, dona nobis pacem.

Lamb of God, who taketh away the sins of the world, have mercy upon us. Lamb of God, who taketh away the sins of the world, have mercy upon us. Lamb of God, who taketh away the sins of the world, grant us peace.

APPENDIX B

GUIDELINES FOR PRAYER LEADERS AND SCRIPTURE READERS

Scripture Reader:

1. For easier reading, type or print passage and put it inside Bible.

2. Read from Bible.

3. In your study, read passages from several versions to see which reads best.

4. If two people read, use two microphones.

5. Practice with the sound technician.

6. If your passage involves dialogue (two or more people speaking), read carefully for natural divisions.

7. *Always* practice reading passage aloud. Hearing your voice is important!

8. Consider taping your reading to hear if you are as expressive as you think.

9. Pay careful attention to main words in the text—nouns, verbs.

Prayer Leader:

Invocation—Leading the people to be conscious of God's presence. Should focus on God in adoration and praise.

Prayer Before the Offertory—A brief dedication prayer for the tithes and offerings. Stresses the total stewardship of life and not simply money.

Benediction—Commending ourselves to God's care and announcing God's blessing upon the people.

Suggestions:

1. Avoid reading a Scripture or "sharing a thought" prior to your prayer.

2. Invite participation from congregation with a phrase such as, "Please join me in prayer." Avoid, "May we pray?"

3. Connect prayers to the season of the year, or surrounding worship elements, such as a hymn; try incorporating hymn phrases or ideas into prayer.

4. To guide your thoughts, consider writing an outline for your prayer.

5. Avoid using clichés in prayers; for example, overuse of "God or Father," "just," "bless the gift and the giver," and "lead, guide, and direct."

6. Remember that each prayer should have a specific purpose; the invocation should not sound like the offertory prayer or the benediction.

7. Address prayers *to* God, not *about* God.

8. Deliver prayer in a clear voice.

Appendix C

Questionnaire on Worship and Preaching

This is a poll to determine how members and other participants view our worship and to identify areas in which they would like to see possible changes. Please consider the following inquiries and give a response to every question.

1. At present we provide a printed order of service for Sunday morning only. In your opinion, this guide is (choose one):

   ❏ important and should be provided Sunday morning only.

   ❏ important and should be provided for *every* service.

   ❏ optional and should be provided only on special occasions.

   ❏ unimportant and should not be provided.

2. Typically, we have included the following elements in most Sunday morning services of worship. Please rate the importance of each as a regular part of worship:

	Creative/ Meaningful	Acceptable	Needs Improving
Organ Prelude			
Processional by Worship Leaders			
Choral or Spoken Call to Worship			
Invocation			
Welcome and Registration of Guests			
Anthem by the Choir			
Pastoral Prayer			
Children's Sermon			
Offertory Prayer			
Offering with Organ Offertory			
Scripture Reading			
Solo, Duet, or Other Special Music			
Sermon			
Invitation to Church Membership			
Presentation of New Members			
Opportunities for Service			
Benediction			
Organ postlude			

3. In each service we use at least one lay worship leader in one of a variety of assignments (for example, prayer, Scripture reading, welcome). How do you rate the importance of this participation?

❏ Important: use laypersons regularly.

❏ Optional: use laypersons occasionally.

❏ Unimportant: use laypersons seldom or never.

4. At present our morning service is scheduled to begin at 11:00 A.M. and to conclude at 12:00; hence, to last one hour. Your preferences:

To begin:	To end:	To last:
❏ 10:30	❏ 11:30	❏ 45 minutes
❏ 10:45	❏ 11:45	❏ 1 hour
❏ 11:00	❏ 12:00	❏ 1 hour & 15 minutes
❏ Other	❏ Other	❏ Other

5. Throughout the year, a number of special emphases are featured in the Sunday worship services. Please evaluate the significance of each:

	Creative/ Meaningful	Acceptable	Needs Improving
Ordination Services			
Youth Week Sunday			
Stewardship Sundays			
Annual Budget Promotion			
Holy Week: Palm Sunday & Easter Sunday			
Recognition of High School Seniors			
Parent-Child Dedication Service, Mother's Day			
Independence Day Sunday, Patriotic Emphasis near July 4			
Mission Emphasis Sundays			
Thanksgiving			
Advent—Christmas Services			

6. Listed below are a number of general characteristics which can be applied to the "style" in which worship is conducted. Based on your understanding of these terms, indicate the direction in which you would like to see our services move in the future:

	More of this characteristic	About the same as at present	Less of this characteristic
Formality—Dignity			
Spontaneity—Extemporaneousness			
Reverence—Holiness			
Congregational Participation—Lay Involvement			
Liturgy—Planned Aids			
Drama—Pageantry/Banners			
Innovation—Experimentation			
Humor—Laughter			

7. There are a number of musical "styles" for congregational singing. Based on your understanding of these types, indicate the direction in which you would like to see our services move in the future (answer each part):

	More of this characteristic	About the same as at present	Less of this characteristic
Traditional hymns that are widely recognized to have a quality tune and text			
Gospel songs largely out of the revivalist tradition that primarily express one's personal testimony			
Contemporary songs whose texts address current issues and whose tunes reflect more recent musical styles			
Brief choruses, usually learned and sung by memory, that typically stand in the tradition of religious folk singing			

8. How often would you like to sing new or unfamiliar hymns in worship?

❏ One per service

❏ One per Sunday

❏ One per month

❏ One per quarter

9. Present practice is to stand and sit equally for most congregational singing. Your preference:

❏ Stand for most congregational singing.

❏ Stand and sit about equally for congregational singing.

❏ Sit for most congregational singing.

10. At present the organ and piano normally accompany congregational singing in the Sunday morning services. Which one of the following do you think would be most effective as a regular practice?

❏ Use organ only.

❏ Continue to use both organ and piano accompaniment.

❏ Use both organ and piano plus other orchestral instruments as available.

11. Currently it is typical to have one non-congregational musical presentation in the Sunday morning service, an anthem by the Sanctuary Choir. As you see it:

    ❏ This is about the right number and balance of special musical presentations.

    ❏ This is too little special music; have even greater variety by using other choirs and by having more ensemble groups to sing, soloists, etc.

12. Many worshipers tend to view choral music as falling into two broad categories: (a) "Classical," by which they mean the kind of music, whether traditional or contemporary, that appeals to those with a cultivated appreciation of musical excellence; (b) "Popular," by which they mean the kind of music that appeals to those with or without an acquired taste for serious music primarily because of its emotional impact upon the hearer. Within the context of those categories, what "mix" would you like in our Sunday morning worship services?

    ❏ Mainly "classical" choral music, with the more "popular" type reserved for Sunday evening and special occasions such as revivals.

    ❏ Mainly "popular" choral music, with the more "classical" type reserved for special occasions such as choir concerts.

    ❏ A mixture of "classical" and "popular" choral music that favors the "classical."

    ❏ A mixture of "classical" and "popular" that favors the "popular."

    ❏ A deliberate balance between "classical" and "popular" that gives each of them equal weight.

13. At present A.M. services are more formal while P.M. are less formal and more spontaneous. Your preference:

    ❏ Keep the same.

    ❏ P.M. more like A.M.

    ❏ A.M. more like P.M.

14. At present we baptize at a convenient time, usually near the beginning of the service. Your preference:

    ❏ Sunday morning, near beginning of service.

    ❏ Sunday morning, near end of service.

    ❏ Sunday evening service.

    ❏ Some other time (i.e., in special service).

15. At present, we celebrate the Lord's Supper four times per year. In your judgment this is:

❏ Too often—observe less frequently.

❏ Too seldom—observe more frequently.

❏ About right—continue present frequency.

16. Taking our Pastor's morning preaching as a whole, carefully rate its effectiveness in the following areas:

	Excellent	Good	Average	Poor	Failure
The sermons show thorough preparation and careful thought.					
The sermons are clearly organized and move to a logical climax.					
The sermons are interesting and well-illustrated.					
The sermons strengthen the relation between pastor and people.					
The sermons address a broad spectrum of human needs.					
The sermons appeal to a wide spectrum of ages and backgrounds.					
The sermons are relevant to current events, community needs, and seasonal emphases.					
The sermons call the lost to new life in Christ.					
The sermons convey an urgency that demands decision and response.					
The sermons sound a prophetic note that convicts of sin.					
The sermons inspire and motivate the hearer to deeper dedication.					
The sermons explain the basic beliefs and practices of our faith.					
The sermons provide practical guidance for daily living.					

APPENDIX D

PARENT-CHILD DEDICATION

A Sample Service

THE CHURCH . . .
. . . GATHERING FOR WORSHIP

The Chiming of the Hour	
Opportunities for Service	Bob Spradling
Welcome to Our Guests	Bob Spradling
Prayer Needs of the Congregation	Bob Spradling

. . . EXPRESSING PRAISE

*Hymn No. 383	"We Are God's People"	SYMPHONY
*Invocation		Randall and Brenda Bradley

. . . FOCUSING ON GOD'S GIFT OF CHILDREN

Responsive Reading

Leader:	God has entrusted you with a magnificent responsibility.
Parents:	We lovingly accept this responsibility.
Congregation:	We will help you.
Leader:	Again God has given the gift of life.
Parents:	We will protect and nurture this gift.
Congregation:	We will pray for you.
Leader:	A child is like a clean slate; it knows no right or wrong.
Parents:	We dedicate ourselves to the teaching of the ways of Christ.
Congregation:	We will be with you.
All:	Praise God, from whom all blessings flow.

Presentation of Bibles
Individual Prayer with Families
Hymn No. 508   "Lord, for the Gift of Children"   NYLAND

. . . FOCUSING ON FAMILIES

Responsive Reading No. 503
Hymn No. 507   "Would You Bless Our Homes and Families?"   NETTLETON
Prayer for the Offering
Organ Offertory   "Because I Have Been Given Much"   arr. Kerrick
(Please join in singing "Jesus Loves Me" as children in pre-kindergarten and kindergarten exit
for Children's Worship Workshop.)

. . . HEARING GOD'S WORD

Scripture Reading: 1 Samuel 1:1–18   Brad and Sherry Carroll
Choral Proclamation   "As a Little Child"   Joseph Martin

Message   "A Gift Given and Returned"   Bob Spradling
*Hymn No. 504   "God, Give Us Christian Homes"   CHRISTIAN HOME
**Benediction   "Would You Bless Our Homes and Families"   NETTLETON
                                  (Hymn No. 507)

Let us reach beyond the bound'ries of our daily tho't and care
'Til the family You have chosen spills its love out everywhere.
Help us learn to love each other with a love that constant stays;
Teach us when we face our troubles,
Love's expressed in many ways.

Organ Postlude   "Festive Trumpets"   arr. Wetherill

*Please stand.
**CCLI #169926. Used by Permission.

APPENDIX E

WEDDING CEREMONY

The Marriage of

CARLITA LOWRY ALMAND
to
R. G. HUFF

The Prelude

"God of Grace, and God of Glory"	Manz
"Sheep May Safely Graze"	Bach
Four Chorale Miniatures on "For the Beauty of the Earth"	Burkhardt
"Cantabile"	Franck
"Jesu, Joy of Man's Desiring"	Bach
"Be Thou My Vision"	Travis
Selections from WATER MUSIC	Handel
"Allegro Vivace"	
"Air"	
"Hornpipe"	
"Minuet"	
"Allegro maestoso"	
"Song of Gladness"	Dobrinski
Aria	Peeters
"Come, Thou Fount of Every Blessing"	Manz

The Service of Worship
Processional of the Choir "Rigaudon" Campra

Solo	"Joyful, Joyful We Adore Thee"	Maddux
Prayer of Invocation		

Choral Praise   "Hallelujah" from the MOUNT OF OLIVES   Beethoven
    Hallelujah unto God's almighty Son!
    Praise the Lord, ye bright angelic choirs in holy songs of joy.
    Man, proclaim His grace and glory. Hallelujah!

Processional   "Praise, My Soul, the King of Heaven"   Hustad

The Reading of the Word of God

Minister:	Praise the Lord! Sing to the Lord a new song! Sing His praise in the assembly of the faithful.
People:	Let us be glad in our Maker. Let us rejoice in our King.
Minister:	Let us praise His name with dancing, making melody to Him with tambourine and harp.
People:	For the Lord takes pleasure in His people, giving victory to those who fear Him. (From Psalm 149:1–4.)
Minister:	Put on then as chosen ones, holy and beloved, compassion, kindness, lowliness, meekness, and patience; be gentle with one another, forgiving one another.
People:	Above all, put on love which binds everything together in perfect harmony.
Minister:	Let the peace of Christ rule in your hearts, and be thankful.
People:	Let the Word of Christ dwell in you richly, teaching and admonishing one another in psalms, hymns, and spiritual songs, singing to God with hearts full of thankfulness.
Minister:	And whatever you do in word or deed, do everything in the name of the Lord Jesus, giving thanks to God the Father through Him. Amen. (From Colossians 3:12–17)

Hymn 14   "Praise to the Lord, the Almighty"
[Please sing the final stanza in unison.]

The Ceremony of Marriage

The Charge
The Vows
The Exchange of Rings
Solo   "O Love that Will Not Let Me Go"   Clawson
Prayer of Blessing
Choral Benediction   "Ascription of Praise"   Schwoebel

    Now to Him who is able to keep you from falling and to present you without blemish before the presence of His glory, with rejoicing to the only God, our Savior, through Jesus Christ our Lord, be the glory, majesty, dominion, and the authority before all time, and now and forever. Amen. (Jude 24–25)

Recessional   "Toccata" from SYMPHONY NO. V   Widor

Officiants	Davis L. Cooper and Wayne Jenkins
Matron of Honor	Carla Lowry Tarrant
Best Man	Billy Coburn
Organist	Jane Martin
Soloist	Cynthia Clawson
Director of Music	David J. Lane
Handbell Director	Donna Jo Butler

APPENDIX F

WEDDING POLICIES

[Note: The following policies may serve as guidelines. Wedding policies should be reviewed and revised regularly.]

INTRODUCTION

Marriage in the church is a worship service; therefore, every element of the service should honor God in a spirit of worship. A wedding deserves thorough preparation. You are encouraged to plan all the details of your wedding carefully and not overlook spiritual preparation. The ministers and staff of this church will assist you as you plan.

Careful thought and judgment have gone into the preparation of these wedding policies and guidelines. They are official church policies and suggested procedures for weddings and wedding receptions. They are intended to assist you in planning a worshipful wedding, to see that the church's property is well-maintained, and to insure the church's belief that all of its services are God honoring.

MAKING THE RESERVATION

The date and time of the wedding should be placed on the church calendar as soon as possible. Tentative dates may be arranged by phone; however, the bride, groom, or their parents must arrange final dates through a personal conference with the wedding coordinator.

A "member" wedding is one in which the bride, groom, parents, grandparents, or guardians are members of this church. All other weddings are regarded as "non-member" weddings. No non-member weddings can be scheduled earlier than sixty days before the date, in order to permit members of the church to have preference of dates.

FEES

Organist—One hour rehearsal and wedding (Amount)

Wedding only (Amount)

Custodian (Amount)

Soloist (Amount)

Lighting and sound operator (Amount)

Building usage fee (non-member only) (Amount)

Sanctuary (Amount)

Chapel (Amount)

Reception (Amount)

[Fee should reflect your local area. If your church has a large number of "non-member" weddings, then your church's fees are too low or you have a particularly beautiful building.]

There is no minister fee included above. This fee is left to the discretion of the couple, but the amount should reflect the important role that the minister plays in the ceremony and planning.

Payment of all fees for the use of the church facilities and services is required at the time the building is reserved.

GENERAL GUIDELINES

- When a non-staff minister is used in the wedding, the wedding coordinator should have a copy of the wedding two weeks prior to the rehearsal.

- Weddings are not scheduled on Sundays or on holiday weekends, including New Year's Day, Memorial Day, Independence Day, Labor Day, Thanksgiving Day, and Christmas Day.

- Evening weddings are not scheduled to begin later than 8:00. (If the reception is to be held at the church, the wedding should begin no later than 7:00.) All rehearsals should be scheduled for 6:00 P.M. on the day preceding the ceremony and should begin on time.

- Church facilities may be used only for receptions of weddings held at the church.

- Receptions must be concluded by 10:00 P.M.

- No nursery facilities will be provided for rehearsals or weddings.

- Church policy prohibits smoking in any area of the building.

REHEARSALS

- Rehearsals should begin on time.

- The wedding coordinator will be in charge of the rehearsal.

- Both sets of parents should be present for the rehearsal.

- The ushers should be present for the rehearsal.

- Wedding rehearsals will not exceed one-and-one-half hours.

DRESSING AREAS

[This section should outline which areas (rooms) may be used as dressing areas by the wedding party.]

PERSONAL VALUABLES

- Dresses, tuxedos, or other clothing delivered to the church must be arranged through the wedding coordinator.

- The church is not responsible for personal items of any type that are brought to the church for the wedding or reception. The church is not liable for stolen, lost, or damaged items.

RECEPTIONS

- Members are encouraged to use church facilities for receptions; however, the caterer or the family is responsible for leaving the building in the condition that it was found.

- Throwing of rice and bird seed endangers the safety of those who are using the halls and walks and is strictly prohibited.

- Alcoholic beverages are never served at receptions held in the church building.

TAKING OF PICTURES

The photographer may take pictures before or after the wedding in any part of the building; however, pictures cannot be taken during the actual ceremony, except available light exposures and natural-light videos taken from the back of the chapel or the balcony of the sanctuary. The photographer may take pictures of the wedding party as they process and recess. Photographs are encouraged before the service; however, they may be taken after the service. Ushers are responsible for informing camera-carrying guests that no photographs are to be taken during the ceremony.

SELECTION OF WEDDING MUSIC

- All wedding music must be submitted to the minister of music as early as possible for his approval.

- The minister of music is available to assist in the selection of wedding music. Music with texts which are not God-honoring and worshipful are not allowed.

- The use of congregational music is strongly encouraged.

- [Some churches have a tape of appropriate wedding music (instrumental and vocal) available for couples to listen to and make selections. Other selections must be approved by the minister of music or wedding committee.]

- The minister of music will assist you in securing soloists (vocal and instrumental). Choir robes are available for participating musicians.

- Musicians who are to play the church organ or piano must be approved by the church organist or pianist or minister of music.

INSTRUCTIONS TO THE FLORIST

- Permanently secured furnishings should not be moved.

- No furniture shall be moved or rearranged without special permission.

- No nails, tacks, staples, pins, or anything that will mar woodwork may be used.

- All candles must be dripless. To protect the floor, plastic covering must be used under candelabras.

- Only holding devices (wrapped wire, rubber bands, etc.) that will not mar the pew ends may be used to fasten bows. Do not use tape.

- One week before the wedding, the florist must arrange for decorations to be delivered to the church.

- The florist is expected to remove all decorations within one hour after the end of the wedding.

- The florist is responsible for any damage to the building or furniture by candles or flowers and is responsible for cleaning any wax from the carpet or furniture that is a result of the wedding.

- No decorative items may be placed on or adjacent to the piano or the organ console.

- The church reserves the right to restrict florists who have previously violated the above policies.

APPENDIX G

FUNERAL SERVICE

THE WORSHIP OF GOD

**In Memory of Hedy Smelcer Huff
Thursday, July 6, 1989
Eight O'Clock in the Evening
First Baptist Church
Pigeon Forge, Tennessee**

The Organ Prelude		Karen Hill
Hymn 521	"On Jordans Stormy Banks"	PROMISED LAND
The Prayer of Invocation		Carl Whaley
The Reading of Scripture from the Book of Revelation		Tim Childers

Leader:	I am the Alpha and the Omega who is, who was and who is to come, the Almighty! (1:8)
Congregation:	To him who loves us and has freed us from our sins by his blood. To him be glory and power for ever and ever! (1:5–6)
Leader:	Do not be afraid. I am the Living One; I was dead, and behold, I am alive for ever and ever. (1:17–18)
Congregation:	Salvation belongs to our God who sits on the throne and to the Lamb. (7:10)
Leader:	They fall down before him who sits on the throne and worship him who lives for ever and ever. They lay their crowns before the throne and say:
Congregation:	You are worthy, our Lord and God, to receive glory and honor and power. For you created all things and by your will they were created and have their being. (4:10–11)
Leader:	Blessed are the dead who die in the Lord. They will rest from their labor and their deeds will follow after them. (14:13)

Congregation: Blessed are they who do his commandments; they have rights to the tree of life and may enter in through the gates into that city. (22:14)

Hymn 161   "Crown Him with Many Crowns"   DIADEMATA

The Welcome and the Reading of the Obituary   W. W. Cope

The Solo   "Does Jesus Care?"   Hall
Dwight E. Maples

The Reading of Scripture from the Book of Proverbs (unison)

A good name is rather to be chosen than great riches, and loving favor rather than silver and gold. (22:1)

The Choral Worship   "The Majesty and Glory of Your Name"   Fettke (from Psalm 8)

Memorial Message: W. W. Cope

The Closing Prayer
Hymn 280   "Jesus, Keep Me Near the Cross"   NEAR THE CROSS

The Benediction (unison)

May the grace of our Lord Jesus Christ be with us all, tenderly loving us, giving us his Presence in this, our time of grief. Now to the God of Hedy Huff be the highest glory and praise from this time forth and forever more. May we trust him fully, all for us to do; they who trust him wholly, find him wholly true. Amen and Amen!

The Organ Dismissal   "How Firm a Foundation"

We have gathered here tonight to say "goodbye" to one of God's saints, Hedy Huff. At the same time, we are here to worship the God to whom she had committed her life; her study of God's Word, and her teaching of it are hallmarks of her days among us.

On behalf of Raymond, Ronald George, and the rest of the family, we thank you for your presence and your prayerful support. Your very presence is witness to your friendship with Hedy and her family. We cannot thank you enough for that.

Graveside services will be tomorrow morning at the Pigeon Forge Baptist Cemetery at 10:00 A.M.

APPENDIX H

COPYRIGHT GUIDELINES: THE UNITED STATES COPYRIGHT LAW

A PRACTICAL GUIDE

AN OUTLINE FOR THE CORRECT USE OF COPYRIGHTED PRINTED MUSIC

This outline is intended to be a guide to the major requirements of the Copyright Law as they apply to users of printed music, to inform those users so that they may maintain proper standards of ethics and seek to protect themselves, their churches, schools, colleges, and organizations from incurring liability or subjecting themselves to the possibility of being sued.

This outline does *not* presume to be a comprehensive summary of the Copyright Act of 1976. It does *not* attempt to deal with all the issues covered by the legislation, nor does it provide answers to many of the legal questions. The purpose of this outline is to inform all users of printed music of the basic provisions of this statute.

A complete story of the Copyright Law of 1976 and further information may be obtained by writing: The Copyright Office, Library of Congress, Washington, DC 20559.

COPYRIGHT—WHAT DOES IT MEAN?

Under the U.S. Copyright Law, copyright owners have the exclusive right to print, publish, copy, and sell their protected works. The copyright owners of the books and music you purchase are indicated on those publications.

The printed music you use reaches you as a result of the collaboration of a number of people:

- the time and creative effort of the composer

- the investment of time and money by publishers

- your local music retailer who supplies your musical needs

Whenever printed music is copied without permission, you *steal* from:

- composers/arrangers

- publishers

- music retailers

It is illegal for you to copy a publication in any way without the written permission of the copyright owner, subject only to the very specific provisions of the Copyright Law.

THE RIGHTS OF OTHERS

The Copyright Law is designed to encourage the development of the arts and sciences by protecting the work of the creative individuals in our society—composers, authors, poets, dramatists, choreographers, and others.

It is essential to the future of printed music that the Copyright Law be upheld by all. Composers, arrangers, publishers, and dealers are losing a significant percentage of their income because of illegal photocopying. This loss of revenue ultimately means that less and less printed music is available, and dealers are no longer able to afford to carry large stocks of sheet music.

Copyright owners have every right to prosecute offenders under the U.S. Copyright Law. To date, there have been a notable number of court decisions against individuals, churches, colleges, and other institutions for violations of the Copyright Law—some involving substantial fines.

WHAT YOU MUST NOT DO!

The following are *expressly prohibited:*

- Copying to avoid purchase.

- Copying music for any kind of performance (note emergency exception in the next section, point 1).

- Copying without including copyright notice.

- Copying to create anthologies or compilations.

- Reproducing material designed to be consumable such as workbooks, or study guides.

- Charging beyond the actual cost involved in making copies.

Copyright ultimately means that no one but the copyright owner has the right to copy without permission.

What you *can* do without having secured prior permission:

1. Copy in an emergency to replace purchased copies that for any reason are not available for an imminent performance, provided purchased replacement copies shall be substituted in due course.

2. Copy, for academic purposes other than performance, multiple copies of excerpts of works, provided that the excerpts do not comprise a part of the whole which would constitute a performable unit such as a section, movement, or aria. In no case may you copy more than 10 percent of the whole work. The number of copies shall not exceed one copy per pupil.

3. Edit or simplify printed copies that have been purchased, provided that you do not distort the fundamental character of the work, alter the lyrics, or add lyrics if none exist.

4. Make a single copy of recordings of performance by students for evaluation or rehearsal purposes. The educational institution or individual teacher may retain a single copy.

5. Make a single copy of a sound recording (such as a tape, disc, or cassette) of copyrighted music from sound recordings owned by an educational institution or an individual teacher for the purpose of constructing aural exercises or examinations, and it may be retained by the educational institution or individual teacher. (This pertains only to the copyright of the music itself and not to any copyright which may exist in the sound recording.)

PENALTIES FOR INFRINGEMENT

The remedies provided by the law to a copyright owner mean that anyone found making illegal copies, or otherwise infringing, could face:

1. Payment of from $250 to $10,000 (statutory damages), and if the court finds willfulness, up to $50,000; and

2. Fines of up to $50,000 or two years' imprisonment or both if willful infringement for commercial advantage and private financial gain is proved.

OUT-OF-PRINT MUSIC

Sometimes music may be erroneously reported to be out of print. If you are in doubt and it is vital that you obtain the music, write directly to the publisher. Only the publisher or copyright owner has the right to confirm that a title is out of print.

Individuals violating the Copyright Law are subjecting their churches, schools, colleges, and other institutions to the same liabilities stated above.

THE MOST FREQUENTLY ASKED COPYRIGHT QUESTIONS

Why can't I copy anything I want?

It's against the law, other than in very specific circumstances, to make unauthorized copies of copyrighted materials.

What if I am faced with a special situation?

If you want to include copyrighted lyrics in a song sheet—arrange a copyrighted song which the publisher cannot supply in regular published form—the magic word is . . . *ask*. You may or may not receive permission, but when you use someone else's property, you must have the property owner's permission.

What if there isn't time to ask?

That makes no difference. Think of copyrighted music as a piece of property, and you'll be on the right track. Plan ahead.

What about photocopies that are now in our church or school library?

Destroy any unauthorized photocopies immediately. Replace them with legal editions.

Can I make copies of copyrighted music first and then ask permission?

No. Permission must be secured prior to any duplication.

What if I can't find the owner of a copyrighted song? Can I go ahead and copy it without permission?

No. You must have the permission of the copyright owner. Check the copyright notice on the work, and/or check with the publisher of the collection in which the work appears. Once you have this information, write to the copyright owner.

As a soloist, is it permissible for me to make a photocopy of a copyrighted work for my accompanist?

No. Permission for duplication, for any purpose whatsoever, must be secured from the copyright owner.

Is it permissible to print copyrighted words only on a one-time basis, such as in a concert program?

No. Permission must be secured prior to any duplication. Using "just the words" makes no difference.

But what about items that are out of print?

Most publishers are agreeable, under special circumstances, to allow reproducing out-of-print items, but again, permission must be secured from the copyright owner prior to any duplication.

Can I make a transparency of a copyrighted song for use by an overhead projector?

No. The making of a transparency is a duplication, and permission must be secured from the copyright owner.

Can I make a record or tape using a pre-recorded instrumental track?

Two permissions are necessary here. One is from the copyright owner of the selection to be recorded, and the second is from the producer/manufacturer of the original record.

Can I make a band arrangement of a copyrighted piano solo? Can I make a flute arrangement of a copyrighted work for clarinet?

No. Making any arrangement is a duplication, and permission must be obtained from the copyright owner.

What about the photocopiers who don't "get caught"?

They force the price of legal editions higher. They enrich the manufacturers of copying machines at the expense of composers, authors, publishers, and music retailers. They risk embarrassment from professional colleagues who understand the law; and they risk fines and jail sentences if taken to court.

Can I make audio-visual copies of worship services?

Only for archival purposes. For other copies, fees must be paid except for limited areas covered by CCLI.

Can I include biblical texts in the church bulletin?

The King James Version is not copyrighted and can be copied. Other versions are copyrighted and, although some copyright holders offer leniency, the copyright holder (not the publisher) must be contacted for permission.

Can graphics and other materials be copied in church publications?

Copyrighted graphics, poetry, cartoons, lyrics, and so forth cannot be used without permission.

CHRISTIAN COPYRIGHT LICENSING, INC.

Christian Copyright Licensing, Inc. (CCLI) offers the following service for church worship use:

1.0 Rights Granted

1.1 Subject to the payment by Church of the Annual fee, and the church's compliance with the other terms and conditions hereof, CCLI, for the terms of one year from the date of this license, grants to Church the nonexclusive rights to the Songs in the Program for the following uses.

a. To print Songs in bulletins, liturgies, programs, and songsheets.

b. To print Songs in bound or unbound songbooks compiled by the Church.

c. To make overhead transparencies or slides, or to utilize electronic storage and retrieval methods for the visual projection of Songs.

d. To print customized vocal and or instrumental arrangements of the Songs, where no published version is available.

e. To record Songs in Church worship services by either audio or audio-visual means.

1.2 The rights licensed to Church by CCLI are subject to the following conditions:

a. The quantity of copies referred to in 1.1a, 1.1b, and 1.1d may not exceed 15% of Church Size.

b. The quantity of copies duplicated per worship service pursuant to 1.1c may not exceed 15% of the Church Size, and the Church may recover up to $4.00 (U.S.), $5.00 (CAN.) per audio tape and $12.00 (U.S.), $15.00 (CAN.) per video tape for copies duplicated up to the 15% limitation without additional payment to CCLI therefore.

2.0 Restrictions

2.1 The following rights are excluded from the Program.

a. Rental or sale of copies created pursuant to 1.1 (a)–(d) for any form of direct or indirect remuneration or consideration whether by way of direct payment, gift, donation, freewill offering, etc.

b. Distribution of copies created pursuant to 1.1 (a)–(d) outside the jurisdiction of Church use.

c. Photocopying or duplicating any choral sheet music (octavos), cantatas, musicals, handbell music, keyboard arrangements, vocal solos, or instrumental works.

d. Language translations of the Songs.

2.2 In addition to those restrictions set forth in 2.1 above, any and all rights not expressly granted to the Church by this agreement are reserved by the Owners.

For information, contact:
Christian Copyright Licensing, Inc.
6130 NE 78th Ct., Suite C11
Portland, Oregon 97218–9972

Some material for the appendix is taken from pamphlets published by Music Publishers of the United States, 711 3rd Ave., New York, New York, 10017. Used by permission.

APPENDIX I

APPLAUSE IN WORSHIP: ARE THERE BETTER OPTIONS?

Applause, within the context of a worship service, increasingly is becoming an accepted practice in many churches. While many ministers and parishioners have accepted this practice as a phenomenon of worship renewal, some have not felt spiritually fulfilled while applauding during worship. Why have so many churches bought into this fairly recent practice with such little reflection concerning its long-term implications? These and many other questions deserve some discussion.

I have often heard people, after visiting another congregation, say, "What we really need here is to get people started clapping so that we can get a little excitement going. We need to liven things up." On the surface, applause does seem to "liven things up," but the question must be posed: "What then becomes the source of the renewed energy?" Applause in worship can easily present a false sense of excitement, whereas excitement in worship must be spiritually generated. The question becomes not whether we should openly express ourselves in worship, for surely we should, but are there more appropriate ways for Christians to express themselves?

Applause tends to bring attention to the messenger instead of the message. Applause usually follows presentations of musical selections, more often solo presentations than choral. Occasionally, congregations, like theatergoers, feel a distinct need to express themselves after they have heard musical presentations (especially ones that have loud and high theatrical endings). When applauding a musical presentation, one must decide, "Am I applauding the message of the music or the gifts of the presenters?"

If congregations do indeed applaud the message, why is it that slow, meditative presentations rarely receive rounding ovations? When such ovations are given, the soloist is thrust into a very difficult situation: "Should I be gracious by acknowledging the applause; and if I do, will I be perceived as accepting the applause for myself instead of giving the glory to God?" Musicians are taught to be gracious in acknowledging applause; but during a worship service, the soloist, conductor, and others involved are in an awkward position, not knowing quite how to be gracious without taking God's glory as their own. As a soloist, I sincerely desire to offer my musical gifts for God's glory; however, I sometimes struggle to keep my desire for personal gratification in check. When my musical gifts are applauded in services of worship, I contend with my public and private responses.

While applause more often follows highly celebrative acts of worship, what then becomes the response for meditative worship? Because of this hard-to-reconcile question, congregations often end up applauding every act of worship rather than risk offending someone. I have participated in worship in which a beautifully meditative act, deserving moments of silence, was lessened by awkward applause either because of precedence or the congregation's fear of offending the presenter. Applause can create competitiveness among various musicians in a congregation so that soloists question their own effectiveness if their applause level is less than that of another soloist.

Is applause always a poor response in worship? The Bible has numerous references to "clapping." However, there seems to be a difference between clapping *for* an act of worship and clapping *as* an act of worship, that is, clapping during music as a physical act of worship. I am much more comfortable with the latter expression.

The connotation of applause, when offered following acts of worship, is most often secular and has been borrowed by the church in an effort to create a theater mentality in which the congregation cheers on the performers who do the worship, instead of allowing the congregation to do their own worship for the singular audience in worship—the Almighty God!

Can it be that our secular theatrical architecture, our TV models, and our obsession with hearing the stories of Christian superstars have thrust us into the applause mode? If so, what do we do to reverse this trend? It is imperative that church leaders not attempt to take away what is sometimes one of the congregation's only response opportunities without first giving it an alternative. Worship must be restored to the people. Worship leaders must become prompters in worship instead of superstars, and they must help congregations to build a new repertoire of appropriate worship responses.

The most obvious biblical worship response is "amen," which I suggest must be restored to its proper place. This will mean that we must see "amen" as a biblical term and reserve it for use in worship instead of in trivial workaday remarks. We must also use the "people's amen" (i.e., "And all the people said, 'Amen.'") more carefully. However, because of the careless use of the people's amen, I have felt manipulated to say "amen" in response to remarks with which I did not whole-heartedly agree. "Amen," as with any other response, can be overused. I encourage the use of the congregational "amen" as a response to public prayer, and the use of phrases such as "The Word of God" and "Thanks be to God" following Scripture reading. Congregations should be equipped and encouraged to use biblical phrases to freely express agreement to any act of worship.

Church leaders must not overlook the response of silence in worship. Some acts of worship are too profound for verbal expression. It seems that our culture is so obsessed with chitchat that we feel compelled to comment on everything—unfortunately, we bring this mentality with us to worship. I often have observed worship leaders who seemed to show by their verbal responses that they were not wholly participating in worship but were thinking instead of their next verbal response. As writer Anne Ortlund states concerning worship, "Less is more."

Worship leaders must realize that applause is difficult to control. After all, one person can begin a "round of applause." Often, other people will join in applause simply to avoid embarrassing the initiator. The platform worship leader is then in a difficult position: Does he or she applaud with the others and violate his or her personal convictions, or refrain from applause and risk being thought of as stiff and cold? To avoid such situations, worship leaders could, through appropriate ways, express their convictions regarding worship responses.

Surely clapping, and perhaps even spontaneous applause, can make a contribution to worship; however, worship leaders need to help congregations develop other appropriate responses too. Worship leaders must model sensitivity in worship that goes beyond a singular rote response to all acts of worship. We must thereby continually seek fresh ways to restore worship to the congregation.

APPENDIX J

BAPTISMAL INVITATION

Front:

Something special
has happened in my life.
You are invited to celebrate it with me . . .

Inside:

As an act of obedience to my Lord and Savior, Jesus Christ and as a testimony of my faith in Him, I am being baptized at Pleasant Valley Baptist Church, Liberty, Missouri.

It would be an honor to have you present to witness this memorable event in my life.

Date: August 22

Time: 10:45 A.M.

Place: Pleasant Valley Baptist Church
             (I–35 & Pleasant Valley Road)
             6816 Church Road
             Liberty, Missouri

Because of Jesus,

SELECTED BIBLIOGRAPHY

Adam, Adolf. *Foundations of Liturgy: An Introduction to Its History and Practice.* Collegeville: Liturgical Press, 1992.

Allen, Ronald, and Gordon Borror. *Worship: Rediscovering the Missing Jewel.* Portland: Multnomah Press, 1982.

Anderson, Raymond and Georgene. *The Jesse Tree: The Heritage of Jesus in Stories and Symbols of Advent for the Family.* Minneapolis: Fortress Press, 1966.

Appleton, George, ed. *The Oxford Book of Prayer.* Oxford: Oxford University Press, 1985.

Bailey, Robert W., Alton H. McEachern, Paul McCommon, John R. Chandler, Harry L. Cowan, and Everett Robertson. *Music in the Worship Experience.* Nashville: Convention Press, 1984.

Baker, Robert A. *A Summary of Christian History.* rev. ed. John M. Landers. Nashville: Broadman & Holman, 1994.

Barna, George. *User Friendly Churches: What Christians Need to Know About the Churches People Love to Go To.* Ventura: Regal Books, 1991.

Barry, James C., and Jack Gulledge, eds. *Ideas for Effective Worship Services.* Nashville: Convention Press, 1977.

Batts, Sidney F. *The Protestant Wedding Sourcebook: A Complete Guide for Developing Your Own Service.* Louisville: Westminster/John Knox Press, 1993.

Best, Harold M. *Music Through the Eyes of Faith.* Washington, D.C.: Christian College Coalition, 1993.

Bock, Lois and Fred. *Creating Four-Part Harmony: Effective Ideas for Ministers of Music.* Carol Stream, Ill.: Hope Publishing Company, 1989.

The Book of Common Prayer. New York: The Church Hymnal Corporation, 1979.

Brown, Carolyn C. *Forbid Them Not: Involving Children in Sunday Worship.* Nashville: Abingdon Press, 1991.

Brown, Paul B. *In and for the World: Bringing the Contemporary into Christian Worship.* Minneapolis: Fortress Press, 1992.

Burroughs, Bob. *An ABC Primer for Church Musicians.* Nashville: Broadman Press, 1990.

Davies, J. G., ed. *The New Westminster Dictionary of Liturgy and Worship.* Philadelphia: Westminster Press, 1986.

Dean, Talmage W. *A Survey of Twentieth Century Protestant Church Music in America.* Nashville: Broadman Press, 1988.

Dix, Dom Gregory. *The Shape of the Liturgy.* London: A & C Black, 1945.

Doran, Carol, and Thomas H. Troeger. *Open to Glory: Renewing Worship in the Congregation.* Valley Forge: Judson Press, 1983.

————. *Trouble at the Table: Gathering the Tribes for Worship.* Nashville: Abingdon Press, 1992.

Edwards, Tilden. *Sabbath Time.* Nashville: Upper Room Books, 1992.

Erickson, Craig Douglas. *Participating in Worship: History, Theory, and Practice.* Louisville: Westminster/John Knox Press, 1989.

Eskew, Harry, and Hugh T. McElrath. *Sing with Understanding: An Introduction to Christian Hymnody.* Nashville: Broadman Press, 1980.

Fisher, Tim. *The Battle for Christian Music.* Foreward by John Vaughn. Greenville: Sacred Music Services, 1992.

Foster, Richard J. *Prayer: Finding the Heart's True Home.* San Francisco: Harper & Row, 1992.

Gills, James P. and Heartlight. *The Dynamics of Worship.* Tarpon Springs: Love Press, 1992.

Gobbel, A. Roger, and Phillip C. Huber. *Creative Designs with Children at Worship.* Atlanta: John Knox Press, 1981.

Hardesty, Nancy A. *Inclusive Language in the Church.* Atlanta: John Knox Press, 1987.

Hardin, Gary, and Martin Thielen, eds. *Biblical Preaching: Using Great Hymns.* Nashville: Convention Press, 1990.

Harding, Thomas, ed. *Worship for All Seasons: Selections from Gatherings for Advent, Christmas, Epiphany.* Volume 1. Toronto: United Church Publishing House, 1993.

Harper, John. *The Forms and Orders of Western Liturgy from the Tenth to the Eighteenth Century: A Historical Introduction and Guide for Students and Musicians.* Oxford: Clarendon Press, 1991.

Hayford, Jack, John Killinger, and Howard Stevenson. *Mastering Worship.* Portland: Multnomah Press, 1990.

Henry, Jim. *The Pastor's Wedding Manual.* Nashville: Broadman Press, 1985.

Hickman, Hoyt L. *A Primer for Church Worship.* Nashville: Abingdon Press, 1984.

Hickman, Hoyt L., Don E. Saliers, Laurence Hull Stookey, and James F. White. *The New Handbook of the Christian Year.* Nashville: Abingdon Press, 1986.

Hooper, William L. *Ministry & Musicians.* Nashville: Broadman Press, 1986.

House, Garth. *Litanies for All Occasions.* Valley Forge: Judson Press, 1989.

Howard, Thomas. *Evangelical Is Not Enough: Worship of God in Liturgy and Sacrament.* San Francisco: Ignatius Press, 1984.

Hustad, Donald P. *Jubilate II: Church Music in Worship and Renewal.* Carol Stream, Ill.: Hope Publishing Company, 1981.

Johansson, Calvin M. *Discipling Music Ministry: Twenty-First Century Directions.* Peabody, Mass.: Hendrickson Publishers, 1992.

Juengst, Sara Covin. *Sharing Faith with Children: Rethinking the Children's Sermon.* Louisville: Westminster/John Knox Press, 1994.

Kenseth, Arnold, and Richard P. Unsworth. *Prayers for Worship Leaders.* Philadelphia: Fortress Press, 1978.

Killinger, John. *Lost in Wonder, Love, and Praise: Prayers and Affirmations for Christian Worship.* Lynchburg: Angel Books, 1986.

Kostulias, Ray. *Character Witnesses: Dramatic Monologues for Christmas and Easter.* Cleveland: United Church Press, 1993.

Langford, Thomas Anderson III. *The Worship Handbook: A Practical Guide to Reform and Renewal.* Nashville: Discipleship Resources, 1984.

Liesch, Barry. *People in the Presence of God: Models and Directions for Worship.* Grand Rapids: Zondervan Publishing House, 1988.

Lovelace, Austin C. *The Anatomy of Hymnody.* Chicago: G. I. A. Publications, 1965.

Lovelace, Austin C., and William C. Rice. *Music and Worship in the Church.* Rev. ed. Nashville: Abingdon Press, 1960.

Lovette, Roger. *Come to Worship.* Nashville, Broadman Press, 1990.

MacArthur, John Jr. *True Worship.* Chicago: Moody Press, 1982.

————. *The Ultimate Priority: On Worship.* Chicago: Moody Press, 1983.

Mapson, J. Wendell Jr. *The Ministry of Music in the Black Church.* Valley Forge: Judson Press, 1984.

Martin, Ralph P. *Worship in the Early Church.* rev. ed., Grand Rapids: William B. Eerdmans, 1989

————. *The Worship of God: Some Theological, Pastoral, and Practical Reflections.* Grand Rapids: William B. Eerdmans Publishing Company, 1982.

Mathson, Patricia. *Burlap & Butterflies: 101 Religious Education Activities for Christian Holidays for Preschool to 3rd Grade.* Notre Dame: Ave Maria Press, 1987.

McBeth, Leon. *The Baptist Heritage: Four Centuries of Baptist Witness.* Nashville: Broadman Press, 1987.

McComiskey, Thomas Edward. *Reading Scriptures in Public: A Guide for Preachers and Lay Readers.* Grand Rapids: Baker Book House, 1991.

McEachern, Alton H. *Here at Thy Table, Lord: Enriching the Observance of the Lord's Supper.* Nashville: Broadman Press, 1977.

Miller, Steve. *The Contemporary Christian Music Debate.* Wheaton: Tyndale House, 1993.

Mitchell, Leonel L. *The Meaning of Ritual.* New York: Paulist Press, 1977.

Mitchell, Robert H. *I Don't Like That Music.* Carol Stream, Ill.: Hope Publishing Company, 1993.

————. *Ministry and Music.* Philadelphia: Westminster Press, 1978.

Moe, Dean. *Christian Symbols Handbook: Commentary & Patterns for Traditional and Contemporary Symbols.* Minneapolis: Augsburg Publishing House, 1985.

Ng, David, and Virginia Thomas. *Children in the Worshiping Community.* Atlanta: John Knox Press, 1981.

Nichols, Randall J. *The Restoring Word: Preaching as Pastoral Communication.* San Francisco: Harper & Row, 1987.

Norén, Carol M. *What Happens Sunday Morning: A Layperson's Guide to Worship.* Louisville: Westminster/John Knox Press, 1992.

Old, Hughes Oliphant. *Themes and Variations for a Christian Doxology.* Grand Rapids: William B. Eerdmans Publishing Company, 1992.

Orr, N. Lee. *The Church Music Handbook: For Pastors and Musicians.* Nashville: Abingdon Press, 1991.

Ortlund, Anne. *Up with Worship: How to Quit Playing Church.* Ventura: Regal Books, 1975.

Ortlund, Ray. *Three Priorities for a Strong Local Church.* Waco: Word Books Publisher, 1983.

Pass, David B. *Music and the Church.* Nashville: Broadman Press, 1989.

Peterson, David. *Engaging with God: A Biblical Theology of Worship.* Grand Rapids: William B. Eerdmans Publishing Company, 1992.

Petersen, Eugene H., Calvin Miller, et. al. *Weddings, Funerals and Special Events.* Waco: Word Books, 1987.

Phillips, E. Lee. *Breaking Silence Before the Lord: Worship Prayers.* Grand Rapids: Baker Book House, 1986.

Piper, John. *Desiring God: Meditations of a Christian Hedonist.* Portland: Multnomah Press, 1986.

Powell, Paul. *Gospel for the Graveside.* Nashville: Broadman Press, 1981.

Rainsley, Glen E. *Words of Worship: Resources for Church and Home.* New York: Pilgrim Press, 1991.

Rayburn, Robert G. *O Come, Let Us Worship: Corporate Worship in the Evangelical Church.* Grand Rapids: Baker Book House, 1980.

Reynolds, William J. *Congregational Singing.* Nashville: Convention Press, 1975.

Reynolds, William J., and Milburn Price. *A Survey of Christian Hymnody.* Carol Stream, Ill.: Hope Publishing Company, 1987.

Robertson, Everett, comp. *Drama in Creative Worship.* Nashville: Convention Press, 1987.

————. *Introduction to Church Drama.* Nashville: Convention Press, 1978.

Routley, Erik. *Church Music and the Christian Faith.* Carol Stream, Ill.: Agape, 1978.

Sailers, Don E. *From Hope to Joy.* Nashville: Abingdon Press, 1984.

Schaeffer, Franky. *Addicted to Mediocrity: 20th Century Christians and the Arts.* Westchester, Ill.: Crossway Books, 1981.

Schaper, Robert N. *In His Presence: Appreciating Your Worship Tradition.* Nashville: Thomas Nelson Publishers, 1984.

Schillebeeckx, E. *Marriage: Human Reality and Saving Mystery.* New York: Sheed and Ward, 1965.

Sparkman, G. Temp. *Writing Your Own Worship Materials.* Valley Forge: Judson Press, 1980.

Stacker, Joe R., and Wesley Forbis. *Authentic Worship: Exalting God and Reaching People.* Edited by Gary Hardin and Martin Thielen. Nashville: Convention Press, 1990.

Stake, Donald Wilson. *The ABCs of Worship: A Concise Dictionary.* Louisville: Westminster/ John Knox Press, 1992.

Stott, Joan, ed. *In God's Presence: Prayers, Poems and Praise for Devotions.* Melbourne: Joint Board of Christian Education, 1989.

Sydnor, James Rawlings. *Hymns and Their Uses: A Guide to Improved Congregational Singing.* Carol Stream, Ill.: Agape, 1982.

Thielen, Martin. *Getting Ready for Special Sundays.* Nashville: Broadman Press, 1991.

————. *Getting Ready for Sunday: A Practical Guide for Worship Planning.* Nashville: Broadman Press, 1989.

To Celebrate: Reshaping Holidays and Rites of Passage. Ellenwood: Alternatives, 1987.

Wainwright, Geoffrey. *Doxology: The Praise of God in Worship, Doctrine and Life: A Systematic Theology.* New York: Oxford University Press, 1980.

Webber, Robert E. *Evangelicals on the Canterbury Trail: Why Evangelicals Are Attracted to the Liturgical Church.* Wilton: Morehouse-Barlow, 1985.

————. *Signs of Wonder: The Phenomenon of Convergence in Modern Liturgical and Charismatic Churches.* Nashville: Abbot Martyn, 1992.

————. *A Workshop on Worship: In the Heart, in the Home, and in the Church.* Grand Rapids: Lamplighter Books, 1985.

————. *Worship Is a Verb.* Dallas: Word Publishing, 1985.

————. *Worship Is a Verb: Eight Principles for a Highly Participatory Worship.* Nashville: Abbott Martyn, 1992.

————. *Worship: Old and New.* Grand Rapids: Zondervan Publishing House, 1982.

————, ed. *The Complete Library of Christian Worship.* Volume 1, *The Biblical Foundations of Christian Worship.* Nashville: Star Song Publishing Group, 1993.

————. *The Complete Library of Christian Worship.* Volume 2, *Twenty Centuries of Christian Worship.* Nashville: Star Song Publishing Group, 1994.

————. *The Complete Library of Christian Worship.* Volume 3, *The Renewal of Sunday Worship.* Nashville: Star Song Publishing Group, 1993.

Webber, Robert E., and Rodney Clapp. *People of the Truth: The Power of the Worshiping Community in the Modern Word.* San Francisco: Harper & Row, 1988.

White, James F. *A Brief History of Christian Worship.* Nashville, Abingdon Press, 1993.

————. *Documents of Christian Worship: Descriptive and Interpretive Sources.* Louisville: Westminster/John Knox Press, 1992.

————. *Introduction to Christian Worship.* Rev. ed. Nashville: Abingdon Press, 1980.

————. *Protestant Worship: Traditions in Transition.* Louisville: Westminster/John Knox Press, 1989.

White James F., and Susan J. White. *Church Architecture: Building and Renovating for Christian Worship.* Nashville: Abingdon Press, 1988.

Willimon, William H. *The Intrusive Word: Preaching to the Unbaptized.* Grand Rapids: William B. Eerdmans, 1994.

————. *Peculiar Speech: Preaching to the Baptized.* Grand Rapids: William B. Eerdmans, 1992.

————. *Preaching and Leading Worship.* Philadelphia: Westminster Press, 1984.

————. *The Service of God: Christian Work and Worship.* Nashville: Abingdon Press, 1983.

Willimon, William H., and Robert L. Wilson. *Preaching and Worship in the Small Church.* Nashville: Abingdon Press, 1980.

Wohlgemuth, Paul W. *Rethinking Church Music.* Carol Steam, Ill.: Hope Publishing Company, 1981.

Wright, Tim. *A Community of Joy: How to Create Contemporary Worship.* Nashville: Abingdon Press, 1994.

NAMES INDEX

SUBJECT INDEX